Yesterday's Warrior

Yesterday's Warrior

~ A MEMOIR ~

Heather Harrison

WORD WARRIORS PRESS

YESTERDAY'S WARRIOR
Published March 2004

Printed in the United States by Word Warriors Press, LLC, Anoka, Minnesota.
www.wordwarriorspress.com
08 07 06 05 04 1 2 3 4 5

The names of all people have been changed to maintain privacy. The names of all places, including cities and counties, have also been changed, with the exception of the Twin Cities.

ISBN 0-9746940-0-2

Library of Congress Control Number 2003115991

WORD WARRIORS PRESS®

COVER ART: Satya Conger
COVER DESIGN: Lance Conger
INSIDE ART: Jeff Peterson and Elicia Blegen

If you receive this book without a cover, you should know that it has probably been stolen, but do not let that stop you from reading it.

For all those in pursuit of the truth.
May you have the courage and the strength
to face and accept what you find.

1

The First Time

I choke on the smell of burning flesh. Flames engulf dismembered hands, arms, legs. Black smoke covers blank faces. My eyes blister.

He's coming for me. I can't see him, but I know. I know I'm next.

A scream rings out, snapping my eyes open. There's water between my legs. A blue alarm clock with red digits comes out of the dark. I finally recognize my bedroom. Throwing off the covers, I run for the door, fling it open, and sprint up the stairs, leaving the darkness of the basement behind.

I furtively look over my shoulder as I walk through the living room and into my parents' bedroom. My dad's throat clicks with each breath as if something is caught there. My mom lies flat on her back with her mouth wide open. I tap lightly on her shoulder, then rush back against the wall. One time when I woke her up, I scared her and she split my lip open. She doesn't move. I step forward and nudge her harder. "Mom . . . Mom . . . "

She opens her eyes, blinks over and over again. Looks to her left, and then speaks. "What . . . Heather . . . Go back to bed."

I whisper, "I had a bad dream."

"It's just a dream," she sighs. "Go back to bed."

"But Mom, it was bad. Real bad. I dreamt I was in hell."

She's quiet for a moment. "Well, you know you won't go to

hell as long as you have asked for forgiveness from your sins. Do you want me to pray with you?"

I don't need any help praying to God for my forgiveness. At the age of six, I'd already been praying earnestly for my soul for years. "No," I reply softly.

Anyway, it wasn't the devil I was afraid of. It was God. God was the one who wanted to send people to hell.

I got saved for the first time when I was three. I told my mom I didn't want to go to hell and she led me through the prayer that would save my soul. I started getting saved on a regular basis. They said you only needed to do it once, but I wasn't taking any chances with burning forever and begging to die with no mercy. Ever. Besides, I already suspected something was wrong with me, that I was not like other little girls.

The first time I ever talked to anyone about it was the summer of fourth grade. I was riding my purple Huffy to the local pool, with the sun burning down on shoulders already peeling from their latest sunburn. I had left my body and was desperately trying to get back into it. It was as if there was a ladder in my head that I could crawl up to get out of myself and watch my body perform from somewhere above me. Once again, I had crawled up my ladder and watched myself ride my bike, looking down at my pink swimsuit with the hole in the middle, wondering when my blond hair had gotten so long. I wanted to get back into my body but couldn't get there. I hated it when I couldn't get back.

Sometimes I crawled up the ladder and was lost there for hours, sometimes for days. I never knew where I went when I didn't watch. It was as if I crawled up the ladder and disappeared into nothingness for a while. The ability to leave my body scared me because I'd lose pieces of time in my life. I had no idea why I did it; I just knew that I did. It dawned on me that afternoon that maybe other people didn't have a ladder. Maybe it was only in my brain. I decided to ask Philip, my older brother, when I got back home, hoping he'd assure me that I was fine and that the same thing happened to him.

Sitting cross-legged on his bed, watching him sort through his baseball cards for what seemed like the hundredth time, I asked Philip, "Do you ever forget where you are?"

He looked up at me. "What do you mean?"

"Well, like you watch yourself do things. But you're not there. You see yourself." It was so hard to explain. I kept trying. "You know you're real but you can't feel it? Like you float. Up above."

He cocked his head to the side, wrinkled his forehead, and frowned. "I have no idea what you're talking about." He went back to his cards.

Philip was my older brother and my best friend. In my eyes, he was wiser than I'd ever be. If he didn't know what I was talking about, then I'd better keep my ability a secret. I had lots of secrets so I figured that one more wouldn't matter. But even if I kept all of my secrets from other people, I knew there was no hiding from God because he was everywhere and saw everything. There was no escaping him.

"He can read your thoughts. He knows what you're thinking," my mother would warn. I'd feel ashamed because my thoughts were anything but pure. They were filled with rage. As much as I loved my brother, sometimes I hated him for the things he did when we were left alone in the house while my dad worked and my mom shopped. He'd terrorize my sister and me, locking me in closets and pummeling me with his scrawny fists while he sat on my chest and spat in my face. He'd force my sister into the dark unfinished basement and bury her inside the antique chest carried over by my ancestors from Sweden. He sat on top of it, listening to her screams.

I could do nothing to save her.

I would think of all the ways I could hurt him. I wanted so much to be able to destroy him with my fists the way he beat my sister and me. I wanted to make him cry and spit in his face the way he spat in mine. Every time we told on him, I hoped my father would punish him severely, but each time our tales were met with laughter and rebuke.

"Quit being a tattletale," Dad would respond. "You kids need to learn to get along."

"Philip's an abuser," Rebecca would say quietly, tears welling in her blue eyes while she stood slightly hidden behind my legs. She was only five the first time she said it. I don't know how she knew the word abuser, much less how to use it correctly. My father found this hilarious, as if she had just performed a stand-up comedy routine.

"Oh, Becca. You're exaggerating," he'd say through forced and purposeful laughter. His wasn't the kind of laughter that comes from the belly and explodes from the mouth. He made noises that sounded like a dry cough while he moved his mouth in an upward sneer.

The conversation always ended there. If my dad decided that a matter was insignificant, that was the end of the discussion. Each time I pushed or pressured an issue, my mother would admonish that I was not supposed to question my father in any way. It was our job to do as he told us. I don't know how many times over the years my mother told me men were above us in the order of things. She explained that there was a hierarchy in which God sat at the very top. Men were next in line, which meant that my father was the closest thing to God.

My father had a working partnership with God and he took his position very seriously. God had rules about everything. If you broke the rules you were a sinner and God punished sinners. He'd make your life miserable until you repented. The same rules applied in my house, only my dad punished the sins that occurred there.

Every time I disobeyed or had haughty eyes, my father threw me over his lap and held my legs down with one hand while his other hand gripped the white paddle that he had carved and painted himself. He'd say, "God loves us so much that he has to punish us. I'm doing this because I love you." He brought the paddle down on my butt over and over again with all his muscular force, extending his arm all the way up and then slamming it down. The longer it took for me to cry, the harder the paddle got and the longer it took before it was over.

If I argued with him about anything, he'd say, "You can't come out of your room until you can quit being angry and giving me those haughty eyes."

Sometimes in my room, when I was really mad, I'd twist the heads of my stuffed animals until I almost ripped them off. Other times I took my scissors and stabbed them in the stomach until white puffs came out and floated around my bedroom. I wasn't let out of my room until I could apologize for whatever transgression I'd committed. I'd apologize through gritted teeth, knowing that I wasn't really sorry and God knew I was lying. There was no way to win. I was a sinner.

Church was the central part of our family life. We went to church faithfully and consistently, but never to the same church for any length of time. Inevitably, my parents would find fault with the church's beliefs or practices and we'd move to a different one. But we always went to church. Sunday morning, Sunday evening, Wednesday night, and to any other Bible studies or church functions that were held during the week. If we couldn't make it to church for some reason, we'd have a service at home where we'd sing songs and Dad would preach a sermon.

I knew I needed to be at church. Us kids never went to

children's church with the other kids who were our age. We sat through the whole adult sermon. Philip hated it and Rebecca always fell asleep, but I never minded sitting through it because I knew I needed to be there. I sang so loud to the hymns that I hurt my throat. During prayer time, I squeezed my eyes shut so tightly that blue spots appeared as I begged God to not let me be scared of all the things I was afraid of. I strained my ears, trying to absorb every word the preacher spoke. I knew each time he talked about bad seeds, he was directing his sermon towards me. He used lots of big words that I didn't understand, but once I got home I looked them up in my parents' big dictionary.

No matter how long we stayed at a church, my parents were seen as upstanding members. My dad led Bible studies, prayer groups, and served communion on Sundays. My mother taught Bible school and stood by my father's side at all church functions. They had the pastor over for dinner and people from the church regularly came to the house to pray with my father in the living room. He was respected and revered. My mother was the picture of a perfect Christian wife, supportive of my father one hundred percent and submissive to his every word. She bustled around taking care of people, always the perfect hostess at dinners.

"You have such a wonderful family," fellow church members said. "Your children are so well behaved."

My mother told us kids that her extended family wasn't saved. We were to look at them as examples of what would happen if we didn't stay on the right path. They all drank, and drinking was something for people who weren't saved. She'd point to her father and say with a warning, "Look at him. You don't want to end up that way."

At family functions, I saw what alcohol did to the adults. Their first few drinks seemed liked fun. They'd get all giddy and laugh about silly things. They paid attention to my cousins and me, impressed with anything we did. Our somersaults and cartwheels, that usually went unnoticed, were suddenly applauded. Sometimes they acted like children: free and careless, playing games with us. But inevitably, there came a time when the silliness disappeared, replaced by angry outbursts. My grandpa would start yelling at my grandma about something trivial she had said or done, like forgetting to get the mail from the end of the driveway. Uncles waged wars against the aunts for unknown reasons. My mother would run in and out of rooms, trying to quiet the storms. Us kids would head downstairs to the basement or outside to hide from the chaos.

Everyone called my grandpa an alcoholic. I didn't understand what that meant so I always studied him carefully. He had a big nose that seemed to take up his whole face. It intrigued me. Sometimes it was purple and at other times it had red squiggly lines running a tangled web through the skin. His eyes always watered. At times the water was so thick it seemed almost solid, like snot that might start moving down his face if he blinked hard enough. And his skin turned color, moving from a yellowish green to a swollen red. His words slurred, like he had a mouthful of marbles that he had to speak around. And even though my grandma was the smoker, he coughed and cleared his throat constantly.

When we went up north to visit, he never met us in the driveway like Grandma did. We'd have to wait for his entrance, sitting around the kitchen table. Eventually we'd see him walking towards the porch door, crooked and hunched over. He'd walk across the porch and into the kitchen with his beer in his right hand, tucked neatly inside an Old Milwaukee coolie.

"Hi, Dad!" my mom would pipe up the minute he was inside. She'd jump up from her seat to stand in front of him, announcing her presence bodily so he'd know she was there.

"Oh, Carol," he'd exclaim, stopping in his tracks, always

surprised to see her. His body swayed back and forth slightly as he fidgeted with things on the table.

Philip, Becca, and I eagerly waited to be given our freedom to play on the farm. But first we had to give our ritual greeting in unison: "Hi, Grandpa."

He'd respond with a hello, looking over our heads towards the window. I don't ever remember a time when my grandpa spoke to me directly or called me by my first name. He'd commence to talk to my mom and it was the same questions every time.

"How's the weather?"

My mom would describe what the weather was like in our town, five hours south. They always seemed to be fascinated with the weather.

"How was traffic?"

My mom would relate in detail all the roads where traffic got thick and our progress had been slowed. Her report included any areas of construction along the way, and she never forgot to mention Interstate 494, which Grandpa seemed to have a keen interest in at all times. Finally, she'd comment on anything that was out of the ordinary, like a deer or an accident.

"How long are you staying?"

It never mattered how long we were staying, my grandpa's response was always the same. He seemed happy that we were staying, whether it was for two days or two weeks. Sometimes I wasn't even sure if he knew that time had passed since our last visit. He seemed oblivious, like he might not have noticed Christmas if it wasn't for the huge tree in the living room. "Where's Mark?"

It was very unusual to see my mother doing anything without my father, but most of the time when we stayed at my Grandma's, my father stayed with his sister who lived a town away. He stopped in occasionally to see us, or to eat supper at the long table piled with food.

My mom never tired of trying to communicate with my grandpa. Every day that we stayed there my mom would get up at five in the morning to sit with him. She said it was the soberest you could ever get him. Every time we left, my mother would give us kids the warning to stay away from the sin of alcohol.

So I was taken by surprise when I took my first drink that it didn't feel at all like a sin. I didn't get the horrible pit in my stomach or the sticky palms that other sins gave me. It was the summer of sixth grade and I was twelve. It happened at my neighbor's house, the Engbergs, the people behind us on our dead-end street. A chain link fence separated our backyards. My parents disapproved of the Engbergs, but then they disapproved of most people. Other people were of this world and our family was not; we were "born-again Christians." The Engbergs attended St. John's Lutheran Church down the block faithfully, but they still weren't saved. My parents had an amazing ability to know the fate of people's souls, and the majority of them were going straight to hell.

Not only were they Lutheran, but Mr. Engberg owned the only bar in town, a heinous crime against God. On the weekends, cars would cover the length of their driveway and extend into the street. My mom would roll her eyes and say, "Looks like the Engbergs are having another party." My dad would nod his head and glare like they were committing murder behind us.

Alexandra Engberg was my age. My parents didn't like for us to play together but occasionally they'd allow it. Every time they relented, my mom would watch carefully, certain Alex would steal one of my toys.

Late one afternoon, my mom let me go to Alex's as long as I promised to be home for supper at five. I was always excited to play with the "bad girl." Trying to be good all the time was tiresome. We jumped outside on her trampoline for a while, though my mom had strict adult-watching rules for that.

After a while we got bored and went inside to rest. As we walked into the kitchen I knew immediately, by the bottles of booze scattered all over the counter, that it was the night of one of their wild parties. I eyed a bowl of the forbidden "parents' punch." Alex's parents were nowhere in sight. We looked at the punch bowl and then back at each other. I don't know who chose to voice out loud what we were both thinking, but one of us said, "Let's drink it."

Alex grabbed two small punch glasses and filled them to the top. We giggled with the excitement born of the fear of getting caught. But we successfully carried the glasses into Alex's bedroom and locked the door behind us. After carefully setting the glasses on the dresser, we collapsed on the bed, laughing hysterically.

"Shh!" I warned through my laughter. I eyed my glass, wondering about this magical potion that made adults act either like silly children or get so mad that they threw things.

I picked mine up, silent now. This was a serious matter. Feeling like Alice in Wonderland, I sipped slowly, slightly scared of what might happen. I swished the punch around in my mouth, savoring the strange taste. It was different than anything my taste buds had been blessed with before, very sweet and thick. I swallowed with more force than was usually required. As the liquid went down my throat, it left a warm trail that went through my veins and all the way to my stomach. Tingles coursed all through my body. I shivered, looked at Alex, and smiled.

It was my first real smile.

I was surprised to see Alex's pudgy face all scrunched up, with her lips turned up towards her nose. "Ick," she exclaimed, "This stuff is gross."

What was wrong with her? I took another drink and another until I emptied my glass and felt the thick sweetness coated inside my mouth. I knew why people drank. This was incredible.

I wanted more of the punch and to stay for the party, but I looked at the clock and saw that I was almost late for supper. If I wasn't home on time my mom would huff exaggerated sighs all through dinner with her lips pressed together tightly, holding back the words and refusing to look at me.

When I stepped back outside, the world looked different. I didn't remember the sun shining so brightly before, but now it was beaming down on me. My body felt like it was humming a tune all its own. I felt wild with excitement.

I had spent my entire life living in fear of doing bad things. I constantly worried about the paddle I'd get across my butt if I stepped out of line, and I knew perfectly well what God did to girls who were bad. But at that moment, none of it seemed to matter. It was the first time I didn't care about being bad and I wasn't scared of God either. I could breathe without feeling as if I'd choke on the air.

I didn't know how much you had to drink before someone could smell it but I didn't want to take any chances. When I sat at the dinner table, I tried to hold my breath. I couldn't put food in my mouth until after my dad prayed, but as soon as the prayer ended, I stuffed my mouth full of food.

Supper was always a troublesome time at our house. We all had to be very careful not to upset my father. He sat at the head of the table, which was appropriate since his moods dictated the event. If he was in a good mood, things ran smoothly. We could all talk and laugh about our day. But if he was in a bad mood, things were entirely different. He seethed anger as he ate. The silent anger was almost worse than the outward bursts. When he brooded, his appearance changed and his movements became robotic, each move made with distinct force and precision. His face tightened and his forehead lined with stress. He looked as if he was in physical pain. My dad's eyes, usually blue, turned dark and cold.

His overpowering silence and demeanor were our cue to be silent during the meal. But sometimes we'd miss the cue. We'd giggle and act like children. Anything could set him off and then someone would get yanked off the chair and pulled into a bedroom for the wooden paddle.

While we screamed and cried, he'd paddle us until our butts stung and burned. When he was done he'd say, "You can come back to the supper table as long as you can behave yourself."

It was hard to decide whether or not I could behave myself since most of the time I didn't even know what I'd done wrong. Were my eyes haughty again? Had I been swinging my legs without knowing it? Or was it nothing? Sometimes I refused to go back to the table just to prove my point that I hadn't done anything wrong. But he'd always return to his spot at the head and the meal would resume as if nothing had happened. Whoever was left at the table would follow his lead quietly.

"Hon, did you get enough to eat?" my mother would ask as he sat back down. "Do you want anything else?"

But tonight was different. Supper didn't bother me at all. I didn't even care if I made him mad. Released from the looming control of his anger, I felt separated from the rest of the family. The usual heaviness that hung over the dinner table wasn't there for me. Light and free, I smiled at my secret.

That glass filled with the shimmering liquid from the punch

bowl had awakened inside of me a hunger that, until that day, I never knew I had. Now I understood that I'd been empty ever since I could remember. I had never fit into this world that looked good on the outside but that slowly killed from the inside. Part of my soul had gone missing, but I didn't know how or when.

For the first time, I felt whole. The emptiness inside me was gone, replaced by a warm glow that made my entire world look brighter and more bearable. I had to have more.

2

The Honeymoon Period

I fell in love with alcohol the same way a young girl falls head over heals for a cute boy. I looked forward to the next time I could get drunk the same way you'd look forward to going out on the next date. Everything about alcohol, from the taste and smell of it to the way the bottle felt in my hand, made me ecstatic about my new relationship.

I was immersed in my honeymoon period with alcohol when Eric Graham moved to town in seventh grade. We called him by his last name and he was never known as anything else. Graham was a short kid whose squinty eyes and shiny, black hair made him appear Asian, though he was as white as white boys come. He entered the small town school and quickly found his place among my crowd, even though he didn't follow the rules for being cool that were a requirement for my group.

My crowd was considered "the popular ones." Our group had been established since elementary school. Every grade has the "cool kids" and we had always been it. There are specific rules for being cool in a small town.

The first and most important rule is that you have to dress cool. You have to wear the best clothes, which at that time meant Girbaud jeans, strategically rolled at the ankles. I saved my babysitting money year 'round to afford my designer clothes, since my mom refused to buy them. Graham wore the standard Girbaud jeans, but his were always two sizes too big and he never tucked in his shirt.

Besides the clothes, being cool meant being attractive and competing for being the best looking. But it was important to pretend at all times that you cared nothing about this competition. The key was to always be a player in the game but to never let anyone know you were playing. The game was hard for me because I never felt like I beat the competition. I wanted to be skinnier and to replace my dirty blond hair with the beautiful, sun-blond hair of the girls I envied. Despite my misgivings, the kids at school thought I was attractive. No one even considered Graham to be competition because he was barely over five feet tall and his feet pointed out to the sides, which made him waddle like a duck when he walked.

To be cool, you also have to be smart and get good grades. I had no problem in that area. I could ace a test without a second of preparation or study. I never had to bring work home to still end up on the A honor roll. Graham, on the other hand, barely got Cs and spent his time in class cracking jokes.

Another rule was that you had to play sports well, and I was very athletic. Sports had always been a part of my family life. I'd spent many hours in the driveway shooting hoops with my dad while he coached me on technique.

"Look up, don't look down. Look at me!" he'd instruct, trying to tip the ball out of my hands as I dribbled past him.

"Practice your free throws. You've gotta make your free throws. So many games come down to the line." One summer, I shot a hundred free throws a day to make sure I never lost a game at the line.

I'd grown up tagging along with my brother and all the other boys on my block who played sports at Jack's, a vacant field at the end of our street. I had to constantly fight to disprove the remark, "She can't play, she's a girl." I made sure I could do everything just as good or even better than the boys.

My mom would map out distances for me to run and then show me exactly where I had to go to achieve the desired miles. When I had a race coming up, she'd take me to the golf course where the meets were held and time me with her watch.

"Run! Go faster!" she'd yell, jumping up and down like she did at the real meets. "You can do it! You're almost there!"

All the practice and hard work paid off. In a school as small as mine, if you're a good enough athlete, the coaches move you up to play on the high school varsity teams. I was one of only two seventh graders on the varsity cross-country team. I played basketball for my school and for a traveling team made up of the elite. I started every game of the season and was the leading point scorer. In the spring, I ran varsity track. My parents rarely missed a meet or a game. They were my biggest fans, as well as my harshest critics.

An entire wall of my bedroom was devoted to my accomplishments. A collection of medals, trophies, and ribbons hung on the shelves. I had trophies and plaques from basketball tournaments where I was named to the All-Tournament Team, a team made up of the ten best players in the area. My gold and silver medals from cross-country meets hung on the wall, waiting for the day they would be pinned on a letterman's jacket. There were pegs that held the blue ribbons I'd achieved in freestyle swimming races.

My entire crowd consisted of jocks. I felt like what I lacked in looks, I made up for in athletics. I never knew if I was going to hold the coveted position of the most beautiful girl at school, but I knew if there was a sport to be played, I'd be the one to take home the prize.

It became a standard joke in our crowd that the only sports

Graham played were the ones on his computer in his bedroom. Despite his sloppy clothes, mediocre grades, and lack of athletic skills, Graham quickly found his place in our crowd. He had a huge house, a teenage paradise. His father owned the local funeral parlor and was always away attending to the town dead. His mom was never there either.

We spent our time in the living room on the main floor. There was a huge TV against the center wall with surround sound, a comfortable black sofa against the wall directly in front of the TV, and reclining chairs placed in both of the corners by the stone fireplace. Through sliding glass doors was another area filled with small tables and chairs. There was an eight-person hot tub in the corner that I got thrown into on more than one occasion. The stereo set up in the living room had speakers strategically placed all over the house, carrying the latest music throughout.

Two stairs led down to the kitchen from the living room. It was an ordinary kitchen with a white tiled floor, white cupboards and the standard appliances. My favorite part of the kitchen was the corner taken up by a fully stocked liquor cabinet that was never locked. The cabinet held every imaginable kind of liquor.

Graham introduced us to the liquor cabinet the first time he had a party, and the format was the same every time. He'd grab tall glasses from the cupboard and set them on the counter. Then he'd grab a bottle of Malibu and pour a small portion into the glass. Next, he'd grab the Windsor Canadian, Absolute Vodka, Blue 100, and Captain Morgan's Spiced Rum, pouring parts of each into the glasses until they were full.

"We've got to switch which bottles we drink out of," he'd instruct us.

I always made sure I got the first glass. Taking a huge drink, my body would shake and twitch as my stomach threatened to reject it. I'd close my eyes and take a deep breath before the next swallow. After the first few gulps got choked down, it was easy to drink the rest.

Inevitably, Alex or one of my other girlfriends would come up behind me to sniff my glass. "That is so gross! I can't believe you drink that."

I'd throw my head back, finishing off the glass, wipe my lips and smile. "I don't care. I just wanna get drunk."

Whichever girl it was would roll her eyes at me and return to sitting in the living room with the rest of the girls, watching as I got drunk with the boys. None of the girls drank except for me, but I didn't care. We quit hanging out anywhere besides Graham's on the weekends.

After the Friday night football game, we'd all go to Graham's. He had two older brothers who, even though they didn't live there, were always hanging around. One particular night, both his brothers happened to be there and had brought a friend. Graham and I were the first of our crowd to arrive and find them sprawled out on the furniture with glasses in their hands and drunken smiles on their faces.

Mike, the second oldest, yelled, "Eric, c'mon in!"

"I'm the one that lives here. Ya don't have to invite me in." Graham laughed. "Did you guys buy booze?"

Nick, getting up from his spot on the couch and stepping down the stairs into the kitchen said, "Yep, no drinking mom and pops' tonight." Grabbing an unopened bottle of vodka from the table and handing it to us, Nick added, "Here, little man. You and your girl can drink this." He thumped Graham on the back with his hand before going back into the living room.

The front door opened. Teenage laughter and voices drifted in as people took off their shoes and hung their coats on the rack.

"Graham," I whispered in his ear, "let's go in your room to drink this."

He smiled and nodded. We ran up the stairs giggling. Neither of us wanted to share our treasure. We locked ourselves in his bedroom and plopped down on the bed, pushing all of his comic books onto the floor. We opened the bottle and passed it back and forth.

"Did you see Derick looking at you?" Graham asked, handing the bottle to me after he'd taken his turn. "I think he wants you."

"Was he the guy standing against the wall, staring?" I asked.

"It's Mike's fr . . . shit!" He had knocked over the ashtray, spilling butts onto the comforter. We started laughing uncontrollably. "Anyways, he's Mike's friend. Nick has been bringing him over to the house lately. I guess he just got divorced or something."

Looking back, I should have thought it was odd that Derick was interested in me. I was in seventh grade and he'd graduated years ago. But I didn't pay it any attention.

"I love you, Graham," I said, as my head started to swim and my thoughts grew fuzzy. "I need a smoke, gimme one."

"I'm out," he replied, picking up the butts and placing them back in the ashtray.

I took the bottle back from him for a pull. "I'm gonna go see if I can talk Nick or Mike into taking me uptown. I'll be back in a minute."

I made my way down the stairs. Then I made the rounds, asking all the older guys for a ride to the gas station and someone to buy cigarettes for me. Derick stood up from his spot on the couch.

"I'll give ya a ride, sweetie," he said. "Let's go."

I followed him outside to his green truck and climbed in on the passenger side. It had gotten really dark and the minute I shut the door behind me, I felt uncomfortable. I tried to act like I wasn't nervous and anxiously played with the loose threads of the fraying mesh seat cover as my stomach did little flip-flops.

When we were a few blocks from Graham's, he murmured in a

husky voice, "Don't sit so far away." I moved closer, within his hand's reach. The space between us was too close. My chest tightened.

He was talking about something. I heard his voice but not his words. One minute his hands were on the wheel and the next minute one of his big hands was underneath my shirt. I'd had a couple of boys' hands underneath my shirt, but this was different. This was a grown-up man's hand. It was big and strong, rough and calloused. He pulled my bra up over my breasts. My face felt hot and my head pounded like there was a bomb inside.

I started chatting and laughing. I couldn't talk fast enough. I talked about football and school. I acted as if nothing was happening, like he wasn't really pinching and pulling at my nipples until they hurt, or sliding his hand over the breasts that were barely more than two small lumps on my chest.

After what seemed like hours, we reached the gas station. As he got out of the truck, he gave me a smile like he was really proud of himself. I moved as fast as I could to the other side of the truck, kicking the empty bottles and papers at my feet out of the way. I pulled my bra down and tried to breathe. I kept telling myself that it wasn't a big deal, like what just happened didn't really happen.

He returned all too quickly with my Marlboro Reds. The journey back to Graham's began. I rhythmically packed and packed my cigarettes on my hand in a long drawn-out staccato beat. Somehow I knew that these cigarettes would keep him away. He wouldn't intrude on my sacred act of smoking. I made an exaggerated production of carefully unwrapping the cellophane from the pack and removing a cigarette. I searched for my lighter, even though I knew it was in my pocket. Finally, my cigarette was lit and in my mouth. I was sure I was almost back to safety.

Then, without a word, he turned away from Graham's, and towards the empty parking lot at a run-down motel.

"What are we doing?" I asked, amazed that I had found my voice again.

"I just want to talk to you." He turned off the engine and the headlights. "I really like you."

In two seconds, he crawled next to me and pushed me back against the seat. His calloused hands were all over my body, pulling and poking. I stared at the pieces of green paint chipping off the ceiling of the cab. He started kissing my neck and covering my face with slobber. I kept moving my head, looking out the stained windows at the shadows moving around in the darkness, so that he would miss my lips. His breathing was heavy against me. My mind told my body to move, to open the door and run like hell, but I was frozen to the seat. My mind told my mouth to scream, to yell, to tell him to get the fuck away from me, but I was mute.

He unzipped his pants and pulled out his cock. It was huge. I closed my eyes because I couldn't bear the sight of it. He grabbed my hand and put it on his cock. I could barely fit my fingers around it. I didn't know what to do with it. It was the most repulsive thing I'd ever touched.

Swallowing back the taste of bile in my throat that threatened to escape from my mouth, I looked at his face. His eyes had turned angry and cold. They'd turned from blue to black stones. I knew I'd seen this look before, but I couldn't remember where or when. I quickly looked back up to the ceiling, concentrating on the design that remained from the missing paint. He took my hand from his cock and spit into the palm of it. Then he put his hand on top of mine and began to move it up and down and up and down on his cock. My head felt like it was about to explode and spray pieces of my brain on the windshield. My thoughts raced so fast I couldn't discern any particular one. I felt the puke rise in my throat and fall back down, over and over again, with the motions he made with my hand. Finally, with a groan that sounded like an animal, he sprayed his putrid white semen onto my stomach. I breathed a sigh of relief. I knew that it was over.

He grabbed a towel from the floor that was crusted with some substance that looked like oil. He wiped himself off and tucked himself back inside his pants.

"Here," he said, throwing me the towel with a look of disgust. "Clean yourself up."

I wiped off my stomach as best I could and he started the truck back up. On the way back to Graham's, he looked straight ahead at the road and didn't utter a word. I lit up another cigarette and inhaled deeply. The booze that was in the liquor cabinet would be waiting for me when I got there.

It never even occurred to me to tell anyone what happened, but my crush on alcohol quickly grew into an obsession. *I want to get drunk* became a pounding thought that reverberated in my head, over and over again. I couldn't drink during the week because Graham was my drinking partner and the one time I asked him to drink on a Monday night, he looked at me like I was crazy. I had no choice but to wait for the weekend, which became harder and harder to do.

At a school dance in eighth grade, my boyfriend broke up with me. It was the first time I'd ever been dumped. I sat on the bleachers waiting for Sean. Instead, his friend Luke appeared.

"Sean doesn't want to go out with you anymore," he announced. I stared at him, expecting him to say more, but his eyes were busy darting around the room checking out the girls wearing tight shirts. He tapped his white tennis shoes together. "Well . . . um . . . see ya." Turning his back, he stepped carefully down the bleachers to the gym floor filled with teenage bodies.

I sat silently on the bleachers, watching bodies move to the music. Sean walked in with his arm around a skinny girl, whose sun-blond hair fell halfway down her back in waves.

I wanted to run down the bleachers and slap his face, but pride held me in place. I felt the lump lodged in my throat but I refused to cry, especially in front of people. It was a badge I wore proudly, that nobody besides my family had ever seen me cry. If you cry, people know they've hurt you. I vowed at a very young age never to let anyone know they hurt me.

But I had to do something. Graham hadn't brought any booze and I was empty handed as well. I got up from the bleachers and walked outside through the parking lot, hoping I would run into somebody who had a bottle to share. I heard footsteps behind me and turned to see Alex running to catch me.

"What's wrong?" she asked, matching my stride.

"Nothin'." She knew by the absence of expression on my face that she shouldn't ask me any more questions.

She walked silently by my side, down the gravel road in front of the school. No cars drove by and we saw nobody. Suddenly a brilliant idea came to me. "Hey, let's go back to the dance and pretend we're drunk!"

She looked at me strangely but refrained from stating the obvious. I grabbed her arm and turned her back toward the school.

"C'mon, it'll be fun!"

I walked back into the gym with a smile on my face and a bounce in my step. I skipped over to Sam, an older guy on my cross-country team, and grabbed his arm.

"Dance with me!" I demanded, pulling him onto the floor, making sure I was close enough for Sean to see. The music throbbed and I moved up on Sam, grinding my pelvis against him seductively. He grabbed my ass and smiled at my aggression.

"Are you drunk?" he asked through a wide smile that showed all his teeth. "Do you ever come to these things sober?"

I giggled, "Yep, I'm drunk."

I finished with him and moved on to the next guy. I threw

myself on him and did my best dirty dancing routine. I was dancing with my third guy when Alex grabbed my arm.

"I've gotta talk to you," she demanded, pulling me off to the side. I stumbled along, letting myself be dragged.

She looked straight at me with her hands on her hips. "What are you doing?"

"Nothin'. Havin' a good time. I'm drunk."

She rolled her eyes at me and let go of my arm. "Whatever." She huffed and turned to walk away, but I caught what she muttered under her breath: "Something's wrong with you."

Alex started to look at me differently that night. It wasn't long after that before the other girls in my crowd started to see me in a different light, too. They started giving each other concerned looks when I'd disappear with Graham and return drunk. They'd catch me sneaking shots and roll their eyes. I started to look at them differently, too. They weren't much fun anymore. Even Alex seemed kind of boring. Their looks towards each other seemed snotty and I felt insulted. They put up with me because they liked boys and wherever I went, boys followed.

One day in English, while we sat doing our homework together, my friend Tracy asked me, "Don't you get nervous around Graham and those guys?"

"Not at all. I'm like one of them."

I never told my girlfriends about what sometimes happened with the guys. I never told them about the night with Derick or the night with Rich, the guy who came next in line and would be followed by others.

Rich was a friend of Alex's older cousin, Dan. Alex had invited Dan and his friend to a party she decided to throw while her parents were out of town. Alex and I were the only girls. Graham brought Peter with him. Alex had a crush on Peter for years. She spent the entire night outside in the camper making out with him. I didn't mind. I was happy to sit in the living room with the guys and drink.

I sat on the couch with Rich next to me. He smelled like a mixture of body odor and Old Spice, which made me want to laugh because the only person I knew who wore Old Spice was my grandfather. He kept looking at me with a lopsided grin, exposing teeth that looked like they'd been randomly stuck in his gums at all sorts of angles.

"So, I hear you used to go out with Rodriguez?" he asked, leaning close to me so that I could smell his rancid breath.

"Yeah."

"What's it like being with a Mexican?" He put his arm around my shoulder. "Is it true they have small dicks?"

I knocked his arm off my shoulder. "Fuck you. None of your business."

I got up from the couch and moved to the floor next to Graham, who was playing solitaire. But every time I moved, Rich relentlessly followed. And every time he opened his mouth, he said something sexual. After he made a comment about my breasts starting to grow, I replied, "God, you are nasty."

Eventually I got tired of shooting him down. He refused to quit and the sound of his voice was beginning to make me want to choke him. I was tired of pushing him away so I decided to curl up on the couch and pretend to sleep, tucking myself into a ball and closing my eyes. For a while I had some peace, listening to the guys carrying on without me.

I lay with my eyes closed but I could feel the presence of someone invading my space. My senses were keen and always on alert, so I knew when someone was near. When I felt a hand begin to rub my thigh, I shook it off.

"Mmmph . . . " I mumbled, trying to sound convincingly sleepy. I rolled over so my head faced the back of the couch.

The hand returned to my leg and caressed it. I lay perfectly still. The hand moved up and tried to get between my thighs. I cringed and locked my knees. I knew it was Rich. It had to be. The sounds of the small party continued on. I listened to the guys' voices talking and laughing.

One of the guys said, "Rich!"

"What?" he said, feigning innocence.

They all laughed.

"You're a dog," Graham said sloppily, which brought more shrieks of laughter.

Unable to speak the words out loud, I screamed in my head. *Tell him to stop. Do something. Don't just sit there. Tell him to leave me alone, for God's sake.*

I fumed inside. What could I do, though? If I jumped up and got mad then they'd know I'd only been pretending to sleep. They'd think that I wanted this and if I said I didn't, they wouldn't believe me. They'd make fun of me like they made fun of all the other girls who acted like girls. I knew I could no longer be one of the guys if I acted like a girl. I decided I had no choice but to lie there silently and wait for it to be over.

Dear God, I prayed silently and earnestly. *I know I'm messing up big time lately, but please don't punish me this time. Please don't let this last long. Make him stop. If you make him stop, I promise I'll start cleaning up my act.*

I lay stiffly while Rich reached under my shirt to play with my breasts. I tried to tell myself that he wasn't doing it. I focused on not feeling his hand. I focused so hard that eventually I didn't feel it. I didn't feel my body at all. It was like my body was asleep but my mind was awake. I listened to the music and let the voice of Steven Tyler carry me away.

"I have to pee." Rich's voice startled me, jolting me back to reality. I felt him leave my side and heard his steps to the bathroom.

The door clicked shut behind him.

I sat up sleepily and rubbed my eyes. I made a production of stretching and yawning, as if I'd just had the most peaceful sleep. Graham and Dan were the only two guys left. Graham was passing in and out on the floor in front of the TV. Dan was lounging on the blue recliner.

"Christ, I guess I was tired." I faked another yawn.

Graham slurred from his position on the brown carpet, "What happened to partying all night?"

"I guess I had more to drink than I thought I did." In my head, I was thinking that I hadn't had nearly enough.

"Hey Heather, I bet I can pee through the whole national anthem," Dan challenged, holding up an empty milk carton. "I drank all this."

Rich appeared from the bathroom. I jumped up.

I said, practically running to stand outside in the hallway, "Let's hear you do it. I'm ready to sing. You gotta leave the door open so I know you don't cheat."

The next morning, I told Alex that I had sung the entire national anthem while Dan peed and that I had finished the entire song and gotten halfway through it a second time before he finished. We laughed and laughed. I never mentioned what happened with Rich. Graham and Dan never said anything to me about it and I threw it aside, telling myself that it wasn't a big deal. I'd just have to stay away from Rich so it wouldn't happen again. After a while, I erased the incident from my mind. When I told the story of that night it went like this: I was just one of the guys who stayed up all night partying at Alex's house while her parents were gone. I watched Dan take the longest pee ever while I sang the national anthem off-key, with my own lyrics added when I forgot the real words.

3

A New Life

"Margarita . . . Margarita . . . " My Spanish teacher, Mrs. Quimby, was calling out my Spanish name.

I shook my head and looked up at her through stoned eyes. "Uh, I don't know?"

She frowned and called on someone else. I looked at the clock and discovered that class was almost over and I'd missed all of it because I was high. Sure, I'd been sitting there but mentally I'd checked out as soon as I sat down. I wasn't in my chair. I wasn't surrounded by the kids who'd given me dirty looks when I walked in late. I wasn't thirteen. I wasn't me. I was somebody else. Somebody who didn't care. Somebody unaffected by others, who couldn't be touched.

Whenever I smoked pot, I experienced the same transcendence I did when I'd climb up the ladder in my head and disappear. I had other head games that I played as well. My favorite one was to create a character for myself, usually an orphan girl, and transport myself to live in her world for a few hours. Whenever I wanted to, I could look down from above at my body and watch myself perform. I'd stare down at myself and wonder why I was that girl, wishing I never had to go back inside the body. It was the body that housed me, but the real me was my mind. Anything could happen to the body, but no one could touch the mind. Pot allowed me to just be the mind anytime I wanted to. I could disconnect from the world like I'd always done and retreat to my special places, but it didn't take any mental effort.

I was in the grip of a downward spiral that felt so much better than any God I had ever known. Since I was already doomed and going to hell, it became very easy to destroy myself completely. I broke all the rules I'd been instructed to adhere to since I was a toddler. I lied so much that eventually I believed my own lies. I couldn't even remember what it was like to be a virgin. I stole to get what I wanted, or sometimes just for the thrill of getting away with something. I started to seriously hate God.

By ninth grade, I'd become a druggie poster child. Although I used to work so hard to maintain my appearance, I rarely wore make-up now, which just made the dark circles under my eyes all the more apparent. Long hair hung in my face and I went days without washing it. I traded in my designer labels for baggy jeans and big T-shirts that hid the weight I was losing.

I was moved from the gifted and talented classes, but even in the regular classes my grades continued to fall. I skipped my classes most of the time and if I happened to be in one, I either fell asleep at my desk or created a disturbance to get myself kicked out. One minute I'd cuss and yell at anyone near me, but the next minute I'd be sullen and depressed, withdrawing from any contact with people. My emotional outbursts were erratic and unpredictable.

The only part of my old identity that I still cared about was basketball. Even though I missed most of my classes, I still tried to make it to practice. My athletic photo from ninth grade is distinctively different from the pictures taken in previous years. My picture from the year before shows me kneeling next to three other players with a wide grin on my face and a ball in my hands. My face is fresh and clear, my hair pulled into a tight ponytail. My body is muscular and strong.

In my ninth grade picture, I'm alone, leaning against a wall with my shoulders hunched over, holding a basketball. My body no longer has the strong confident muscles of an athlete. My eyes are red and the lids heavy. My head cocks to the side and the marks of a fading hickey bruise my neck. The left side of my lip rises in a half-hearted attempt to smile.

When I brought the pictures home, Mom sighed, "You look high in this picture."

I ignored her comment. "Tomorrow I find out if I get moved up."

A few days earlier, the ninth grade coach had gathered the team together and informed us that the varsity coach would be choosing a few players to be moved up to play on his team. I had a sinking suspicion that I wasn't going to be one of the chosen few.

"I don't think I'm gonna make it," I said. "I'm pretty sure the coach hates me."

"Well, let's say a prayer about it." My mom moved from her seated position on the couch to kneel beside it. I kneeled beside her. I figured she was on much better terms with God than I was. Maybe her prayers would be heard.

"Dear heavenly father," she began. "We come to you today to ask that you would be with Heather. Help her to be able to play varsity. You know how much this means to her. We ask these things in Jesus' name. Amen."

She waited a few minutes with her head bowed to see if I wanted to pray out loud. When I kept my mouth shut, she stood up. I turned to look at her. "If I don't make the team, I'm giving up on God forever."

She laughed nervously. "Oh Heather, don't say that. You know he loves you." All I really knew was that he watched every move I made and laughed at the punishments I got each time I screwed up.

The next day at practice, I stood in line next to the rest of the players, listening as the names of all the girls I'd always played with were called. I was left standing with the girls who had been substitutes for me. They'd sat on the bench, only playing when one of us needed a break. Now, I'd be playing with them. I stormed into the varsity coach's office.

I demanded, hands on my hips and my chin pointed out, "How come I didn't get moved up?"

"It's simple," he said, pulling basketballs out of the wire container. "I can't have someone who skips school and uses drugs on my varsity team."

"That's bullshit!" I yelled. "I still play ball just as good as I ever did. I've played with Paige and those guys since third grade. We've always been a team. They can't play without me."

He set the balls down and looked me directly in the eye. "I think they'll do just fine without you. But I'll tell you what. You start going to school, get your grades up, quit messin' around with drugs, and we'll see if you can play on my team. How's that?"

"How's this?" I replied, kicking a ball in his direction. "You can take your basketball and shove it up your ass! I ain't playin fuckin' ball anymore."

I turned and walked away, slamming the door behind me. *This can't be happening.* I slowed down, listening for his voice to call out to me, to tell me it was all a mistake, a big misunderstanding. His voice didn't come. God had just taken away from me the last thing I cared about. "Damn you, God!" I grunted out loud, heading for the locker room to clean out my locker.

Everyone I knew had turned against me. They were all part of a big conspiracy to get me to change back into the compliant, good girl that they wanted me to be. Everyone was in on it: my parents, my teachers, my friends, the school principal, and my brother. God sat at the top of the hierarchy, orchestrating it all.

I'd spent my childhood years in a prison of thou-shalt-nots, and for the first time I felt free. Drugs had opened my eyes and my mind to a freedom I didn't know could be mine. There was no way I was going to let anyone take it away. I was determined to defend my newfound freedom at all costs.

Despite my protests, I was sent to see the school guidance counselor, Mrs. Rush, whose job usually consisted of helping people plan their careers. I slouched in the chair in her office with my arms folded across my chest, glaring at her, ready to do battle. Her blue glasses were too big for her narrow face. She nervously pushed them up her nose and then folded her hands on top of her desk.

"Heather, do you know why you're here?"

"Nope." *Is she an idiot?*

"Well, people are concerned about you . . . "

"Yeah, right. Nobody gives a shit."

"Now Heather, you can't use language like that." She pushed her glasses up her nose again and moved back in her chair.

"Whatever." Defiantly, I unfolded my arms and began tapping my fingers on the wooden armrest.

In the voice a kindergarten teacher uses when she tells her students not to run in the hallway, Mrs. Rush admonished, "Let's try to use nice language." I laughed out loud.

She cleared her throat. "This isn't funny."

I folded my arms again and crossed my legs, watching the tips of her ears get red. "I think it is."

"Well, you seem to be a different student this year. You've always gotten good grades but now you are in danger of failing ninth grade. Do you know why?" She sat straight up in her chair, obviously trying to gain some control of the situation.

"Because I don't go to class and I really don't care."

She blinked a few times in rapid succession. Then she continued, "We've also noticed that you've changed your group of friends. Did something happen between you and your friends? Did you get into a fight?"

Did we get into a fight? C'mon lady. What are you gonna do, make us sit down with cookies and milk to talk it over? I retreated into silence, staring at her with angry eyes as she nervously poked at her glasses and rearranged papers on her desk. Finally, she inhaled deeply through her nose and let it all come out slowly through her mouth.

She returned to her kindergarten teacher voice. "I'm just going to ask you . . . Are you on drugs?"

I laughed.

"Well . . . uh . . . we just want to help you."

I leaned forward, resting my elbows on her desk. "Ya know, you keep saying 'we' and I don't get it. Who the hell is we?"

"Your parents. Your teachers. Your old friends. Mr. McKinnsey."

"Oh, yeah. I bet Mr. McKinnsey really wants to help me," I snorted. Mr. McKinnsey was the principal and I'd spent lots of time sitting in his office. "He just wants me to quit making my teachers cry . . . "

This time she interrupted me. "This is getting us nowhere. I just want to let you know that I'm here for you if you need me."

I rolled my eyes. "Whatever. Can I go now?"

She nodded and I jumped up from my chair.

As an afterthought, she instructed, "Go back to class."

I stepped out in the hallway and saw my friend Jesse walking toward the gym. I hurried to catch up with her.

"How'd that go?" Jesse asked, turning around at the sound of my footsteps.

"It was incredibly stupid. I've got a bag. Do you wanna get outta here?"

She followed me out the doors of the school to the parking lot, then behind one of the storage sheds on the far side, a place where we could get high. Jesse was a new friend, Graham's neighbor from across the street, the blue house on the corner. We'd connected one night when I was behind Graham's garage smoking a joint. She spotted me as she was walking through the neighbor's yard to get to her house.

"Hey," she called, walking over to where I stood.

"Hey," I replied, cupping the joint in my hand.

She sniffed the air. "It smells like weed." I expected her to react like my girlfriends, rolling her eyes and walking away. Instead, she surprised me. "Do you get high? I was with Bobby and Red earlier. They're these guys from Pinsla. Bobby is so hot. Anyways, I'm like so baked right now, I can't think straight."

I smiled widely and opened my hand to reveal the joint still burning.

"Cool!" She took it from my hands and lifted it to her lips.

I watched her take a hit and smiled again. I'd been worried about finding new friends since my old crowd had turned their backs on me. When I drank, they had tolerated it, but smoking pot crossed some invisible line with them. They looked at me with contempt, although Melissa tried talking to me.

One night, while we were walking home from Graham's with Alex and Paige, Melissa said, "You're really going kinda nuts. You don't seem like the same person anymore. It's kinda starting to freak me out."

Stopping in my tracks, I snapped, "Whatever. Don't be saying anything to James about me."

"I'm not even talking about James. This has absolutely nothing to do with your boyfriend. I'm just saying . . . "

"I saw you talking to him tonight. You probably told him all kinds of shit about me," I ranted. Alex and Paige moved to stand behind Melissa. "I know you want him. You've always wanted him. Sorry to burst your little bubble, but he's never liked you!"

"Ya know what? Forget it, Heather. This is exactly what I'm trying to say. You don't make any sense. I say something about you and suddenly you're yelling at me about James." She shook her head. "Not only that, you're being mean . . . "

"Mean? You think I'm mean? Whatever. First I'm nuts, then I'm fuckin' mean. What else do you have to say about me? Huh?" I stepped closer to her.

"Nothing. I'm done. This is pointless." She stepped back from me and I responded by moving forward again.

"No, really. Go ahead," I continued. "You might as well get it all out. I mean, Christ, all you do is talk about me behind my back. You might as well tell me to my face. Or maybe you don't have the balls, do ya?" Her silence angered me further. I stepped directly in front of her face, within inches of her nose. "C'mon, speak to me. Get it all out. I knew you didn't have any balls."

Alex yelled from behind her, "Knock it off!"

"Shut-up, Alex. This isn't any of your business." I maintained my position in front of Melissa. Then I grabbed Melissa's purple windbreaker and pulled it up around her neck tightly. "Listen, I don't care what you have to say about me. Stay the fuck out of my business and my life. You don't know anything. You ever mess with me again and I'll kick your ass!"

I let go of her jacket and shoved her backwards into Alex and Paige. I turned and walked away, wishing I had punched her in the face. Who did she think she was?

No one dared confront me after that. My old friends avoided

me at all costs. When I caught their eyes, they looked away. When I approached them in the halls, they turned their backs. I told myself I didn't care, that we had just grown apart. That way, I could remain unaffected by the gap that continued to widen between us until we were completely separate.

I turned to the people I'd barely spoken to in the past because I had always considered them to be losers. Suddenly, the greasy haired guys who wore leather jackets or Grateful Dead T-shirts seemed very attractive to me. They always talked about having wild parties. Most of them had gotten kicked out of regular school and went to alternative school. They stood in the hallway outside of their special classroom, arms crossed, intimidating us with their presence. I wanted what they had.

Keith Bennett was the baddest of the bad boys who went to alternative school. He stood in the hall most of the time, making lewd comments to the girls passing by. He called me "sweet cheeks" whenever I passed by and I blushed every time. He was seventeen, almost three years older than me. His long blond hair rolled down the back of his leather jacket, and he drove a red truck. I knew he'd been in trouble with the law and had heard rumors that he sold pot. He got into fights and bragged about his conquests with older women. I set my eyes on him, determined to make him mine.

Our first date was very simple: we planned to get drunk together. I told my parents I was staying overnight at a friend's house so that I could stay out all night with him. Keith picked me up at the park a block from my house. His hair was bright and shiny, flowing down his back, and he smelled like Cool Water cologne, my favorite. He held up an unopened bottle of vodka.

"Where'd you get that?" I asked, lighting up a cigarette. I was always curious to find a new connection. There was no such thing as having too many of them.

"My mom," he replied, bringing his cigarette to his lips.

"Your mom?"

"Yep, she's a drunk. She's so wasted, she don't care. Now, are ya ready to get wasted or what?"

My answer was to grab the bottle and take the first pull. I was out to impress him with my capacity to drink, to show him I wasn't one of those girls who got drunk and stupid after one beer. I emptied out a bottle of 7-Up and refilled it with vodka, like he did. We headed out of town.

Keith belonged to the subculture of people that spent hours in their cars drinking on the back roads outside of town. He and his buddies raced their cars, side by side, spewing gravel down the roads. Sometimes they crashed into each other. It was a dangerous game. Keith took me on my first ride.

He yelled, "Hold on!" and pressed his foot down hard on the gas pedal. I gripped the strap above the window and watched the speedometer jerk back and forth.

Trees and fields flew by. He raced towards a four-way stop.

"Watch this, wooooo!" he yelled, blowing through the stop sign. The truck sailed into the air as if we had just gone off a jump. We landed with a scrape and a thud. He pulled the emergency brake, whipping us sideways before coming to a stop.

"Shit!" I yelled through laughter. "We caught some serious air!" I grabbed my bottle and took a huge gulp. "Let's do it again!"

"Whoa girl, you're crazy!" he said, turning the truck around.

I laughed giddily, feeling the immediate effects of what I just drank, mixed with the adrenaline of driving so fast and carelessly. I'd show him just how crazy I was. I filled my bottle up again and drank it just as fast as I had drunk the other bottle.

"We're gonna have to find more booze," he said, holding up the nearly empty bottle. We hadn't even been driving for an hour. That's the last thing I remember. I blacked out, which is what usually happened when I drank. I wouldn't pass out. I just couldn't remember things. The conscious part of my brain would shut down because it couldn't handle the poison, but my body would continue to function. Tonight was no different.

I came back to conscious awareness lying on Keith's lap in the backseat of a strange car. He was talking to me about something. There was someone else crammed next to us in the back seat. Stoney Miller, Keith's best friend, was driving and someone occupied the passenger seat. The car had an incredible stereo system that bounced and shook the entire car with its power. I could feel the bump of the bass, and each time it thumped my stomach heaved and my head swam. I couldn't move my body or even lift my head. I knew I was going to be sick. I wanted to tell Stoney to pull over, but when I opened my mouth, vomit spewed out instead of words. My mashed potatoes from supper splattered on Keith's lap.

"Fuck! Pull over, she's puking!" Keith yelled.

Stoney pulled the car over to the side of the road. Keith jumped out before the car was completely stopped and pulled me out behind him. I hunched over on the road, puking until my stomach was empty. Keith held my long hair away from my face while I heaved.

When I finished, I stood back up. I felt better, like I always did after I puked. My head quit spinning and my stomach calmed. Then I realized I had just puked on Keith on our first date. "Ohmigod, I'm so sorry." I stood on the side of the road as he used snow to wipe off his pants.

"Don't worry about it. It's nothin'." He smiled. "It happens to the best of us. C'mon, let's get outta here before someone calls the cops."

He grabbed my hand and helped me back into the car. He put his arm around me and I snuggled close to him, inhaling his scent. I felt warm and safe.

Keith leaned forward to talk to Stoney. "Drive to Kwik Trip so we can clean up."

"Man, that was so fuckin' nasty," Stoney said, laughing. "I've never seen Bennett move so fast in my life."

"I knew she'd puke but man, you should see this chic drink," Keith replied. I beamed proudly. "Remember that one time, when that one chic . . . what was her name?"

Stoney tried to help. "Shauna?"

"No, it was . . . God, who the hell was it?"

I drifted off into my own thoughts, oblivious to the conversation around me. I closed my eyes, feeling the warmth of Keith's body next to mine and smelling cologne mixed with the sweet scent of alcohol. I knew at that moment that he was the one. He had held my hair while I puked. It was a sign that he was my Prince Charming.

4

Trapped

During this period, it became glaringly obvious to my parents that I was drinking and getting high. I was done hiding and pretending to be the girl they thought I should be. Any evidence of the child they once knew was gone. My mom was convinced Satan was attacking me and trying to disrupt our family structure. My dad was simply infuriated with me at all times. However, I had lost the fear of his anger, and without that fear he had lost the ability to control me.

Whenever I got caught skipping school, staying out all night, or getting high, they would attempt to ground me. But my bedroom was in the basement and I had a window at ground level. It was easy to remove the screen. I placed my dresser directly underneath the window so that all I had to do was climb up on my dresser and head through the window to my freedom. Keith would be waiting in the driveway in his red truck, the lights turned off.

One night I came home to a surprise. I crawled through my window after having been with Keith all night. I stepped onto the dresser and hopped down. I maneuvered my way through the darkness to the light switch above my bed and flicked the switch. The room filled with light, revealing my parents sitting on my bed.

"Where have you been?" my dad demanded, walking over to stand in front of me, peering into my eyes.

I looked right back at him. "Nowhere."

"She's drunk, hon," my mom announced quietly, her eyes welling with tears. She blinked rapidly to keep them from falling down her cheeks. "I can smell it on her."

My dad pinned me tightly against the wall, his forearm pressed against my collarbone and his other hand gripping my shoulder. "Have you been out with Keith? Did he come get you?"

"Get away from me!" I pushed him back and turned away. He grabbed my arms and jerked me back around to face him.

"Who do you think you are?" His eyes bulged and his nostrils flared with quick breaths.

"What are you gonna do? Spank me?" I laughed.

"You think you're so smart. I'll show you what I'm gonna do!" He grabbed my arm and squeezed.

"Hon, stop. Leave her alone. She's just drunk." My mom got up from her spot on the bed and stood beside him, tapping his arm. "Let's just go to bed. We can't do anything about it tonight."

My dad released his grip slowly. He narrowed his eyes to slits, peering at me before opening the door and leaving my bedroom. My mom remained behind. We stood in silence, listening to the sound of his footsteps on the stairs.

"Why do you do this, Heather?" Her face creased in worried wrinkles and she had bags underneath her eyes.

"I'm not doing anything. Just leave me alone," I retorted. She tried to hug me, but I pushed her away. "Get out of here. You're on his side."

As if I had slapped her, she brought her hand up to her face and touched her cheek, searching for a physical mark. She moved away from me with her eyes wide open, still fighting back tears. She said good night softly, hanging her head down low to stare at the blue carpet before opening the door and following my father upstairs.

It wasn't long until they nailed my screen shut and placed boards over the window. I just switched to the back door leading to the garage instead. There was no way they'd nail that door shut. My nighttime routine of waiting for them to fall asleep, sneaking out of the house, and running off into the night to get drunk with Keith continued.

They sent me to a Christian psychologist, Dr. Hawkins, an old man in his sixties who looked more like a minister than a counselor. He wore three-piece black suits with red ties. He talked slowly and purposefully as he asked me questions. I got high before every session and stared aimlessly out the window at branches as I sat on his leather sofa.

He never asked me about my life. He focused his questions on saving my soul. "Do you pray any longer?" he'd ask, moving his chair closer to me.

"Nope."

"Heather, Jesus is the only person who is going to help you get through this difficult time. You have turned your back on him, but you can go back to him at any time. He wants you to come back to him. He does not want to lose you to Satan."

"Satan already has me," I snorted. "Nothing anyone can do about it."

He'd ask, his eyes grown huge, "Have you been worshipping him?"

Now he's really gonna try to save my soul. What a fuckhead. I refused to answer his question. Let him worry about it.

Eventually, he told my parents that if I continued to come high, he couldn't see me any longer. My mom made the mistake of telling me what he'd said. I made sure that I was so wasted for my next appointment that I could barely walk, let alone talk.

He took one look at my red, watery eyes as I shuffled through his door and said, "I cannot see you anymore unless you're sober."

I'd already sat down on his leather sofa. "Well, I'm never gonna be sober," I slurred, standing up and heading back out the door.

Dr. Hawkins called my parents and told them our sessions were over. As a punishment, I was grounded again. Trying to keep me in the house, my dad resorted to standing in front of the door, his arms stretched out and resting on both sides of the doorframe. I tried to grab the doorknob. He clutched me by my wrist.

"You are not going anywhere, young lady."

I reached for the doorknob again, quickly opening the door. He pushed back against it with his body as I struggled to keep it open. I planted my feet, pulling on the door, as he remained braced in front of it. I knew I just had to get it open about six inches and I could slide my body through.

Usually he'd grab me, pulling me back into the house, slamming the door behind us. An all-out wrestling match followed. He threw me down to the ground, pinning me underneath him. He sat on me with his legs on top of my legs, my wrists held back with his hands.

"Get off me!" I'd yell.

My sister would begin to cry in the doorway of the kitchen.

"Go to your room," my mom would instruct her from her spot at the kitchen table, where she sat working on her latest cross-stitch project. Becca would run into her bedroom, slamming her door.

Eventually, I'd quit fighting so he'd release his hold on me. As soon as he stood up, I made a frantic dash for the door once again. I'd fling it open and take off at a dead sprint, like I'd just heard the gun being fired at the starting line of one of my cross-country meets. Sometimes he ran after me. He was a former cross-country star as well and could catch up quickly. He'd tackle me to the ground, throw me over his shoulder, and carry me back into the house as I kicked and screamed, pounding on his back with my fists. We'd return to the house, where the battle would continue until he finally gave up.

Then I'd run the four blocks to Keith's house, looking frantically over my shoulder. We'd been together for a few months now and Keith was officially my boyfriend. In the beginning, I'd spent all of my time with him because I was madly in love. He was obsessed with my every move, which I found incredibly flattering. He wanted to be with me at all times, and if he wasn't, he wanted to know where I was and who I'd been with. He really cared about me in a way that nobody else did. He understood me.

"Are you high?" Keith demanded one night, opening the screen door before I even knocked. He had his muscular arms stretched out, bracing both sides of the doorframe.

"No," I lied, looking at my feet and trying to get my gums unstuck from my front teeth.

"Look at me!" he ordered.

I looked up to meet his brown eyes, rimmed with thick black lashes that any girl would kill for. They could look so doll-like when they weren't filled with anger.

I silently instructed myself. *Open your eyes. Look at him. Don't look stoned. Look sober.*

He grabbed my chin with his hand, lifted it up, and leaned forward within inches of my face.

"You're wasted," he declared, raising his upper lip in a disgusted smirk. He grabbed my arm and jerked me through the doorway. "Get in here."

I followed him through the small patio filled with miscellaneous tools and empty cardboard cases of beer and liquor. In the kitchen, the radio was tuned to classic rock, Lightning 107.1, as it always was. Leftover dishes from supper stank in the sink. Rocky, the small gray poodle, lay in her designated spot next to the stove. Keith's mom, Donna, sat at the small table by the window in her gray sweatpants, with a cigarette burning in the ashtray in front of her and a can of Old Milwaukee in her hand.

When she saw me behind Keith, she exclaimed "Heather!" The weary frown lines in her face straightened into a smile that showed her decaying, yellowed teeth from years of drinking and chain-smoking. "How was your night?"

"Shut-up, Mom. Don't talk to her!" Keith ordered, walking through the doorway on the right to the pantry.

"Oh, Keith, I'm sorry," she slurred, making Keith sound more like "Keef." I heard the sound of aluminum being moved around in the fridge.

"I told you to get me more beer," he reprimanded his mother, walking back into the kitchen with one of her beers in his hand. He cracked it open.

She apologized quickly, looking at the orange-carpeted floor left over from the 70s. "I'm sorry. Gee, Keef. Big Keef didn't get home till late. I couldn't go to the liquor store."

Keith rolled his eyes and took another drink. "You're so fuckin' lazy! Can't you ever get off your ass and do anything? Oh yeah, I forgot. You're too drunk."

"I'm sorry." She still looked at the same imaginary spot on the carpet. Her shoulders tightened and her head hung low. She pulled her arms forward as if she wanted to disappear into her own body.

"Get out of here!" Keith ordered, pointing to the doorway that led to the living room.

"Oh, oh, oh . . ." she stammered, picking up her cigarettes and then dropping them on the floor. She bent over to pick them up, her hand shaking and her body swaying. I wanted to tell Keith to leave her alone, but I knew I was already in enough trouble.

She shuffled through the door and clicked it shut behind her without looking back.

"Sit down," Keith ordered. I sat. I hung my head and copied Donna's gaze on the carpet. He sat across the kitchen table from me, setting his beer down. "I told you to stay home tonight."

He'd worked tonight in the kitchen at Stub's Pub, the only bar in town. He usually didn't get off work until the early hours of the morning. Lately, he wanted me to sit at my house until he got home from work. But the walls in my bedroom closed in on me and would have swallowed me whole if I stayed.

"I know you did and I was going to, but . . . "

He cut me off. "There are no butts! You never listen to me." His fist slammed down on the table, knocking over his beer and spilling it into his lap. "Dammit, look what you made me do!"

I jumped up and grabbed the towel from the rack.

"I'm sorry," I apologized, setting his beer upright. I wiped off the table and then his lap. I threw the towel in the sink and sat back down in my chair. He was still silent, looking out the window and tapping his fingers on the table. The beat was deliberate: tap, tap, tap. The silence made a buzz start in my head that sounded like radio station static. I hated his silences.

"I hate sitting at home," I blurted out. "I go crazy."

"All you had to do was wait for me to get off work," he said, turning to look at me. "I would've come got you."

I knew he would have. He always did, but it was always late at night and each time he left my driveway he peeled out, spinning his tires, and leaving the black skid marks behind. The sound woke my parents every time, alerting them that I was gone.

I said in a voice more whiny than I had ever used in childhood, "But I didn't want to sit there till two."

"I don't care! I know you're out there getting high and whoring around with other guys when I'm at work."

"I'm not!" I wouldn't dare. Even if I wanted to, he had a way of finding out everything I did. If one guy even looked at me too long, Keith would punch him straight in the face. I'd seen him do it on more than one occasion. "I just sat in Jesse's basement all night getting high with her. It was no big deal."

He snorted and ground his teeth back and forth. "She's a fuckin' loser. I don't know why you hang out with her."

He hated everyone I hung out with. It never mattered. He'd introduced me to lots of his friends and he hated me to hang out with them as well. I didn't get it. There was no way for me to win unless I just gave in and only hung out with him. I used to want to spend every single minute with him during the first few months we were together, but lately I couldn't stand it. I could never do anything right and I was beginning to feel like I was suffocating.

"I've gotta go home," I declared. "It's two thirty and I was supposed to be home at midnight."

"See what I mean?" Now his voice sounded whiny. "If you just would've waited, your parents would've been in bed by the time I was done. We could've had you back by the time they got up. Now your mom is probably all freaked out again. God, you piss me off."

"But my parents . . . "

"Fuck your parents!" he snorted, raising his beer to his lips. It was his favorite thing to say whenever I mentioned doing anything they wanted me to. It was easy for him to say. He'd never had a curfew or parents like mine.

I rubbed my hands on my face, trying to clear my head. I was so sick of arguing and defending myself. He got up and walked over to stand behind me. My body tightened. I'd learned to prepare for the blows. How long had it been since the first time? Only about a month but God, it seemed like forever since he'd pushed me down the stairs after I threatened to leave him. He put his arms around me and I cringed, gripping my chair with my hands. His arms were loose and he began to kiss my neck. I relaxed my muscles and my hold on the chair.

I turned my head and brought my mouth to meet his. He stuck his tongue in my mouth and kissed me hungrily. I tasted the Old Milwaukee. He pulled back and took my head, cupping it in his hands.

"I just get so pissed 'cause I love you so much," he said, his eyes finally soft.

"I love you too," I replied and gave him another kiss. He pulled my chair back and moved in front of me. I heard the sound of his zipper going down. I automatically reached down to pull out his penis and began to stroke it, up and down. He groaned and responded by unzipping my pants. I lifted my butt off the chair so that he could pull my pants down to my ankles, panties and all.

His voice was muffled as he licked my neck with his wet tongue. "You drive me crazy."

I turned my head to look at the numbers on the microwave: 2:42. Christ, I had to get home. He grabbed my shoulders and pushed me back in my chair as I spread my legs. He entered me and began his frantic thrusting. I counted his strokes: one, two, three, four, five, and then he sprayed his come inside of me. I smiled at my knowledge. I knew that from the time he entered me, he'd never last more than five strokes. It made the task a lot easier. He went limp on top of me. The smell of fried food wafted up. Looking out the window, I noticed that Donna had put up a new bird feeder. My eyes returned to the clock: 2:45.

"I've gotta go, for real," I said, moving my legs underneath him.

He grunted. "I'm so tired. Can't you just sleep here with me?"

"Not tonight. My parents are still pissed about the last time I stayed out all night. Technically, I'm still grounded."

He laughed. "Yeah, that works real well."

"Maybe this weekend I'll stay here. Now, c'mon, seriously, I've got to go."

"Oh all right, fine." He stood and pulled his jeans back up. I stood quickly and did the same. He grabbed his beer and finished it off. "Call me when you get home. Don't forget, I'm picking you up at eleven tomorrow. Don't bother going to school."

"I'll be ready." I leaned over and gave him a peck on his check. "I love you. I'll let myself out." I walked away without waiting for a response. I didn't want him to change his mind and become adamant that I stay. I didn't want to sleep next to him.

"Heather . . . " He called out, just as my hand was on the door.

"What?" I braced myself.

"I love you, too. Don't ever forget that."

"I won't." I smiled with relief, opened the door and walked into the crisp air, snow falling down around me.

It hit me with the brisk cold. *What am I doing? How did I get myself into this?* I was running away from a father who had lost control over me and into the arms of a man who wanted to gain control of me.

I lit up a cigarette and continued walking. Maybe it wasn't as bad as I was making it out to be. Sure, my dad was an asshole, but Keith wasn't as bad as he was. I mean, Keith loved me. Our love was so powerful that it made him lose control. But a soft voice from inside me spoke up: *Look how he treats his mom. He hits her and he's started to hit you. He'll do it again. It's only gonna get worse.*

I shook my head, trying to erase the thoughts. I threw my cigarette onto the ground and grabbed a joint from my pocket,

bringing it to my lips, lighting it, and inhaling the sweetness. I held the smoke in my lungs as long as I could before releasing it back into the air. Then I sat down on the cold curb on the side of the road, smoking my joint, instructing myself to quit thinking until I felt the familiar peace come over my mind.

It was going to be okay. I was going to be okay. I mean, Keith could be mean, I wasn't gonna deny that. He could also be controlling, but it wasn't that bad. This was nothing that I couldn't handle. He had perks. He was introducing me to all sorts of new connections and people. Just a few days ago, he'd even brought me to the place where he bought the pot that he sold.

It was a beat-up trailer off a gravel road with a cornfield on each side. The woman who answered the door weighed about three hundred pounds and didn't have any teeth in her mouth. She smiled at us, all gums. As she welcomed us into the trailer, a black rottweiler ran up to sniff my crotch. We walked into the kitchen and Keith motioned for me to sit down. He followed the fat woman to a room in the back of the trailer and shut the door.

The kitchen was a mess and smelled like rotten food. My feet stuck to the floor. Dirty dishes piled in the sink and lined the counters. Empty beer cans and bottles overflowed the garbage can and spilled onto the floor. At the table next to me was a pudgy brown-haired boy playing solitaire. Across from him was a big man with a belly and muscular arms who eyed me quizzically. His intimidating presence filled the room.

Then he stuck his hand out. "I'm Ryan Hedstrom. They call me Strom."

"Hey, I'm Heather," I responded, shaking his hand.

"Do ya wanna drink?"

"Sure." I reached down to pet the dog that was still sniffing me cautiously.

"That's Sasha," the little boy said. "I'm Zeke."

"Hi, Zeke."

"I'm six," he declared proudly.

"Wow, that's pretty old," I humored him.

Strom grabbed the bottle of Windsor Canadian that was in front of him and mixed me a drink at the counter. He kept looking at me with a sideways smirk on his face. "Don't you go to school?"

"Not today."

He laughed. "I've heard about you."

I didn't know what to say. What had he heard and who told him? Was it good? I was a new person in this circle and I knew how important it was to be trusted.

He pulled out a bag of pot and loaded a pinchie. I watched him smoke it as he joked with Zeke. I wanted to get high because I hadn't been all day, but I said nothing. When we walked up to the door Keith had given me very specific instructions: "Be quiet and don't ask for anything."

I didn't have to ask, though, because as soon as he finished smoking, Strom packed it again and handed it to me. I took it gladly. He watched me carefully as I smoked it and then gave me another. I knew he wanted to see if I'd start laughing uncontrollably like beginning pot smokers do, but I'd passed this stage long ago. We didn't talk much. Keith was taking a long time. Right as I started to get paranoid, he returned and I followed him out the door.

Sitting on the curb in the cold at nearly three in the morning, remembering this, I realized Keith really trusted me. Maybe I was blowing his controlling behavior out of proportion. It wasn't like our troubles were just his fault. I was always doing things to make him mad. I could try harder to do what he asked me to do. He loved me and I loved him. None of the other stuff really mattered as long as we loved each other. Besides, I needed him as much as he needed me. I got up from the curb with a renewed determination to make our relationship work.

5

Access Granted

I got kicked out of school in the middle of ninth grade, after a long drawn-out game of being given "last chances" to behave. I skipped my classes almost every day and had quit making up stories or pretending to be ill. When I was at school my time was spent in the principal's office, waiting to be given punishment for being wasted on school grounds, for getting into fights, for stealing money and cigarettes from lockers, or for whatever else I had done the last time I'd been in school. The principal, Mr. McKinnsey, was running out of ways to punish me. I didn't show up for detention and suspending me just gave me a legitimate reason not to go to school.

Mr. McKinnsey, my teachers, and my parents decided I would be put on a zero tolerance policy, another "last chance." But this time Mr. McKinnsey led me into his office and ordered me to sit down. I sat in front of his long metal desk that was covered with papers and yellow post-it notes. Sprawling my legs straight out in front of me, I crossed my arms and rested my head on the back of the chair.

He looked directly into my eyes. "Heather, this is it. We've done everything we can think of to try to keep you in school. Nothing seems to work. You don't seem to care." He paused, keeping his eyes on me. "I've decided, along with the school board and your parents, to give you one final chance to stay in school."

"What if I don't wanna stay?" I challenged, cocking my head to the side.

"Well, then I guess that is a choice you will make, because frankly we don't care anymore. This is a sad situation. See, there's some kids that you know are gonna struggle to get through school and some of them you know probably won't make it. They struggle their way from kindergarten on. You've never been one of those kids, Heather. You're smart, creative, a natural athlete, and you excel at everything you try." I'd never heard him speak so softly. "The only reason that you're still here is because we all crossed our fingers and hoped one day you'd snap out of this and realize how badly you're screwing up your life. But I'm gonna be real straight with you. No one believes that's going to happen."

He paused again, letting his words sink in. I shifted my gaze to a brown stain on the gray carpet as a lump lodged itself in my throat. I refused to meet his eyes.

"Here's the deal, it's real simple. You're on a zero tolerance policy, which means you screw up once and you're out. No questions asked." He picked up a piece of paper from his desk and handed it to me. "This is your list of rules. All of your teachers have the same list. You break one of these rules and you're gone. For good."

I took the paper and skimmed the words without reading what they said. *Why do I feel like crying?*

He leaned back in his chair. "Got any questions?"

I shook my head. I couldn't speak around the lump in my throat. I just wanted to get out of there.

"All right, then. Get out of here." He picked up his phone and punched in a number.

The policy stated that I had to be in class on time every day. Once I was in class, I couldn't leave for any reason, not even to go to the bathroom. I wasn't to cause any disruptions. I couldn't get caught smoking on school grounds, be under the influence of any drugs, or have any drugs on me. Last of all, I couldn't talk to any of my teachers outside of the classroom without Mr. McKinnsey being present.

It dawned on me as I walked into school the following Monday that I didn't know what I'd do if I got kicked out of school. I was only fourteen. I was supposed to be playing varsity basketball, going to school dances and football games, writing papers, taking tests, and making my girlfriends laugh at lunch. Instead, I was failing all of my classes, not playing any sports, not involved with any school activities, and none of my girlfriends even spoke to me. How had I gotten here?

I shook my head, trying to clear it of serious thoughts. *Relax, Heather. Just follow their silly rules for a while. They'll relax, and then you can do what you want to again.*

The first day of the policy, I made it to all of my classes on time and didn't leave. I got through by laying my head on the desk and going to sleep. By the time my last period came, I felt rested and pretty proud of myself for having made it through the day.

My last class of the day was English. The teacher, Mr. Cameron, was my favorite teacher to harass. He was such an easy target, a first-year teacher who wore brown polyester pants that hung on his hips and dragged on the floor. He also wore a white shirt with brown vertical stripes that he tucked into his pants. I don't know if he never washed his clothes or if he had ten identical outfits, but every time I saw him he was dressed the same. His short, squatty body carried a small neck and a big head. He wore thick glasses that made his already large eyes look even larger. He looked like a turtle that was in the process of evolving into a human, but hadn't quite made it there.

Halfway through his class, I started to get bored. I ripped pieces of paper out of my notebook and folded them into tight triangles. I had a small pile on my lap. I waited until Mr. Cameron turned around to write on the blackboard and then threw one at his back. It connected. His hand stopped writing, and then he continued. "When you conjugate a . . ." Another one of my triangles hit his leg. The class started to snicker as he turned around.

"Who did that?" he demanded, hands on his hips. This only brought more laughter. "Quit it. Quit laughing." He sounded like a whiny young boy begging his older brother to leave him alone. He waited until the laughter subsided. I decided not to push my luck.

At the end of class, he wrote the homework assignment on the board and turned to look at me. "Heather, I need to see you after class."

"Is Mr. McKinnsey gonna be here?"

"No." The bell rang and everyone grabbed their books, jumped up, and headed out the door. He walked over and stood directly in front of my desk, crossed his arms on his chest, and peered down at me through his thick glasses. I stood up and stepped around him.

He grabbed my arm, demanding, "Where are you going? I said I wanted to talk to you."

I declared, walking toward the door, "Look, Shit Pants, Mr. McKinnsey isn't here. You know the rules."

"I don't care," he retorted, keeping his hold on my arm and matching my stride.

"Well, you're just gonna have to wait." I pulled my arm away and walked faster towards the door.

Mr. Cameron moved in front of me again. "No." The tips of his ears turned red. "You sit down now!"

I stepped around him. "Why don't you sit down, Shit Pants? I'm leaving!"

He hurried to block the doorway with his body. "You insubordinate little brat!"

I pushed him aside and stepped into a hallway filled with students slamming their lockers and hurrying out of the school.

"See ya!" I smiled, looking over my shoulder. I started pushing my way through the other students. He came up behind me and grabbed my arm. I jerked away and continued walking. He grabbed me again and pulled me backwards.

My head started to pressurize as if it was a balloon being stretched to the limits. It was my signal to fight or run. I turned around to face him. Through gritted teeth, I spat, "Get your fuckin' hands off me!"

I started walking, moving faster, but I heard his footsteps behind me. Suddenly, he grabbed me again and shoved me up against a row of lockers.

A female voice yelled, "Get Mr. McKinnsey!"

Mr. Cameron held me against the locker, the red from his ears moving into his face. I shoved him and he flew backwards into a student. But he lunged back at me and before I knew it, he'd grabbed me again. He wrestled me to the other side of the hallway, threw me into the Science room, and shut the door behind us. I broke free and ran to the teacher's desk at the front of the room, grabbed the electric pencil sharpener and threw it at his head. He ducked and it smashed into the wall.

The air in my head threatened to explode. "Fuck you!" I yelled.

He moved towards me through the rows of desks, yelling, "No, fuck you!"

I stood at the front of the room, by the first row of chairs. Picking one up by the legs, I brought it over my head and threw it in his direction. I picked another one up and did the same. The chairs toppled on their sides and upside down. He shoved the chairs out of the way and kept strutting towards me. Suddenly

Mr. Dixon, the three hundred pound Science teacher, burst through the door, ran up behind Mr. Cameron, and held him in a tight bear hug.

"Knock it off!" he ordered. "You need to settle down!" Mr. Cameron jerked forward and shook his head back and forth before going limp in Mr. Dixon's arms. He breathed in and out rapidly, as if he had just finished running a marathon.

"Looks like you're not so tough now," I laughed, giving him the finger and holding back the urge to spit in his face. He sprung back to life, kicking and wiggling to free himself from Mr. Dixon's hold.

"Heather, get the hell out of here!" Mr. Dixon ordered without releasing his hold. "Go!"

I turned and stormed back into the hallway. It was filled with students and teachers who had gathered to watch. When I caught their eyes, they looked away. They moved to the side as I marched through the stony hallway. I looked down at the floor, a sinking feeling in the pit of my stomach. I was officially one of the kids that other kids were scared of, but it didn't feel like I'd always thought it would. I'd thought that being the one who was angry and the one to inflict pain meant being in control, but instead I felt completely out of control. People's eyes bored into my back, questioning what the hell was wrong with me in the same way I questioned my dad's anger.

I shoved open the heavy doors and walked into the parking lot. Quickly spotting Keith waiting for me in his truck, I hurried over, opened the door and slid in.

"What took you so long?" he asked, giving me quick peck on the cheek.

I tried to shut off the leftover anger pounding in my head. "You don't even want to know. I don't think I'll be going back to school."

By the end of the week, a school board meeting was held.

I was expelled and Mr. Cameron lost his job. With my expulsion, any semblance of a normal teen life disappeared. My emergence into the adult world of drugs and desperation was complete.

Keith was happy I was done with school. He saw it as an opportunity to spend more time with me. But I was growing more and more tired of his possessive demands for my constant presence and attention. I no longer found his relentless questioning about my whereabouts flattering. All we did was argue about where I'd been when I wasn't with him, who I'd been with, and what I'd done. Our arguing always ended in fights that were growing increasingly more violent.

I started spending less and less time with Keith and more and more time with Strom, the drug dealer Keith had introduced me to a few months earlier. I became a frequent visitor at the trailer in the country between two cornfields. I didn't know who owned the trailer, but Strom spent a lot of time there, along with the toothless fat lady who turned out to be his sister.

Keith's connection for pot was slowly becoming my own. Strom was beginning to trust me. Before long, he started carefully schooling me in the mathematics of splitting up large quantities of pot into smaller amounts for selling. Pot was scattered all over the house. It was on every table, counter, and the bathroom sink. He even fed the dog green buds for doing tricks. I was in awe. He was a great teacher and I was an even better student, eager and willing to learn everything he had to teach me. His school replaced high school but now I showed up every day on time. The only reason Strom trusted me was because I was Keith's girlfriend, but the title only got me limited access into his world and I wanted complete access to everything that went on in the trailer.

Strom and I would sit on the plastic chairs around the white table in the kitchen, with pot and booze spread out in front of us. Throughout the day people would knock at the door and Strom would peek through the faded yellow curtains before he hollered for whoever it was to come in. If the person was uninvited or unknown, we sat in silence until they were gone.

Most of the time, people walked in and pulled up a chair next to us. Strom would take their money and give them what they came for. If anyone ever questioned his dealing, they were cut off.

One afternoon after an exchange had been made, a guy with a pair of khaki pants and a tucked-in white shirt asked Strom, "Do you have a scale?"

Strom snorted and grabbed back the bag he had just handed the man. "It's a fuckin' half. Don't you trust me?" Strom opened his eyes huge, moving his jaw quickly.

"No . . . I mean . . . yes . . . I just . . ." The man was flustered. "It's just ya know, sometimes people . . . "

"I'm not one of those people." Strom dug into the pocket of his blue jeans and pulled out the wad of bills the man had given him. He tossed them in his direction.

"Man, shit, I didn't mean nothing. I still want it. I trust ya." I noticed a bead of sweat forming on his forehead.

Strom ordered, "Get the fuck outta here, dude." His low voice made grown men act like dogs tucking their tails between their legs. It was direct and cold, with every syllable enunciated perfectly; in such a way that no one questioned his authority.

The man stood up, took his money from the table, and let himself out without saying another word.

I saw how Strom treated people, saw how people treated him, and stored what I saw in my memory. I wanted to be one of the people he trusted and respected. I watched everything going on to determine how I needed to act and talk in order to be that person.

Other times when people came, Strom would immediately stand up when they reached the kitchen. These people were different from the potheads. They were usually skinny men with long hair and eyes that darted around the room.

"Answer my phone if it rings," Strom would instruct as he turned to walk down the hallway with the others following. I'd hear the click of the door as they shut it behind them and strain my ears, but I could only hear muffled whispers and occasional outbursts of laughter. I'd sit at the table, anxiously chewing my fingernails and chain-smoking. They'd never stay in the back bedroom long. When they returned, they were animated and lively, talking so fast that I couldn't follow their conversations. Their pupils became large black circles. I'd seen enough movies and been around drugs long enough to know that they were on some kind of speed. I'd watch them through eyes that were covered with a blanket of stoned numbness. They seemed so energized and full of life. I wanted to feel like they felt.

I never said anything, never asked to come along, or what they did behind the door. You needed an invitation and I knew better than to ask for one. But I knew there was an entire world of drugs to use. Pot and booze had become old and boring. There was no excitement in them any longer. Smoking and drinking were just habitual routines that I performed over and over again, like brushing my teeth.

Keith was holding me back from getting what I wanted. I was his girlfriend, so I was associated with how he was known to be: erratic and unpredictable. You never knew when he was going to get angry and just start destroying things. Since I was his girlfriend, it was assumed that I was the same. I didn't want to be known as Keith's girlfriend anymore. I wanted my own identity and my own place in Strom's world.

I began to plan how I'd break up with Keith with the least amount of difficulty. I'd try to make it seem like the breakup was entirely about me, focusing on the fact that I was young and stressing that it had nothing to do with him. If I made any references about him being at fault, I knew he'd promise to change. Each time I tried, he either cried like a baby, begging me to stay, or else got so mad that he hit me. It became harder and harder for me to get the words out. I started trying to avoid him, but that was impossible. He'd call constantly until I answered my phone, or simply show up uninvited wherever I happened to be.

Strom and I didn't talk about my relationship with Keith. He wasn't the type to delve into anyone's personal life. But one day he brought it up while we were parked on the street outside his parents' house in his beat-up Chrysler LeBaron. I was smoking my Marlboro Reds, blowing the smoke through the window crack. The driver's seat was moved back as far as it would go, but even so his big belly still pushed against the steering wheel when he moved. I didn't understand how his stomach could be so big while his arms looked like the muscles I'd seen on bodybuilders on TV.

"Where are ya headed to now?" he asked, giving me a bag.

"I'm supposed to go to Tara's. She's having people over, but Keith doesn't want me to go." Tara was a friend I'd met at a party a few weeks before and we'd been spending a lot of time together.

"Keith doesn't want me to go," Strom mimicked in a little girl voice, rocking his head back and forth.

"Shut up!" I said, punching him in the arm as he laughed. I loved his laugh because it came up from his belly and shook his entire body.

"Christ, it's like he's your dad. Don't you ever get sick of it?"

"Fuck, yes!" I replied hurriedly. "You don't even know how tired of it I get. I'm gonna break up with him."

"Yeah, right!" Strom snorted. "I've heard that one too many times before."

He was right. I was always announcing I was breaking up with Keith, but a few days later I'd admit we were still together.

"I mean it. This time it's for real. I don't care what he does to me." I took my pinchie and loaded it with pot.

"What do you mean, you don't care what he does to you?" Strom jerked his head up from the pot he was sorting on his belly.

"Never mind." I looked out the window at the empty baseball diamond across the street and started smoking my purple one-hitter.

"Listen kid, I kinda like you. I don't like too many people but I take care of the ones that I do. I'm gonna ask ya a question and I want ya to tell me the truth. Does he hit you?"

"Yes." As soon as the words were out of my mouth, I wanted to take them back. I looked at girls who let men hit them as being weak and pathetic. I didn't want to admit that I was one of those girls, and I certainly didn't want Strom to think of me as one of them.

"If that motherfucker ever lays a hand on you again, you come to me. I'll take care of his stupid ass. After I'm through with him, he'll be too scared to come near you again. Seriously. Fuck him!" He punched the steering wheel. "You got that?"

Startled by his reaction, I nodded my head quickly. I'd heard a rumor that Strom had killed a man and I didn't doubt it. For the first time in a long while, I felt powerful. I had Strom on my side. I could do it. I could get rid of Keith. I didn't need or want him anymore because as long as I had Strom, I had power.

I opened the door. "I've gotta go."

"Are ya gonna go to Tara's?"

"Well, her and Troy are supposed to pick me up at the park at nine," I added with determination. "I'm gonna stop at Keith's and dump his ass before I go out there."

"All right." He started up the car. "Ya know where to find me."

I got out and shut the door behind me, waving to Strom as he drove off. It was only a few blocks to Keith's and I rehearsed what I would say as I walked.

First, I'll tell him I only have a minute 'cause I'm supposed to be meeting Troy and Tara. I'll tell him I love him but I can't be with him right now. I'll tell him I'm too young to be in a serious relationship. It's not a lie. I'm telling the truth. I don't wanna feel like I'm married at fourteen. I need to be free. That's all I'll say. Then I'll just say that I've got to go. He'll probably think I don't mean it. But this time I do. I do.

As I strutted up Keith's driveway, I saw him sitting on the front steps with a bottle between his legs. I hoped he hadn't been drinking all day. My heart started to beat faster.

Just stick to the plan. Just stick to the plan. I slowed at the sidewalk. His eyes bore into me, the pupils dilated with anger already. *Don't be scared. You can do this.*

"Hey," I said, looking down at my feet and taking a deep breath.

"Where ya been?" he asked, swaying to the left as he stood up.

"I drove around for a while with Strom." I took my cigarettes from my pocket.

"God, I wish I'd never introduced you to him. He's nothing but trouble." Keith took a swig from his Captain Morgan.

I didn't say anything. I didn't want to get into this argument we'd already had many times before. I just wanted to say what I had to say and go meet Tara and Troy.

"I've got to tell you something."

"What? Are you cheatin' on me?" He stood up and put his hands on his hips.

"No, I . . . "

"You are, aren't you? You little slut, I knew it!" He ground his teeth together.

See, you're doing the right thing, Heather.

"Keith, listen. Just sit down and mellow out." I chose my words carefully because I knew how easily he could be set off. "I am not cheating on you. I just want to tell you something."

"What?" He stepped directly in front of me and peered into my eyes with his teeth clenched tightly together.

You can do this. You can do this. I lit my cigarette and took a long drag before speaking out loud. I spoke the words as fast as I could, without giving him a chance to interrupt. "Okay, this is it. I love you, Keith. I really do. Don't get me wrong. This has nothing to do with love. But I'm young. And I wanna do lots with my life. I don't wanna be tied down. You're ready to be so serious. I'm not. Not that I never will be. But right now, I just can't. I don't wanna have to worry about hurting you all the time and I always seem to hurt you. I don't wanna do that. So, please don't hate me, but I'm breaking up with you. I don't wanna be with you anymore."

I turned around and started down the sidewalk, holding back an urge to sprint. I didn't want to give him an opportunity to somehow change my mind, like he'd done so many times before. I needed to stay calm and focused.

He yanked my arm from behind. "Where do you think you're going?"

Without turning around to face him, I said, "I'm leaving. It's over and I don't wanna talk about it anymore. I'm going. I've gotta be somewhere."

He snorted. "You don't get to just break up with me without me saying a word. You really think you can get away from me that easy?"

"Keith, please!" I whined. "Let go of me. I have to go. People are waiting for me. I don't want to talk about this. I'm done."

I took a step forward. He grabbed me again and jerked me around to face him.

"You're not going anywhere. Not until we talk." His nostrils flared in and out as if he were a bull waiting to be released from the pen. His breath smelled like rotten cheese, the way it often did after he'd been drinking for days. I held back the urge to gag.

"There's nothing to talk about. I've made up my mind." It wasn't until I tried to turn around to leave that I realized he was gripping both of my arms tightly. I'd been so focused on saying what I needed to say and not being affected by his words that I'd forgotten he'd use his physical strength to control me when his words couldn't.

Here we go again. I tried to free my arms. *I can't believe I thought I could do this so easily. I can't go back on my words. I have to stay strong this time.*

He said flatly, "Don't . . . fight . . . me, Heather."

As my head filled with pressure, I forced myself to look him in the eye. "Listen, if you let go of me, we can talk. Just let go of me so that we can talk about this, okay?"

"Promise?" he bargained, cocking his head, his dirty blond bangs falling over his right eye.

"Yes."

"Okay." He slowly released my arms.

I stood there for a second then turned on my heels and ran. I only made it a few strides before he tackled me and threw me onto the concrete.

He jumped on top of me screaming, "You bitch!" Then he sat on my stomach, pinning my arms down. The faces of my dad and my brother crossed his face, contorting into a three-headed monster as the pressure exploded in my head with a violent rush. I arched my back, brought my knees up and smashed them into his back with as much force as I had.

He cried out, releasing his hold on my arms. I sat up and shoved him off me, scrambling to my feet, but not fast enough. He quickly shoved me back to the ground. I fell on my hands and knees. He brought his foot up and slammed his steel boots onto my small hands.

I screamed, "Get off me! Leave me alone!"

He reached down and grabbed a handful of my long hair with his hands. His pull made my head snap back. I was afraid he'd tear the hair right out of my head.

Like an army general, he ordered, "Get up!"

I stood slowly, trying to keep my head steady. He dragged me by my hair to his steps, pinned me against the side of the house and looked into my eyes.

He's crazy. He's out of his mind. I closed my eyes, wishing him to disappear.

"Nobody loves you like I do. Nobody will ever be able to put up with your shit like I do. You're a no-good junkie." He narrowed his eyes to slits.

"Fuck you!" I snapped back. "You're crazy!"

Suddenly the door opened. Donna peeked her head outside. "What's going on?" she asked meekly.

Without turning around, Keith ordered, "Mom, go back in the house. Don't come out again."

"Help me!" I cried, turning to look at Donna. She looked away, refusing to meet my eyes.

"GET IN THE HOUSE!" Keith yelled, raising his fist up toward my face.

"I'm sorry, Heather," Donna said softly, turning back into the house. She began to cry as she shut the door.

"Please Keith, just let me go," I begged. "I love you. I do. I'm sorry. I didn't mean it. Really, I didn't."

The tension in his face eased slightly. "If you are fuckin' with me this time, I swear to God, you'll regret it."

"I'm not."

"I'm warning you, you better not be." He searched my eyes.

"I love you. I don't know what I was thinking. Just let me go. You're hurting me. I'll stay. I will. I promise."

He eased his hold slightly and moved back a step away from

me. "I mean it, Heather. You don't understand how much I love you. If you leave me, nobody loves you. I'm all you've got. Think about that."

"I know. I know, Keith," I pleaded, keeping my voice steady even as my heart pounded in short, quick spasms. "We can work this out."

He let go of my hair and took another step backwards. I smashed his chest with both hands. Then I swung at him with my fists, connecting with his face and continuing to punch any part of him that I could. I kicked at his knees and ankles. I heard the sound of my voice screaming but couldn't understand my words. I flailed my arms and legs against him in a fury, as he became every man who had ever touched me in a way that they shouldn't.

He grabbed me by my hair again, jerked my head back, and slammed it against the stucco siding on his house. A loud crack resonated though my head, as if it had split in half. Blackness covered my eyes.

I came to sitting on the steps, holding my pounding head in my hands. I brought my fingers away from my head and saw that they were covered with a sticky substance.

My head is bleeding. What is happening? What just happened?

I winced in pain as I turned my head to find Keith sitting next to me. His arm was around my shoulders. His own shoulders shook with sobs that wracked his whole body. He peered at me with tears streaming down his face and snot running from his nose into his mouth.

He whimpered like a small child in pain. "I'm sorry, baby. God, I'm so sorry. I didn't mean to hurt you. I just love you so much that I lose control. I can't help it. You don't know what you do to me. I can't live without you. I'm sorry."

"What . . . Where . . . my God . . . I . . . " My thoughts wouldn't come together. *Leave. Just leave. Go.*

I stood up, swaying to the side and trying to regain some sort of balance. I took a step forward as if I was in a trance. Keith grabbed me and pulled me back down to the steps. I cried out because the sudden movements made my head feel as if it was being split all over again. He brought his fingers to my neck and wrapped them tightly around it.

"I'm sorry, baby. I'm sorry, baby," he cried, beginning to squeeze my neck. "I didn't want to hurt you. I love you."

His grip tightened, shutting off air. I kicked my feet and waved my arms in one final attempt to fight back before I just let my body go limp. I felt like I'd been shoved underwater and was drowning. My head swirled as I looked up at him from someplace warm and fluid in my mind, watching the vein on his forehead pulsing while he squeezed.

He's finally going to kill me. Then darkness again.

When I came to, I was sitting on the front steps of Keith's house and I heard yelling. The voices came from the yard and one of them was Keith's. I turned my aching head to the side to see Keith pinned to the ground by a man who held him down in the same manner that Keith had held me down so many times. Keith kicked and struggled to get up. I felt a hand on my shoulder and turned the other way to see Tara sitting beside me.

Her blue eyes filled with the concern of a mother, she asked, "Can you get up? Caleb is gonna take care of Keith."

"I think so." It hurt to talk. I barely knew Caleb, a friend of Tara's, but he had just saved my life. My head was filled with a thick blanket of fog. Tara stood and offered her hand. I grabbed it and she pulled me to my feet. She brought her arm around me and, leaning against her, I took a few steps. I felt disconnected, like my head wasn't part of the body that was beginning to walk across the yard.

"C'mon. Troy is parked around the corner." She turned me towards the street on the side of the house.

I looked behind me to see Caleb still sitting on top of Keith. We walked slowly and silently to the car where Troy, Tara's best friend, waited in the driver's seat with the car still running. Tara opened the front passenger door for me and I slid in, leaning my head back against the seat.

"You okay?" Troy asked, turning to look at me.

I felt like I was in the middle of a dream, trying to force myself to wake up. "Yeah . . . What the hell happened?"

Tara leaned forward in the back seat. "Well, we waited and waited for you but you didn't come. I knew you probably stopped at Keith's so I thought we'd come get you 'cause I know how hard it is for you to get away from him."

My laugh came out like a dry, raspy cough. "Obviously."

Caleb came running to the car and jumped in the back seat.

"Let's get the hell out of here!" he called to Troy, who quickly put the car in drive and headed down the block.

"He won't bother you again, Heather," Caleb said, patting my shoulder from behind.

"Thanks."

"Heather, your head is bleeding," Tara remarked. "We should probably take you to the hospital."

"I'm fine," I snapped. "Did you guys get my bottle?"

"Are you serious?" Tara asked.

"Yeah, did you get it?" I grabbed Troy's cigarette that was burning in the ashtray and brought it to my lips.

Caleb reached into a bag and grabbed my bottle.

"Don't let her drink. That's like bad when your head is all fucked up," Tara exclaimed, stopping Caleb's arm.

"Don't worry about it, Tara." Caleb pushed her arm away and handed me my bottle. "She needs a drink."

"Hell, yes!" Troy interjected.

I took the bottle from Caleb as Tara sat back in her seat and let out a huff. I unscrewed the top and brought it to my lips, taking a huge pull. I drank from it as if I hadn't had a drink in weeks. Nobody spoke. No one knew what to say. Keith had almost killed me and I knew it was over. This time it was really over. I was no longer his girlfriend.

I yelled out coarsely, breaking the awkward silence, "Let's party!"

Caleb raised his bottle into the air. "I'll drink to that!"

6

Virginity

The first rule in the world of junkies is that there is no moral code. Anything is acceptable, and even if it's not, you keep your opinions to yourself. Junkies who don't follow the rules of the game don't get to play. So if you value being a player, you keep your mouth shut. The only junkie moral is the unspoken understanding of the need to get high and stay high, no matter what. I understood unspoken rules because my family was filled with them. So I was not the least bit surprised that no one ever spoke about the night Keith almost killed me. It was simply understood that Keith and I broke up.

With Keith out of my life, I began to find the place I had longed for in Strom's life. I could spend all of my time with him without having to worry about upsetting Keith. Shortly after the breakup, Strom let me into that backroom world of his. That night was also the first time I got into trouble with the law.

The night began in Strom's brown LeBaron. Justin, a short, stocky kid with unruly black hair, was in the passenger seat next to Strom. I wanted to occupy that seat, but for the time being I felt content to just be in the car. Justin snuck looks at me in the rearview mirror. I caught his glances and quickly smiled back at him knowingly. Whenever Justin and I partied together, a weird chemistry ignited between us. We played a game of flirting that included sly smiles and suggestive glances–not leading to sex but instead to doing something wild. We both got excited and turned on by stealing cars, picking fights, trashing houses, destroying property, and anything else that was illegal. I could tell by the look that had already been exchanged that tonight was going to be one of those nights.

I was stuck sitting next to Tim Meek in the back. We called him Rocket Man because his girlfriend told us he wasn't circumcised. He thought it was a reference to Elton John. Rocket Man thought he was tough, the worst sixteen-year-old around because he'd spent six months in juvenile detention. But I didn't mistake the fat rolls underneath his white T-shirt for muscles. He annoyed me by teasing me about being younger than him.

We were on our way to a party. The images of parties at Graham's were gone, replaced by dark basements and rotten smells. Our parties consisted of cramming as many people as possible into the basement of a house or trailer somewhere in the country. Most of the time the party space lacked furniture or effective plumbing. We'd squeeze in on the few pieces of ratty and torn furniture, which looked worse than any furniture at the Salvation Army. Once the furniture was occupied, the bodies of people lined the walls. A mixture of alcohol, pot, urine, body odor, and puke permeated the air. After a while though, I didn't even notice the smell. There was always a radio tuned to the classic rock station. We drank and passed around drugs until the room exploded into meaningless conversation.

Tonight, there was a strange excitement in the car. I could sense it in my stomach, a sort of gnawing like I used to get before a big game. I chewed on my fingernails, anxiously watching up front as Justin grabbed a Fleetwood Mac CD from the glove compartment. He put it on his lap as Strom turned the car onto a gravel road, out of sight from the highway. The car stopped and

Strom reached under his seat, pulling out a Ziploc freezer bag. The bag was filled with chunks of white the size of miniature Snickers bars. He took out a chunk and handed it to Justin. Justin took a razor from his pocket and began to chop it up, forming long trails of powder across the CD. My heart started to beat faster in anticipation and my palms started to sweat. I watched them snort the powder up their noses, holding my breath, hoping to get in on it.

As Justin handed me the CD covered with the powder, Tim warned, "I don't think you should do this."

I looked up at Strom in the rearview mirror. He winked at me and I smiled back. I don't know how I knew the way to do a line. I just did. It seemed completely natural. I took the rolled-up dollar bill, brought my face down to the powder, stuck the bill at the beginning of a thick, long trail of white and plugged my left nostril. After putting the rolled-up bill in my right nostril, I started at the top of the line and snorted all the way to the bottom. My nose burned terribly, my eyes watered, and I gagged as I felt a putrid drip down the back of my throat. I kept sniffing over and over again as my nose tingled and burned all the way up to my head. I held back the urge to sneeze.

After passing the CD to Tim, I waited for something to happen. It wasn't long before my heart started to beat faster and my mind became crystal clear. Thoughts flew through my head with a clarity that hadn't been there for so long. I could feel my hair growing. I was light and free, completely energized. My feet moved back and forth. I hadn't run in years, but I felt like I could run a marathon now if I got out of the car. I wanted to jump up and down, screaming and laughing hysterically. I felt as if the excitement might burst through my chest at any moment.

I looked up front and caught Justin and Strom exchanging wide smiles with each other. Strom elbowed Justin, "Told ya she'd love it."

He was right. I loved it. I'd been in a stoned numbness for so long that having clarity in my mind made me ecstatic. Ideas rushed through my head and I couldn't get words out fast enough. We spent the night driving from basement to basement, dropping off crank and filling our noses with the magical powder. I realized I could drink booze like it was water. Smoking pot was just like smoking a cigarette.

I followed Strom in and out of all the rooms at the strange houses. My nose started to bleed and he dropped chunks of powder into my Captain Morgan so I could give it a rest. Strangers sitting on a bed showed me how to lay a long line on tinfoil, hold my lighter underneath it till it smoked, and then bring my face down into the smoke. The smoke filled my brain with sweetness. I would have put the powder anywhere.

At around three in the morning, we dropped Tim off at his grandma's. On the way to our next stop, cherries appeared behind us.

Strom looked in the rearview mirror. "Fuck!"

Justin flipped open the glove compartment and began pulling out baggies and folds of powder. He frantically handed them to me.

Strom ordered, "Crotch 'em."

Strom began slowing the car down while I hurriedly shoved the crank down my pants and into my underwear. We came to a stop. Squeezing my knee, Strom instructed, "Be cool. Don't worry. They can't search your crotch 'cause you're a minor and a chic."

I didn't care if they did search my crotch. Strom and everyone he had introduced me to had all been arrested. I wanted Strom to know that if it came down to me getting into trouble for him, I would do it. He rolled down his window as the officer peered into the car. He shone his flashlight into Strom's eyes, my eyes, and finally Justin's. I squinted in revulsion.

"Where you guys been tonight?"

Strom responded, "At a friend's house."

"Doing what?"

"Hangin' out."

"Been drinking?"

All three of us shook our heads. I turned around to see another squad car pulling up behind us. My heart beat faster and I felt like I was in a movie.

"I smell alcohol and I'm gonna ask you to get out of the car, one by one." The cop pointed to Justin. "You first."

Justin stepped out and the cop walked over to meet him. He put Justin's arms on top of the car and started to pat him down. Strom quickly rolled up his window.

Looking straight ahead, he whispered, "Whatever you do, just don't let that shit fall out of your crotch. They're gonna know you've been drinking but they can't prove anything else. Whatever he says he knows, he doesn't know shit. Just keep your mouth shut and you'll be cool."

I kept nodding my head up and down. *He trusts me. He really trusts me.* When my turn came to step out of the car, I looked over at Strom one last time to assure him not to worry. I followed the cop's instructions. I stuck my tongue out for him to feel, followed his light with my eyes, stood on one foot, said my ABCs, walked ten steps forward, and took a breath test.

"You're drunk," he declared. "What else are you on?"

"Nothin'."

"I'm going to ask you to empty your pockets." I pulled the inside of my pockets out and my one-hitter clanked to the street. The officer picked it up. I shrugged my shoulders. "Turn around." I turned and heard the sound of metal jingling. Then I felt the pressure of the cuffs going around my wrists and heard the clicks. He turned me around and walked me back to the squad car.

The crisscross wire mesh was close to my face and my knees

smashed up against it, but I didn't care. I smiled. I'd kept the drugs safe. I felt like I had just earned a badge symbolizing that I was officially a bad ass.

The cops brought me down to the station and called my parents to come get me. I slid into their blue minivan and neither of them uttered a word. We walked into the house as the sun was coming up. I ran downstairs to my room and called Strom.

"I didn't expect you to answer," I gushed when he picked up.

"Hamilton bailed me out."

"There is no way I am going to be able to sleep tonight."

Strom laughed. "Nope. You got that right. So, we took away your virginity tonight."

"What do ya mean?"

"Wait and see," he answered.

A couple years later, when I was sixteen, I took away a twelve-year-old girl's "virginity." By this time, I was fully immersed in the court system. I had a probation officer, a social worker, and a judge that made decisions for me and ruled my life. I had just been put on a court-ordered curfew after being charged with my third minor consumption, possession of marijuana, possession of paraphernalia, and failing all of my drug tests.

The conditions of my curfew were very clear. I was to be at my parents' house every night by ten and couldn't leave until eight the next morning. If I didn't make it home or left during the night, my parents were court-ordered to call the police. Every time I broke my curfew, it was a probation violation that moved me closer to spending at least nine months in a juvenile detention center.

I hated being sent away, so I decided to comply with the curfew. I'd come home at my assigned time and hang out downstairs in my bedroom. My mom would get up periodically and come downstairs to check on me. By this time I was hooked on crank, so sleeping was rarely an option. Most of the time I was too wired. I'd lie in my bed with my eyes closed, wishing to go to sleep and knowing it was no use. I sipped on the vodka hidden in Mountain Dew bottles on the nightstand next to my bed. My CDs repeated themselves over and over again as candles burned down to nothing on my dresser. I'd stare at my blue alarm clock's red digits, counting every minute until I could leave again.

I alternated between lying in my bed and sitting in the bathroom with the door locked. My dad had remodeled the old storage room into a small bathroom. It was cramped with the necessary toilet, sink, and shower. There was a small space between the sink and the wall where I'd sit cross-legged on the white tiles. I snorted my lines off the top of the closed toilet lid. The only sound was the overhead fan, whirring constantly in a vain attempt to clear the air of my endless pot smoke.

My only company for hours was my own mind. The bathroom seemed to grow smaller and smaller as voices ran through my head, growing louder and louder. I'd plot ways to burn the house down, or fantasize about killing myself with the pink razors in the shower that I used to shave my legs. The small blue flowers on the wallpaper seemed to talk to me, encouraging my plans and harassing my weakness for being compliant to the rules.

On one of these nights, I stepped outside to smoke a joint. I knew that it would do no good for the madness in my mind, but it was a comforting habit nonetheless. My body ached for sleep, for some sort of a rest, but my mind ran on in circles. My thoughts were stuck on a treadmill that never slowed down.

The garage was attached to the left side of the house and I walked around the corner to stand beside it. I noticed a dark figure making its way through the field across from me. As the figure got closer, I saw it was Tom, a friend of mine. He carried a case of beer. All of my friends knew about my restrictions and every now and then, when nothing else was going on, they'd show up. It was a welcome break from my solitude. However, I wasn't happy to see Tom. He was one of the loudest and most obnoxious people I knew.

The minute he got near enough to hear me, I said, "You gotta go."

"C'mon, girl. Just have a beer with me." He leaned next to me on the garage, hitting a garbage can and causing it to clang.

"Shh! I'm going inside," I said, finishing my joint. "You can leave me a couple beers, but I've gotta go in."

"Man!" he yelled. "This is fuckin' bullshit! You shouldn't have to put up with this shit! They can't trap you here. You've got rights! Mother . . . "

"Tom, shut up! You're gonna wake . . . "

He yelled, "I don't give a fuck! I'll . . . "

"Shut . . . up!" I hissed through gritted teeth, stressing every syllable. "I mean it. Get outta here!"

"I don't have to . . . "

My dad's voice broke into the night. "Heather?"

"Shit!" I snapped. "Get outta here!" Tom grabbed his case of beer from the ground and took off running back through the field.

I walked around to the front of the garage. My dad marched towards me. He reached me quickly, took my chin in his hand, and peered into my eyes. "What are you doing out here?"

I kept my voice low, so as not to anger him further. I didn't want to fight tonight.

"Smoking before I go to bed."

"I'm so tired of your games," he hissed, flicking my chin with his other hand, making my teeth hit each other. "You think you're so tough."

"Dad . . . "

He paid no attention. He kept flicking my chin with the top of his hand. "You aren't so tough. What? What? You wanna go a couple rounds?"

"Dad, leave me alone. I'm not doing anything. I was just getting ready to go in the house." I didn't move from my spot. He pushed me backwards and then jumped in my face again. "Dad please, I don't wanna fight," I pleaded. I looked at the ground, away from his angry eyes.

He sneered, "Oh yeah, let's see how tough you are. C'mon, tough girl. Let's see what you've got." With both hands, he grabbed me by the shoulders and shoved me backwards. I moved around him. He jerked my shoulders from behind, snapping me back. My mom opened the front door and stood on the front steps with her pink bathrobe tucked around her.

"Hon, leave her alone," she called out weakly.

He ignored her. I felt his fingernails digging into my arm, pulling me towards him. I pulled away and ran down the driveway, hearing his steps behind me.

He called out, "You leave this yard and I call the cops. You're not so in control now are ya little girl?"

"Leave me alone!" I yelled. I stopped at the end of the driveway and turned to face him.

He marched towards me, grabbed my head in both of his hands, and jerked me within inches of his nose.

"You are not tough! You are not in control!" His spit hit my face.

"Leave her alone. Come inside," my mom pleaded from the steps.

Before I could respond, he slapped me hard under my chin with the back of his hand. I bit my tongue as my jaw snapped closed. Pure hatred and rage seethed through my body as a rush of air exploded in my head.

"I hate you!" I screamed, swinging at him with my fist and connecting with his face.

"I'm calling the cops, you little brat." He turned around and strutted towards the house.

I wanted to leave, to run across the field and find Strom, but

I was trapped. My heart thumped against my chest. I took out a cigarette, brought it to my lips, and lit it. *I hate him. I hate this house. I hate this bullshit.* I brought my cigarette in and out of my mouth, taking hurried drags and blowing the smoke out rapidly. *Calm down. Don't leave. He's gonna go to bed. You didn't do anything wrong. He's not gonna call the cops.* Slowly, my heart quit thumping and my breathing returned to normal.

I was filled with a mixture of surprise and anger when I saw the red lights making their way down my street. "Shit." I tossed down my cigarette and ground it out with the tip of my shoe.

Three squad cars arrived. One pulled into the driveway and the other two cars parked on the street. Two cops stepped out of the car in the driveway. I recognized the short fat one, Walt Mitchell, because he had arrested me before. I didn't know the tall bald guy.

"What's going on here, Heather?" Walt asked, shining his flashlight into my squinting eyes.

"Nothin'."

My dad burst through the front door, running across the yard. My mom followed behind, still clad in her pink bathrobe. "Take her away. She's out of control." He pointed to the red mark underneath his eye. "She attacked me."

"I did not!"

Walt moved behind me and took hold of my arms. I knew the routine.

"What the fuck. You can't take me away. I didn't do anything wrong," I yelled as the handcuffs jingled. I jerked away, but he held tight.

My dad said, in a calm voice that infuriated me, "See, told ya she's out of control. This is what we have to live with."

"Fuck you!" I screamed, kicking at Walt's legs.

As I struggled to get free, Walt said firmly, "Calm down, don't make this hard."

"Ask my mom!" I yelled. "She saw the whole thing. He started it. I was just defending myself." I heard the click of the cuffs behind me.

Walt turned me around with him to look at my mom. "Is she telling the truth?"

Mom replied softly, staring at the ground, "I didn't see anything."

"Let's go," Walt ordered. He pushed me towards the squad car while the tall cop opened the back door for me. I slid in, staring at the floor, refusing to watch my parents walk back into the house. The police scanner crackled in the background as Walt and the tall cop took their places up front. The other two squad cars pulled away. I watched their red taillights disappear down the street.

"We've got the juvenile in custody," Walt spoke into the CB. "We're en route."

Walt looked over his shoulder at me as he backed out of the driveway. "Kid, you just keep digging a bigger hole for yourself."

Normally, I would have given him some sort of an angry comment, but I didn't have it in me. If only my mom would have spoken up for me. I looked out the window at the stars in the sky, shining brightly because the moon wasn't in sight. When it came down to my mom choosing between my dad and me, she'd always choose him. What did I expect? She'd told me since I was a little girl that he was the man of the house and she would do whatever he instructed her to. She'd explained to me many times in the past, "The Bible tells wives to submit to their husbands and I have to do what the Bible says. Your dad has to come first."

I stared at the stars, wishing there was some way I could disappear. If I held my breath long enough, maybe I could just vaporize into the empty black spaces between them. It seemed like we drove forever before pulling into a driveway.

I looked out the window at a two-story house with stairs leading up to the front door. "Where are we?" I asked.

"Mrs. Morrison's house. She takes in foster kids. You'll be staying here tonight." Walt opened his door and stepped out. He unlatched mine, releasing me into the driveway.

"C'mon, let's go." He pointed to the house.

"Can't you take the cuffs off?" I asked.

"Nice try, kid. Move it." He held my arm and walked me up the steps. Just as he was about to knock, the door opened.

She was an older woman with a long red nightgown and a face lined by stress and tension. Wrinkles formed at the corners of her mouth from years of frowning. Her eyes were small and pointed, hidden by round glasses. She ushered us inside, telling Walt, "I'll call her probation officer in the morning."

"Okay." Walt turned me around and undid the cuffs. Mrs. Morrison shut the door behind him.

"Are you on birth control?" Her voice was high, like she had to squeeze to get it out.

I stared at her. *What does that have to do with anything?*

"Not gonna talk to me, huh? You come into my house in the middle of the night and don't have the decency to answer my questions." She snorted. "You kids are all so ungrateful."

She turned around to punch in numbers on a pad next to the door. I noticed the huge varicose veins wrapping themselves around her calves, which peeked out from underneath her gown. I couldn't help but wonder what would happen if I poked one with a pin.

She turned around. "What are you smiling at?"

"Nothing," I mumbled, still grinning.

"The alarm is set. If you try to go out the door or any of the windows, it's wired directly to the police station. Don't even try it." I didn't understand how her voice could be so high and so forced at the same time.

Annoyed, I said, "Can I go to bed now?"

"Normally you'd be sleeping with Molly, but I'm not going to disturb her just because you're here." She pointed to a couch in the living room. "Sleep there."

I walked over and sat on the couch, directly in front of a large window. The couch was hard and smelled like old people. It was too small for me to stretch out completely. I looked up to see Mrs. Morrison hovering over me. She had shoulders the width of football players. She dropped a folded blanket on me.

"Here." She sighed as if I had just required her to run ten laps around the house. "Oh, and by the way, don't expect to be sleeping until noon. In my house, the kids get up early to work."

I heard the sound of her feet shuffling away and then a door being latched. I rested my head on my arms and closed my eyes, hoping I'd be able to sleep. Birds were beginning to chirp. I must have dozed off because the next thing I knew, my shoulder was being shaken.

"Get up," her high voice broke in. "Molly and Tony have been outside for half an hour. You are going to do your part."

I grunted and rolled over. She grabbed the blanket and tossed it aside.

"God," I moaned.

"I said get up," she hissed. "You will do as you're told. I don't have time for your games. Move."

I slid off the couch to get away from her voice ringing in my ears. I walked out the front door and the sun shone in my eyes, making me shrink in revulsion. I was in the middle of nowhere. A gravel road ran in front of the house and I could see one little white house down the road. The only other thing I saw was miles of endless trees and cornfields. I walked around to the backyard, noticing the form of a boy by the side of a red shed. A pudgy girl bounced up to me.

"Hi, I'm Molly," she announced. Her cheeks were chubby, as if she hadn't lost all of her baby fat yet. Her short brown hair looked like pieces had been randomly hacked off. "Who are you? Mrs. Morrison told me this morning we got a new girl. I'm so happy. We never get girls, always boys. Boys are so stupid. I hate them. Don't you?"

"I'm Heather and I'm not staying," I replied.

"Oh." Her big brown eyes drooped. "I've been here for six months. Tony's been here for like a year or something. Mrs. Morrison loves him. He's like her pet. I guess his dad almost killed him. He doesn't talk about it, though. I've asked him. He just says never mind."

I grunted and walked a few steps over to a big oak tree. I recognized Molly because we rode the same bus in elementary school. She was twelve, the same age as my sister. I plopped on the ground, sprawling out in the shade.

"We're supposed to pick up sticks in the yard," Molly instructed.

"Go ahead." I closed my eyes.

"She's gonna get pissed. You don't want to piss her off."

"I don't care," I snapped.

Molly whispered, as if somehow Mrs. Morrison might hear her from the house, "Really? Doesn't she scare you? She scares me. She just freaks me out when she's mad. You should see her. Her eyes get all huge and her nose flares out. And she yells, which makes her face look so red. Oh my God, she could like yell forever."

"Well, if you're so scared, then you better go pick up sticks."

"Okay." She grabbed her black garbage bag and skipped off. It wasn't long until I fell asleep in my spot underneath the tree.

"She's coming. Get up!" Molly kicked my shoe.

I opened my eyes to see Mrs. Morrison marching across the yard. She was yelling and waving her hands in the air. "Your P.O.

is going to be here in five minutes. And don't think I haven't seen you doing nothing. I wish they'd warned me about you."

"Yeah, it's too bad," I replied, standing up. "It's too bad I'm not some twelve-year-old kid that you can just boss around."

I didn't wait for what she had to say. I turned on my heels and walked to the front of the house to wait for Rubin. He arrived shortly in a navy blue car with an Aines County sticker on the side. He wore his usual button-down dress shirt, tucked into black pants.

"Hello, Heather," he said, as he always did, drawing out the syllables in hello.

"Hey," I replied. "Are you taking me to my parents?"

"You're going to be here awhile." He cleared his throat, preparing for the verbal assault.

"You've got to be kidding me!" I shrieked. "First of all, last night was not my fault and second of all, she is a nut job."

He laughed. "Always so dramatic."

"Don't patronize me. I'm serious. She's whacked." I tried to stay calm. "How long?"

"I don't know. We're not sure. You'll at least be here for the weekend . . . "

"That's three days!" I interrupted. "I don't have any of my stuff. Nothin'. Not even clothes. I'm not stayin'."

He crossed his arms. "You don't have a choice."

I knew he was right. I didn't have any choices because the court system made them for me. *I have nothing. I can't get high. I can't smoke.* Anxiety gripped my mind, the way it did every time I was faced with having to be without chemicals.

"Your mom is gonna bring your clothes down to the courthouse and I'll drop them off."

"Why can't she just bring them here?" I questioned, anxiously running my hands through my hair.

"She doesn't want to. She knows you're mad." He was so calm it made me want to tear the hair out of my head to get some sort of a reaction. "I'll bring you your stuff sometime tomorrow. While you're here, you follow her rules."

"Not a chance," I declared.

Rubin shrugged his shoulders and then stood up. "We'll be in touch."

He was on his way to the next number on his list. I'd become a case number he filed away at the end of his workday. I stood frozen to my spot; wanting to run but knowing I had nowhere to go. The weekend dragged. I lay in the room I shared with Molly, staring at the cracks in the ceiling, wanting to crawl out of my body. My body yearned for drugs in the same way a new mother yearns to hold her newborn infant in her arms.

Finally, Monday came. I didn't care where I was going as long as I got to leave. I didn't even care if I was going to get locked up because at least then I could stop by my house first, where drugs were stashed underneath my mattress. Sitting on the front steps, I watched the few cars drive by, disappointed each time it wasn't Rubin. After a while, Mrs. Morrison opened the door and handed me the phone. I was shocked because she was the only one who got to use the phone. No one else could receive calls, and you couldn't dial out without the code that only she had.

"Hello," I said.

Rubin's drawn-out greeting was on the other line. "Hello, Heather."

"What's going on?"

"Well, it looks like you're going to be staying awhile longer. Your parents both agreed this was the best thing. I . . . "

"Fuck!" I threw the phone on the ground and stormed outside. This was my dad's way of letting me know he was still in control. He always gained the upper hand. I started punching and kicking the siding on the house until my knuckles bled and my toes ached.

Since I was going to be there for a while, I was allowed the privilege of going to work at the Dairy Queen. I'd worked at the Dairy Queen since I'd gotten kicked out of school. The only reason I still held the job was because it was so easy to steal money from the cash register, and it wasn't hard to make ice cream cones when I was high. If I was too messed up to be at the counter, my manager just put me back in the kitchen, where I flipped burgers for my shift. I was never so happy to be able to go to work.

Immediately, I got on the phone in the office and called Strom. By this time, he was my closest friend and the only person I trusted. He'd become like a big brother to me. I'd earned my treasured spot next to him, always riding in the passenger seat of his car and on the back of his motorcycle. It was a spot I held proudly.

I hurriedly told him where I'd been for the past week. I told him I didn't have any pot or cigarettes to get me through. As usual, he promised to come through for me and I knew he would, because he always did. Within a few hours, I heard his familiar voice in the speaker at the drive-through. He requested me to take his order, pulled up to the window, and we made our exchange. I gave him a vanilla cone and he gave me two packs of cigarettes. One held Marlboro Reds and the other held tightly rolled joints.

"It sucks that you're there," Strom said. "Hopefully you'll only be there for a few more days. Stay out of trouble and don't do anything stupid."

"I won't."

He smiled. "Let me know if you need anything. Hang in there, kid."

"I always do."

I ran outside afterward, telling my manager that the trash

needed to be taken out. I lit up a joint behind the dumpster, carefully watching for anyone. The sweetness tasted so good. My nerves relaxed as the familiar numbness crept into my body and filled my head. After work, I returned to the room that Molly and I shared with a smile on my face.

"What happened at work?" she asked. "I haven't seen you smile since you got here."

"I'll tell you tomorrow," I promised. She looked at me with a glimmer of excitement in her eyes as we got ready to go to bed. I slept peacefully for the first time since I'd been brought to Mrs. Morrison's.

The next morning, Molly was anxious to discover what had put a smile on my face. We told Mrs. Morrison we were going for a walk, then we went about a mile down the gravel road and into a thick area of trees. I made sure we were far enough away from the ever-present eyes of Mrs. Morrison before I pulled out the box of Marlboro Reds that held my joints.

"Have you ever gotten high?" I asked her, lighting the joint and bringing it to my lips.

"No, but my sister does. She's always smoking pot. You probably know her. Rachel? Anyways, she gets high. She lives with her boyfriend." Molly watched me inhale the smoke, hold it in, and then exhale. She cocked her head to the side, her gaze fixed curiously on me. I didn't want to push her. I knew this had to be her choice. I wanted her to get high, though. If she got high, I knew there was no way she would narc on me. If she didn't, I didn't know what I would do to keep her quiet. I didn't want to have to resort to threatening her.

"What does it feel like?" she finally asked.

I chose my words carefully, fully aware of the manipulation that lay behind them. "Well, it's kind of hard to explain. You don't really know until you've tried it."

She spoke the magic words eagerly. "I wanna get high. I'm not scared. They say drugs are bad, but whatever. Who cares? I don't. God, you're so cool. My sister never lets me get high with her."

For a moment, I had a sick feeling in the pit of my stomach. I showed her how to smoke a joint in the same way someone had taught me. I showed her how to hold it, how to put her lips around it, how to hold the smoke in her lungs for as long as possible before releasing it back into the air. Then I handed it to her. She took it and focused on her performance. She brought it to her lips and began to inhale. She coughed and choked on the smoke as it escaped her nose and mouth in thick clouds.

"Hold it in," I instructed, giggling.

She kept on smoking it, eventually being able to hold the smoke in her lungs. We smoked two more joints before she finally started to feel it; it's difficult to get someone high for their first time. I watched the transformation take place. Her eyes grew bloodshot and her lips grew heavy. They drooped down, as if she had a slight case of Down's Syndrome. She had a goofy smile on her face and started to laugh uncontrollably.

"I . . . think . . . (giggle, giggle, giggle) . . . I'm . . . high," she announced, bursting into laughter that made her clutch her stomach. "Ohmigod. Mrs. Morrison . . . We are so in trouble." She burst out laughing again.

I watched her with a smile on my face, reliving my first time ever getting high. I missed the silly goofiness it used to bring. I wished I could still feel the way that she was feeling. The closest I'd ever get to my first experience was to watch her have hers. I was thrilled inside for introducing her to this miracle. She wasn't scared and I could tell that she liked it.

"Do you . . . (giggle, giggle) . . . have any more?" she asked, trying to get her lips unstuck from her teeth. "I'm thirsty."

She was just like me. She'd want more and eventually never

be able to get enough. She'd chase this moment from here on out, just like I chased mine. It was then that I understood what Strom and Justin had felt the day they gave me my first line of crank. They had taken away my virginity in the same way I had just taken away Molly's. Doing a new drug is just like first-time sex, because even though you'll have sex hundreds of times, you'll always remember your first.

I knew at times Molly would hate me, at other times she'd love me, but at all times she'd remember me. She would remember, love and hate me in the same way I remembered, loved and hated those who had taken away my virginity.

7

The First Brainwash

I was fifteen the first time I got sent to treatment, and I don't remember the first three days I spent there. The last thing I remember before coming to in a treatment center was walking through my neighbor's field. I was going home to come down after being strung out on crank and tripping on acid for days. I had just left Strom's house, where I'd been sitting on the brown couch underneath the window, grinding my teeth and trying to remember the last time I'd slept. Strom sat on the floor next to the couch, staring at the dirty white wall across from us. Neither of us talked because our brains were mush and we'd run out of things to say. Thoughts were difficult to formulate and speaking out loud was almost impossible.

The events that happened in the next few hours are not my own. They're the stories my mom has told me to fill in the blank spaces. I recall them in the same way you remember childhood events that have been told to you. You can picture yourself and try to put yourself into the memory as it has been told to you, but no matter how hard you try, the real experience is out of reach.

I stumbled through the door at eight Monday morning. My mom met me at the front door in her pink bathrobe. She hadn't seen me since Thursday, when I'd told her I was going uptown to get a pack of cigarettes. Although she hadn't heard from me, she'd heard from others about me. A woman had called her that very morning, refusing to give my mom her name. "Your daughter is going to die. I saw her last night. I don't know if you know this, but she hangs out with a 26-year-old guy, Ryan Hedstrom. He's the biggest drug dealer in Oxford. He's been in lots of trouble with the law. Your daughter is always with him and she's hooked on crank."

"How do you know all this?" my mom had asked. "Are you sure?"

"Positive. I can't tell you how I know, but I can assure you that I'm telling the truth. When was the last time you looked at your daughter? Look at her eyes, her pupils are huge. Look at her nose and the way it drips constantly. Those are all signs of using crank. She's so skinny she looks like she's about ready to fall through her own asshole."

I can imagine how upset my mom was that an outsider would interfere in our family. She replied shortly, "Look, I appreciate all of this, but I can take care of my daughter."

"I called her probation officer . . . "

My mom interrupted, "How do you know her probation officer?"

"I know a lot. Let's just say I'm involved with the police department. I've been dealing with Ryan Hedstrom for a while. Don't worry; he'll be going to jail. But I just think it's so sad to see a little girl running around with him. I felt compelled to call and tell you how much trouble your daughter is in. If you don't do something quick, you're gonna lose her."

As soon as Mom hung up the phone, it rang again. This time it was my probation officer, Rubin Harris. He informed my mom that it was true the woman worked for the police department, and that arrangements had been made to bust Strom and a few others involved in our circle. They'd be going to jail but I wouldn't because I was a juvenile. He suggested I be taken directly to treatment.

So when I got home that Monday morning, my mom noticed my huge pupils, the outline of my bones underneath my clothes, my sunken face and yellow skin. She had no choice but to accept that the woman had been telling the truth, and that I was doing a lot more than smoking pot. According to my mom, I stumbled past her and went directly downstairs to my bedroom and lay on the bed. She followed me into my bedroom and started throwing some of my clothes into a bag.

"What's going on?" I demanded.

"We're taking you to get some help."

"I'll be fine. Seriously. I've been like this many times. No need to worry." I must have thought she was talking about taking me to see a doctor.

"We're gonna take you to treatment. The people there will help get you off drugs."

She says I went hysterical, twisting and turning on my bed as if I was having a seizure. I alternated between screaming hysterically and bawling like a small child. One minute I was screaming, "You can't take my drugs away! You can't! Stay the fuck away from me! I'm not going! Fuck! You can't do this!" The next minute I was crying, "Please, ohmigod, you can't do this to me. Please! I'm going to die."

My mom just kept throwing clothes into a bag, praying quietly.

"There is no God," I declared, sitting up in bed, and looking right at her. "Don't you dare try to tell me to believe in God. He hates me and I hate him."

I don't remember any of this, or the drive to New Hope Treatment Center in Princeton. My next conscious memory is three days later, standing next to Lindsey, a brown haired girl, in an unfamiliar bathroom. I knew who she was because I had partied with her before. But I didn't know where I was, how I'd gotten there, or what day it was. None of this was very unusual for me. I was losing more and more chunks of time and I'd come to in the middle of a conversation I was having with somebody.

My mind was a blur, overloaded with chemicals and booze, coupled with starvation because the very thought of food made my stomach heave. I checked in and out of consciousness and I'd gotten used to it. In fact, I liked it. It was as close to death as I could get without physically dying.

I looked around me at the toilet, sink, and tub made of shiny white porcelain. I stared at Lindsey, who was leaning over the sink and spitting out wet brown slime. I'd gotten good at not letting anyone know I didn't know where I was or what was going on. Sometimes I could put the pieces together and figure it out. But most of the time I didn't even try to figure it out because I knew it was only a matter of time until I'd black out again.

"C'mon," she said. "You can't go to group with chew in your mouth, dumbass."

I realized I had a thick wad of chew in my mouth. I did what I was told and dug it out from my mouth, spitting my brown slime into the sink next to hers. *Why am I chewing? What in the fuck have I gotten myself into?*

"What's group?" I asked.

She giggled. "Shut up, let's go."

She thinks I'm kidding. I followed her out of the bathroom and walked through a small room with a bed and a desk. She opened the door and we stepped out into a long hallway. The hallway was lined with doors on both sides. There was a big desk at the front of the hall. Nurses dressed in white scurried around it, answering the phone and talking to each other. *I'm in a hospital. How did I get here? What's Lindsey doing here? Why am I in jeans if I'm in the hospital?*

Right before we reached the nurse's station, Lindsey opened a door on the left. I followed her through into a big room.

Windows with thick black trim lined an entire wall. There were about fifteen kids sitting on chairs arranged in a circle. Behind the chairs was a table covered with playing cards and a Scrabble game. At the front of the room stood an entertainment center with a TV and VCR.

Lindsey sat in one of the chairs in the circle and I sat in the empty one next to her. I eyed the girl across from me. She was curled into a ball with her legs tucked underneath her. Short red hair haphazardly framed her face and freckles sprinkled across her nose. With her pale skin and rosy lips, she reminded me of a Strawberry Shortcake doll. She clutched a big white teddy bear in her arms. I laughed out loud when I noticed her Grateful Dead tie-dye.

I didn't have time to finish my observations before the door opened. A woman walked in with big brown hair neatly curled and sprayed in place. She wore a red sweater stretched tightly across her chest. Her upper body was slender but from her waist down she ballooned into wide hips and a huge ass. She wore red lipstick and make-up that looked like it took hours to perfect. She smiled at everyone and stood next to me.

"Should we open?" she asked cheerfully.

Everyone stood up from their chairs and grabbed hands with the person standing next to them, so I stood as well. Lindsey and the woman each grabbed one of my hands. I jerked them away.

"Heather," the woman said, frowning at me. "Let's not go through this again."

She knows my name. This is fuckin' weird. I took her hand. They all recited some sort of a prayer together. I'd never heard it before, which surprised me because I'd spent so much of my childhood in church. I looked at Lindsey. She had her eyes closed and a smile pulled at the corners of her mouth. *What is she doing? Where in the hell am I?* As soon as the prayer ended, they dropped hands and sat down. Everyone else seemed to know what was going on and acted like this was a perfectly normal activity.

"Let's do introductions," the woman said cheerfully. Her voice annoyed me. It was one of those fake voices where you can hear the forced happiness behind it.

The boy with long hair, dressed in black, announced from the right-hand part of the circle, "I'm Jeremy. I'm an alcoholic and a drug addict."

The Latino-looking kid next to him said, "I'm Rick. I'm an alcoholic."

I listened and watched as each kid in the circle took a turn saying their name and announcing that they were a drug addict or an alcoholic. *Oh my god. I'm in treatment. Jesus Christ. How did I get here?*

I knew I was in treatment because my friend Bobby had just gotten out of treatment a few months before, and he'd told me all about it. He'd told me stories about everyone sitting around in circles, just like we were doing now. He said the counselors tried to brainwash you into getting sober by getting you to cry about your life and then trick you into believing that getting sober would make you feel better. They'd almost succeeded in brainwashing Bobby. He'd sworn he was done doing drugs after he got out. But I knew he'd just had some sort of a nervous breakdown after Red died.

Red had been Bobby's best friend and one of my close friends, too. Strom had introduced all of us—we were the only high school age kids in the group—and we soon became a threesome. We spent lots of our time together selling drugs at all the high schools in our area. Six months ago, Red had died from an overdose, which the papers reported as undiagnosed heart failure. I always did my best not to think about his death but the memories flooded back as I sat in the circle of chairs, surrounded by strangers.

The night Red died, the phone rang outside my bedroom

door. It stopped and then started again, waking me. I was annoyed to be awake because I only went home to sleep when I needed to come down for a while, and I didn't like to be disturbed during it. I rolled out of bed and walked to the phone.

"Hello," I said groggily.

"Heather! Heather! I'm comin to get ya. I'm coming to get ya."

"Huh? Bobby, no. Not tonight. I'm tired."

"But Red, Red. He's on the driveway . . . "

"My driveway?"

"Nonono. The driveway. His driveway. I'm coming. There's lights, everywhere. I'm telling ya. Lights! Red! Red, ohmigod!" Bobby was crying.

"What are you talking about?" I asked. "Did you drop again tonight?"

"Yes. No. The cops. All the cherries. My brother saw. He's dead. They say he is. I'm coming," he wailed.

"Whoa, hon, slow the fuck down," I ordered. "You need to chill out. Are you tripping?"

He stammered, "I don't know. Acid. Yes. Red."

"Okay, you listen to me, are you listening?"

"Yes, but Heather . . . I . . . "

I said calmly, "Just listen. You're gonna take a few deep breaths. You're havin' a bad trip. You just need to settle down." Bobby had bad trips a lot but it was usually pretty easy to talk him down. "Red is fine. I just talked to him last night. He's not in anyone's driveway. He's okay. You're okay. Do you hear me?"

"Yes." He sounded like a little boy.

"You're gonna be fine. It's just the drugs messing with your mind. You can't let them take over. You control the trip, the trip doesn't control you. Okay, are ya with me?"

I heard him take some huge gulping breaths. "Yes, yes, I am. Are you sure?"

"Positive. Everything is fine," I said adamantly. "Listen, you've been up for too long and are starting to wig out. You've just gotta come down for a while."

He said, "I do. I do. Can I come sleep with you?"

"Now you sound like yourself," I giggled. He was always trying to get down my pants.

He laughed. "I guess so. Still, can I?"

"Darlin', you are never gonna get in my bed," I sighed. "Are you gonna be okay? 'Cause I really wanna go back to bed."

"Yeah." The hysteria in his voice was gone.

"Okay, I'll call ya tomorrow."

"Promise?"

"Promise."

"I love you, Heather. Thanks."

"You, too. Talk to ya tomorrow." I curled back up in bed.

But the next day I discovered that Red had really died on his driveway. His heart had stopped and paramedics had been unable to revive him. It wasn't just acid, of course. When we did drugs, it was never just one. It was crank, booze, pot and anything else that was available.

My mom drove me to the funeral. She was my mom and I expected her to comfort me because I'd just lost a friend, and I was sad and confused. But she only spoke once through the whole ride. "Was he saved?" she asked. I shrugged my shoulders. She let out a deep sigh. "Well, I hope he was." What she really meant was that she hoped he wasn't burning in hell. I wanted to punch her in the face.

Shortly after the funeral, Bobby started to go nuts. He'd burst into tears for no reason at all and not be able to stop. He'd always gotten into fights, but now he started to freak out and get violent without being provoked. At parties, he'd suddenly jump up and grab someone's head, smashing his head against theirs. He punched walls and crashed his car into stop signs. He started to call me up in the middle of the night, talking about Red and how he wished it had been him. I didn't want to think about Red and talking to Bobby made me do that. I blew him off, trying to get him to talk about something else. Shortly after one of our late night conversations, I didn't hear from or see him for three days. I kept calling his house.

Finally, on one call, I recognized his mom's voice on the other end, which was unusual because his brother was the one who always answered the phone. "Is Bobby there?" I asked politely.

"No. Is this Heather?"

"Yes."

"Listen to me. Bobby is in treatment. He's getting off drugs. You stay away from him. He doesn't want to talk to you and I don't want you anywhere near him. You tell that friend of yours, that unemployed loser Strom who sells drugs to little kids, to stay the hell away from my son, too. You people are evil." She hung up on me.

I blew her off. I was used to parents not wanting their kids to hang around me. About a month later, I ran into Bobby at a gas station.

"Hey!" I called, running through the parking lot to his car.

He turned around. "Hey."

He looked different. His eyes were bright blue and shining. His skin glowed and he had gained weight. He looked like an actual high school student in his clean blue jeans and neatly tucked in T-shirt.

"What's up? I didn't even know you got out. What are ya doin' tonight?" I asked.

"Goin' to a meeting," he replied softly.

"A meeting? For what?"

"It's for treatment. I go to AA meetings." He tapped his feet against each other.

"Okay. Well, do ya wanna get high before ya go?" I asked, motioning to the car I was in.

He glared at me. "I don't get high. I'm sober." What had they done to him?

I didn't know what to say. We stood there, staring at each other. The silence was awkward. We never used to have a hard time making conversation. He finally spoke. "Look, I can't talk to you. It's not good for me."

"You've got to be kidding me," I snorted. "Since when are you better than me?"

"I'm not. You wouldn't understand. Just leave me alone." He opened his door and jumped in without looking at me, leaving me standing next to his empty space by myself.

I didn't understand then, but once I was in treatment I could see how he'd been brainwashed. The counselors and staff were very good at trying to convince you to get sober. They promised that you would be happy if you did. They said you needed to stay away from your old friends because they only used you to get high. The counselors tried to find your weak spot and break you down. They called it "getting through your denial" but I thought it was one big mind game.

Staff members told me over and over again, "Heather, you're going to die. You're a chronic alcoholic and drug addict."

I knew what they said was true. I was hooked and most likely I would die. But their death threats meant nothing to me. In order for a death threat to be effective, the person threatened has to want to live. I'd been intent on destroying myself for a long time.

The whole treatment structure seemed foreign and bizarre to me. I was furious because not only did I not have any drugs, I wasn't allowed to smoke cigarettes. My head pounded and my stomach rotated between waves of nausea and shooting pains. I wanted to crawl into bed and sleep until it was time for me to get out of there. Much like everything I wanted to do, this wasn't allowed.

I was awakened each morning at 7:00 and instructed to get out of bed. They expected us to eat breakfast in the cafeteria by 8: 00. I couldn't get my body out of bed. It ached and shook. It hurt to lift my head off the pillow. While the other kids filed down to the cafeteria, I lay in bed, pulling the pillow over my head whenever the staff came to wake me up.

After hours of staff coming to my room and waking me up, I'd grudgingly get out of bed. I didn't bother to shower or even get out of my pajamas. Mornings were spent listening to different people lecture about the effects of drugs and booze on the body and mind. I wasn't interested in anything the speakers had to say. Of course I knew drugs were poison and messed you up permanently. Wasn't that the point? I'd curl into a chair in one of the corners of the room and fall back to sleep.

After lecture, I plodded in my pajamas upstairs to a makeshift classroom. This infuriated me because I didn't go to school anymore on the outside, and I certainly didn't see any reason why I should have to go to school while I was there. The two teachers could be better classified as advanced babysitters. They passed out worksheets and tried to get us to do schoolwork.

Next came lunch. We walked through an underground tunnel that connected the treatment center to the regular part of the hospital. Filing in line with our trays, our nametags announced to everyone else that we were the kids in treatment. We ate in a room off to the side of the cafeteria, away from the doctors and nurses. I couldn't eat. Every time I tried to put something in my stomach, I ended up running up the stairs and throwing it back up into the toilet. It had been about a year since I started to throw up blood. I hated the way it would hang from my throat before it dropped in thick globs into the toilet. It was easier not to eat.

Group therapy filled the afternoon. This is where the mind games took place. The main counselor, Dave Bateman, led group. He was a short, stocky man with long black hair slicked back into a tight ponytail at all times. He wore jeans and T-shirts and looked young enough to pass for a patient. Long, dark lashes framed his huge blue eyes. His eyes were striking, as if they could look right through you. His face was serious, but easily broke into smiles and laughter. He introduced himself as a drug addict and an alcoholic. I felt threatened by him, but I made sure not to let on to this fact.

He opened the brainwashing sessions with, "Let's go around the room and check in."

One by one, we'd go around the circle, introducing ourselves and talking about any issues that had occurred since the last group. It didn't take long for me to learn that "issues" were a big deal in treatment. They were the things we needed to talk about to feel better. Supposedly, we all had them and anything could qualify as one. The Strawberry Shortcake girl, Amy, always went first and it was the same routine every time. She'd immediately burst into tears after she identified herself as an alcoholic.

"What's wrong, Amy?" Dave would ask.

"I can't talk about it," she'd sniffle. Her short, chubby friend, whose name was also Amy, would put her arm around her and hand her a Kleenex.

Dave would encourage her. "C'mon. You can talk about it. Talking about it takes the power away."

I didn't understand what he meant when he'd give his speeches about taking the power away from our issues. What kind of power could our issues possibly have? And how could talking about our feelings change anything? I couldn't see the point to all the whining and crying.

I'd roll my eyes and slump in my chair whenever Amy cried her ugly-face cry. It wasn't the sort of crying that allows you to still hold on to some of your dignity. It was the cry that scrunches up your face in a way that looks like you've been constipated for years, as the tears fall and the snot drips. Amy always said she couldn't talk about what was bothering her, but it was always just a few minutes before she starting rambling. She always had some sort of problem. Some days it was a letter she'd gotten from a friend or boyfriend, other times she'd had a bad dream, or she wanted to get high. The list of her problems was endless. To me, her problems seemed extremely trivial and juvenile. I figured she was just some spoiled rich girl whose parents found out she smoked pot and put her in treatment immediately. I felt the same way about most of the other kids. I had my own routine for checking in when my turn came around.

"Heather, how are you today?" Dave would ask, turning the focus to me.

"Fine," I'd reply, crossing my arms across my chest.

Inevitably, the next question from his mouth was, "How are you feeling?"

"Just waiting to get outta here. This whole thing is stupid."

Silence would follow while everyone stared at me. I stared back at them with no expression on my face. I worked hard at making sure my face was a blank slate. Slowly, they'd all look away, except for Dave. His eyes remained glued to me.

"Anyone have any feedback for Heather?" Dave would break into the silence, still staring at me, watching for any sign of weakness that he could jump on. I gave him none.

Usually one of the Amys would speak up. "I don't like Heather's negative attitude. All she talks about is getting high. It threatens my sobriety."

"Why don't you tell her?" Dave would instruct. "Tell her how it makes you feel."

This was such a comical part of group. The kids would talk about people as if they weren't sitting right there. Everyone spoke to Dave first. It was as if they needed his permission to speak to the person they had a problem with. The focus was always on feelings. It nauseated me. I lived to get as out of touch as possible with my feelings and I saw no good reason to feel them at all. The only feeling I was in any way comfortable with was anger, and that was the one feeling we weren't supposed to express. Supposedly, it wasn't a real emotion but rather a cover-up for other emotions.

I laughed at the Amys who were so threatened by my negative attitude. "Too bad. If you really wanted to be sober, you wouldn't be bothered by me talking about getting high. I can't help it if you still want to do it. Maybe it's your problem. Anyone got anything else to say?"

My challenge was always met with silence. The other kids were scared of me and didn't like me. I felt powerful. However, everyone had to meet with Dave a few times a week on an individual basis, and it was much harder to remain cold and aloof when we were alone. His office was small, with two windows behind his desk. His desk was always covered with papers and the big thick binders that counselors and staff wrote in. There were two blue chairs in front of his desk where patients were supposed to sit. Every inch of wall space was lined with bookshelves overflowing with titles like *Of Course You're Angry* and *Learning to Live with Addiction.*

The door would shut behind us and instantly I felt as if there wasn't enough air for me to breathe. Dave would lean back in his chair behind the desk, arms folded behind his head. His eyes bored into me. I'd sit in the chair in front of his desk, wanting to jump through the window behind him and run as fast as I could down the street. I knew I couldn't, which only increased the panic of being trapped. I hated these sessions, but there was also a part of me intrigued by Dave for reasons I couldn't understand.

In one of our sessions, he began, "The others on the unit are threatened by you. Do you like that?"

I shrugged my shoulders. "I really don't care. It's not my problem."

He leaned forward in the chair. "Doesn't it ever get tiring trying to be so tough all the time?"

I shook my head. *Don't trust him. Don't trust him.*

"You know being tough is going to kill you, right?" His eyes filled with a sadness that looked genuine.

"I don't care." I stared out the window, watching oak branches flap in the wind.

"Well, I happen to think you've got a lot to live for." He stood up. "You want to know what I think? No, I don't care if you want to know or not. I'm going to tell you. You don't fool me for one second. I don't buy your tough girl routine. I think you're in a lot of pain and inside of you is a little girl whose heart is breaking."

My head began to swim. I felt dizzy. I looked down at the floor. He walked to the front of his desk to stand directly in front of my chair. *Stay unaffected. He's just trying to break you. This is what he does. It's his job.*

"I care about you. I'm not just saying that. I think there's a huge part of you that just wants someone to listen and understand you, but you're too damn afraid. You've been hurt a lot, huh?"

"You don't even know me." I switched my gaze to the carpet on the floor, trying to disappear into the gray design.

"I think I know a lot more about you than you think." He laid his hand gently on my shoulder.

I wanted to pull away, but I was frozen. His touch scared me. That lump lodged in my throat. I didn't know what to do. I wanted to pull away, but there was a small part that wanted to start to cry and let this man hold me. But I knew enough about men to know they couldn't be trusted. His touch had to mean something. He pulled his hand away and walked back to his desk. I breathed a sigh of relief, but for a moment I had the urge to tell him to come back.

"What do you want to talk about?" he asked, sifting through the papers on his desk.

"Nothin'," I replied softly, having a hard time speaking around the lump in my throat.

"All right. You can go then." He motioned towards the door.

I got up, turned away, and shut the door behind me. Then I froze there, my head swimming and swirling around. I wanted to open the door and yell at him that I hated it in this place and wanted to leave. I wanted to tell him that I didn't want to live and that I'd felt that way long before I started doing drugs.

Instead, I walked down the hallway and wandered back to my room, feeling as if I wasn't connected to the body carrying me there. Without drugs, it was as if I was only a mind racing and running wild, disconnected from my body. I watched myself perform from up above. My head raced, my heart pounded, and I couldn't sleep at night. I had to get high or I felt as if I'd explode into a million pieces and no one would ever be able to put me back together again.

Getting high was difficult because everything in treatment is structured to prevent it. I had to steal glue from the arts and crafts room when staff had their backs turned. When I met with the psychiatrist, I rummaged through her desk while she was out of the room and found White-Out in her drawer. For some reason, the nurses gave me pills every day. I'd pretend to put them in my mouth and then quickly drop them into the pockets of my jeans. I didn't know what the pills were for but I figured they had to do something. I chopped them up as best I could with a knife I'd stolen from the cafeteria. Whenever a new patient got admitted, they had to have their bags searched. The nurses would pull out any product that contained alcohol and set it aside. I'd stand by the nurses' desk, watching and waiting to make my move. When they turned their backs, I'd grab the aerosol hairspray or mouthwash.

I accumulated a stash of household products that I hid by pushing up one of the tiles on the ceiling of my room, tucking things into the space above it. At night and during the day when I couldn't get caught, I'd take something out and go into my bathroom. I'd never inhaled chemicals before, but it was my only option. Dousing paper towels with whatever chemical I had, I'd stick them in the bottom of an empty toilet paper roll, put the cardboard roll into my mouth and take big, deep breaths. It was a cheap buzz that made a vacuum sound in my head, but at least I was getting high. Then I felt somewhat normal and the sense of an impending breakdown lessened.

On my third week at treatment, a new guy, Bryan Black, was admitted to the unit. I came out of my room on the way to group and met him in the hallway. He had long blond hair that hung in his face, a Grateful Dead T-shirt, baggy pants and sandals.

"Hhheeeeeyyy." He drew out the word like a pothead.

"Hey."

"How long you been here?"

"Too fuckin' long," I grunted.

The door next to us opened and the two Amys appeared, their arms linked together. The Strawberry Shortcake doll shot me a dirty look as they walked past. I flicked them off.

"I hate them," I reported.

"You're not too happy to be here, huh?" Bryan laughed.

"Are you crazy? I hate this place. It's a fuckin' waste of time and space. Everyone trying to mess with your head and shit. I can't wait till I get out of here so I can get wasted."

A wide smile spread across his face. He leaned towards me to whisper, "I've got weed."

I grabbed him by the shoulders. "Are you serious?"

He nodded his head. I grabbed his face and brought him towards me, kissing him on the cheek. "Dude, you are my new best friend."

That night I waited until after the second bed check before I inched along the wall to his room. We crammed ourselves into his bathroom, which was the size of a small closet. I stood on the toilet while he sat in the sink. He'd rolled a joint using a piece of paper torn out from a Bible. I'd done a lot of things with God's words, but this was the first time I'd ever smoked them.

We smoked quietly, listening for anyone coming. We blew our hits upwards but, with no fan, the smoke quickly filled the bathroom in thick clouds. We coughed and before long tears streamed down our faces.

"See, this is all they needed to do to get me to cry!" I joked.

But I was disappointed. Because I hadn't smoked any weed for three weeks, I expected it to feel like the first time I smoked. Instead of uncontrollable giggles, the numbness took over my mind and dulled my senses.

We no sooner stepped out of the bathroom when there was a knock at the door. I hid underneath the bed. A nurse walked in.

"I see your feet underneath the bed," she announced, hands on her hips. It's the same stance every adult has when they've just caught you doing something you're not supposed to be doing. "You've been smoking pot in here." She walked over to the bathroom door and opened it. Smoke rushed out. I burst out laughing and crawled out from underneath the bed, running back to my room.

The next morning we were both kicked out. I found myself in the office of the counselor with the big ass, signing my discharge papers. I screamed at her, shaking my fist. "God, you are a bitch. All of you people! You say you care about me? Fuck you. You people don't care. Nothin' but lies!"

She looked up at me from her papers. "Heather, you've been wanting to leave since you got here. Now you've got it. I just hope you don't die out there."

"Shut up!" I screamed. "You don't care if I die. Fuck you and fuck this stupid place!"

I stormed out of her office, slamming the door behind me. I stomped to my room where my bags lay on my bed, then climbed up on the windowsill, hugging my knees to my chest and staring out at the trees.

What's wrong with me? What just happened? Why am I so pissed? I'm getting out. I've counted every single minute since I've gotten here until I could leave. Now I am. I should be happy. C'mon Heather, pull yourself together.

I wanted to cry and couldn't understand why. As much as I hated treatment, there was a part of me that liked having people say they cared about me. There was a sense of comfort knowing that if I ever chose to talk about what my life was really like and how I really felt, they would listen. For a brief instant, I felt as if there might be another way to live my life. I quickly pushed the questions away and assured myself that I had just been brainwashed.

8

Splitting

After I got kicked out of New Hope, I was released into the care of my parents. As soon as our blue minivan was parked in the driveway, I ran into the house, threw my bags on my bed, and took off in search of Strom. I told my mom I was going for a walk to enjoy my new freedom. At the other end of the park, I spotted Strom's Chrysler LeBaron on the street outside of his parents' trailer. I ran across the street, knocked on the door, and sprang into the trailer before he answered. He was sitting on the brown couch underneath the window in the living room.

"I'm back." I plopped down on the couch next to him.

"Hey kid, I missed ya," he replied, tousling the hair on top of my head. "Like five minutes after you left that morning, the cops showed up at my house."

"Did you get busted with anything on you?"

"I only had like a half on me. Lucky we got rid of the last of our shit to Charlie. His place got raided, too. He'll be goin' to jail for a long time. Sucks for him, but my ass is free." He was rolling a joint on the coffee table in front of the couch.

I laughed. "Did you know some chic called my mom and told her that all of this shit was going down?"

"Yep, some stupid bitch is a narc. That's how they got a search warrant." He threw me the joint. "If I find out, I'll bust up her face. I don't care if she is a chic."

"I'll do it," I cried out. "So, what kind of trouble you in?"

"Well, the pigs brought me down to the courthouse and I had to piss in a cup. Let's just say I failed." He laughed. "I did ten days in jail. My court date is coming up. I think I'm gonna use the treatment card. Just go to outpatient or some shit."

I lit up then said in that short, choppy way you talk while holding in a hit, "I'd rather be in jail. Seriously. They try so damn hard to sober you up. It's just like Bobby said. A lot of whining and crying."

"Was it really that bad?"

"It sucked. I don't even wanna talk about it. Can ya chop me up a rail?"

Crank had become my favorite drug since I'd done my first line. It brought clarity to my mind and made me feel like I was invincible and untouchable. I'd dreamt about it many times while I'd been away. I'd awakened many nights covered in sweat and tasting the familiar putrid drip in the back of my throat. I needed it now. I'd find some answers once I was high. Everything would become clear while the tingling energy flowed through my body.

I sat next to Strom on the couch, doing lines while we watched TV. I kept waiting for the startling clarity to hit, but it didn't. My mind moved faster and faster, but none of it made sense.

You can't even stay sober for two hours. Big deal, I never said I was gonna try. The cops are gonna come. They're out to get you. Everyone is in on it. Talk to Strom. I don't know what to say. It's Strom. You always know what to say. What's wrong? I'm paranoid. It's been a long time since you were this high.

I tried to quiet my mind by focusing on the TV, but it was useless. The images from the screen passed by my eyes without registering at all. Strom chatted on as if nothing was unusual, telling me stories about who'd gotten into trouble while I was gone. I couldn't concentrate on anything he was saying. After a few more hours, I decided I had to go home, even though I didn't want to. It wasn't a good idea for me to disappear right away. Also, while I was in treatment, my parents had received lots of education on drugs and the signs to watch for. I had a sinking suspicion that it wasn't going to be so easy to fool them anymore.

Strom brought me home, dropping me off a block away, like he always did. I cheered myself on as I walked the block. *Act sober. Don't look at her. She doesn't know you're high.* My plan was to make my parents trust me again and eventually be able to do whatever I wanted to.

"You're high," my mom declared, looking into my eyes. "You just got home."

"I'm not high."

"Oh, right," my mom huffed, walking away. I looked at the ground and walked down the stairs to my bedroom, flopping on the bed.

I can't stay here all night. I'll go insane. I looked around at my familiar walls and the candles burned down to the same familiar spots. I stared at my Jerry Garcia picture, wishing I'd been born twenty years earlier, when doing drugs was more acceptable. After a knock on my door, my mom stuck her head in and handed me the phone.

I took it from her and waited for her to shut the door behind her before I answered. "Hello?"

"Hi, Heather," a deep voice responded. *It's Dave Bateman! Ohmigod! Why is he calling?* The silence stretched out before he spoke again. "I was upset when I came to work today and found out you were gone." *What do I say? Should I just hang up? What does he care?* "I was really hoping that if you stayed long enough, you'd begin to trust me. You might have even started to believe that life could exist without drugs. I wish you would have given it a shot."

"I did." *Why did I just say that?*

"Did you stay clean and sober today?" he asked.

"Pretty much. I just drank a little and got high a couple times," I said quickly. *Why am I lying?*

A long pause followed. As usual, I couldn't deal with silence.

"I'm gonna stay off the hard stuff," I blurted out. "Just a little weed and I'll probably drink some, but I'm not gonna get all strung out again." *You're already wired.*

"Hmm," he said softly. "Well, good luck to you, kid. I care about you and I'm not going anywhere."

I responded quickly, "Thanks, bye," and hung up the phone.

The night dragged on endlessly. I paced my bedroom back and forth with the music of Courtney Love turned up in an attempt to silence my thoughts. I lay on my bed trying to sleep, but it was no use. I felt as if I was going crazy. For the first time, I wanted to come down. *I want to cry. What's wrong with me? They messed you up.*

As soon as I heard the sound of footsteps upstairs, I jumped out of bed. I trudged up the stairs to find my parents sitting around the table in the kitchen eating breakfast. They looked rested and refreshed.

"Eat something," my dad instructed. "We're going for a drive after breakfast."

"I'm not hungry." My stomach was in knots, twisting and turning. I didn't think I'd be able to swallow. I went outside and sat on the front steps smoking cigarettes until they were ready to leave. *I wonder where we're going? Probably to get a piss test. Great.* It wasn't long until we piled into the minivan.

"Where are we going?"

"You'll see," my dad answered.

We drove straight out of town. I looked over my shoulder and saw my black duffle bag on the seat behind me.

"Hey, wait a minute. What the hell is going on? Where are we going?" I demanded.

My dad stared straight ahead, refusing to speak. I turned to my mom in the passenger seat. "Mom?" I pleaded.

"You need help," she answered softly.

"I don't need help. I just need to be left alone."

We kept on driving, hitting the interstate and heading north. I wanted so much to jump out of the car, but I was trapped. We drove all the way to the Twin Cities, parked in a ramp and walked across the skyway into a hospital. The elevator took us to the fourth floor. When the doors slid open, there was only one metal door in front of us. The sign on the door said to press the intercom to be let in. The sign above the intercom said "Redview Adolescent Locked Unit."

My dad spoke into the intercom. "We're here with Heather Harrison." There was a buzz and the door swung open, leading into a room with a receptionist's desk. The walls of the small room were lined with doors, all leading to places I didn't know.

A big Latino woman stood in front of us. "I'll take her with me," she announced. She took my bag from my mom.

"Can't we even see the place?" my mom asked, looking around at the cold gray walls.

Without an ounce of emotion in her voice, the woman said, "I'm sorry. You'll have to go now."

My mom reached towards me, wrapping her arms tightly around me. I stood there, unmoving, with my arms at my sides. My dad touched her shoulders and pulled her away. "C'mon," he instructed. "Let's go."

They left me standing there with the big Latina. She punched a code into a pad next to the door and let them out.

My mom looked over her shoulder at me, waving her fingers in a meek gesture. Tears filled her eyes as the door snapped behind her.

"Come with me," the woman ordered, leading me through one of the doors on the left and into a hallway. She opened a door on the right with a key. The room was a small bathroom with pea green tiles. It had a bench against the wall and a shower with a flimsy white curtain pulled around it.

She immediately ordered, "Take your clothes off."

"Take *your* clothes off."

"Listen, we will sit here as long as it takes for you to get undressed." She sat down on the bench and stared at me. I stared back at her defiantly. I don't know how long we stayed locked in our stare-down before she spoke, but it seemed like forever.

"If you are not dressed, you will spend your first day here in the seclusion room," she informed me.

"What's that?" I asked.

She explained, smiling, "A very small room that's completely empty. It's just you in there. You can't see, talk, or hear anything other than yourself. How's that sound? You'll just stay in there until you can follow the rules. I don't know where you've been before, but in here we follow the rules."

I sat there contemplating my choices, then started to undo my pants.

"Can you at least turn around?" I asked, sliding my jeans down to my legs.

"Nope," she answered with a grin. "Gotta make sure you're clean."

I stripped down to my bra and underwear, covering my chest with my arms.

"Take it *all* off," she ordered.

"You have got to be kidding me," I declared.

She shook her head. "We don't play games."

"You don't have to be such a bitch." I wanted to slap the grin off of her face. *She is enjoying this way too much.*

I decided to do as I was told, pretending that being completely naked didn't bother me in the least.

"There." I put my hands on my hips. "Pretty damn sexy, huh?"

She frowned. "Turn around and bend over."

I turned around and bent over. "How do you like this view, lady?" *This is so fuckin' humiliating. This has to be against the law.*

"Spread your cheeks."

I want to die. Right now. "Do you want to lick me where I pee too, dyke?" I answered hotly.

She looked me over from head to toe and in every crack while I willed myself to disappear into the nasty green tiles. Once she finished, I had to take a shower while she watched. She handed me a towel as I stepped out. I wrapped the towel around me. She handed me a pair of blue scrubs like surgeons wear at hospitals.

"You can get your clothes back when you earn them," she sharply informed me. I spent the next few weeks in my blue scrubs.

Every door in the place locked. Every room we entered had to be unlocked by a staff member, and we had to knock and wait for a staff member to let us out of any room we were in. We went to bed at eight and woke at six in the morning to file into a long hallway. We stood in a line while we were ordered to do jumping jacks, sit-ups, and push-ups for the next half hour. We were locked in our rooms at all times except for meals and groups.

Each room had two beds bolted to the floor and a long cabinet to hold our clothes. Every wall was completely bare and painted white. My roommate was also named Heather. The sign on our door read "Heathers." She laughed at me the first time I met her, when I asked if there was any way to get high.

"Girl, the most high you'll get is flushing bananas down the toilet with me." She laughed. "And another piece, don't go 'round askin' people 'bout getting high. No one wants to be here, and talking 'bout that shit makes ya stay longer."

I trusted what she said since this was her third time here. There were twice as many staff members at Redview than there had been at New Hope. The staff were either big black men who looked like bouncers at a club or white men who looked like washed out hippies. Whenever we were out of our rooms, they circled us like vultures, waiting to catch us doing anything that was against the rules or that mimicked "street behavior." Street behavior was acting like we did on the outside. Any gesture, speech, or clothing could be labeled street behavior and increase your stay.

"Pull your pants up, Marcus! That's street behavior."

"Put your hands down, that's street behavior."

"You're being threatening, that's street behavior."

It went on and on. If you didn't quit doing whatever you were doing, you were only asked one more time to stop. If you still refused, you were thrown into the seclusion room. The big Latina had told the truth. It was a padded room with no windows. You weren't allowed to eat while you were in there. You stayed in the seclusion room until you repented for whatever bad thing you had done. One time a kid spent six hours locked in there, screaming and cussing at the staff. I admired him for his determination.

Most of the kids locked up with me were in gangs. This was new to me because there are no real gangs in small towns. When staff wasn't looking, they flashed signs to each other and threatened to kill each other on the outside. I was pretty much ignored and left alone. Except for once, when I doodled GD on my notebook during group. On the way out from group, a large girl with wild bristly hair grabbed my arm.

"What you claimin', white girl?" she hissed in my ear.

"I ain't claimin' nothing." I jerked my arm away.

"You claimin' GD. I seen you write it on your notebook. Don't be lyin' to me, bitch," she sneered.

"Look, Maleeka or Makeela, whatever the fuck your name is. GD means Grateful Dead. The band? Jerry Garcia?"

She stared at me through her big brown eyes, trying to figure out what I'd said, as if I'd spoken a foreign language. Finally, she threw her head back and started laughing. "That's some funny shit. You white chics are strange." She thumped me on the back with her hand. "Anyways, the name's Maleeka."

I spent the majority of my time sleeping in my room or staring out windows with mesh and black bars. I daydreamed about getting high. After a few weeks, the staff members decided I'd be transferred to Park Meadow. Park Meadow was a treatment center focusing specifically on chemical dependency, not like where I was at, with kids who had stabbed other kids and were just waiting to get placed somewhere. I felt lucky to be getting sent to treatment because I was sure most of the other kids' fates would be a lot worse.

Park Meadow was a huge mansion at the end of a long gravel road with trees surrounding it on all sides. It was painted red with white trim and if I hadn't known better I'd have thought I was being brought to some sort of vacation home. But the inside of the facility was anything but homelike.

The house had three levels. The main level had a massive room in the center, lined with cafeteria tables and a huge window that took up an entire wall on the north side. To the left of the big, open room with the window were two rooms where group was held. The group rooms were filled with couches and soft padded chairs, a welcome break from the hard aluminum chairs at Redview. Across from the group rooms was a medicine room where a nurse worked. To the right of the main room, a hallway led to all of the girls' bedrooms. The upper level of the house, where girls were never allowed to go, was where all the boys stayed. Downstairs was a game room with a pool table, a makeshift classroom for school, and the counselors' offices.

The room where I stayed was big and had a huge sliding glass door that couldn't be opened but that let in a lot of sunshine. There were five tall, wooden bed frames with mattresses on top of them. Two of the beds had teddy bears lying on the pillows and the others seemed to be unoccupied. I chose the bed in the corner.

I shared with Goldie, a tall Native American girl who was only twelve. She'd never done any other drugs besides huffing spray paint, but she already had enough brain damage to make her eyes cross and roll around involuntarily. My other roommate was Inés, a short, chubby Latina girl who always had a smile on her face.

By this time, I'd been sober for almost a month. I felt like I was coming out of a deep sleep and was halfway between waking and dreaming. The longer I stayed sober, the more awake my brain became. It seemed strange to remember my days, endless with so much awake time. The nights were terrible because my body had become rested and I couldn't sleep. My mind replayed things that had happened during the day and fragmented pieces of my past. My thoughts whirled, trying to somehow make sense of it all. I didn't let anyone know what was going on in my head.

To all outside appearances, I was the same angry, defiant girl. I walked around cold and defensive at all times, ready to do battle. I didn't let on to the fact that I didn't mind some of the parts about being there. We got to go outside. Spring had arrived and the air smelled fresh and clean with the promise of summer. Birds chirped and squirrels chased each other up and down trees. I realized it had been a long time since I'd noticed these things.

There was a paved court with a basketball hoop and the guys

let me play with them. It was the only time we were allowed to push and shove without getting reprimanded. I discovered I still had a pretty good shot. For the first time in a long while, I thought about when I used to play basketball, but it made me sad.

My mind became a battleground of thinking and at the same time trying not to think. Without drugs, it became harder and harder for me to push away and ignore the thoughts that were serious or disturbing. Because of this, I hated group. My ability to check in and out was difficult to accomplish in the midst of such intensity. I was uncomfortable when people cried.

Hank, the counselor, was a big man with a short brown beard and fake teeth that clacked together when he talked. He took his job very seriously and rarely smiled. He'd perfected the art of intimidation, but I refused to let him intimidate me. The focus of group at Park Meadow was the same as it had been at New Hope and Redview: our "issues."

"What are you running from, Tyler?" Hank began one day.

I crossed my arms and slid down in my chair. It was like he was talking to all of us, even though he used Tyler's name.

"Nothin', I don't think." Tyler twisted his long blond ponytail.

"Really?" Hank leaned forward in his chair. "What about what we were talking about in group earlier today?"

Tyler shrugged his shoulders and stared at the floor. His lower lip quivered. Hank scanned the room.

"Do you guys remember?" he asked.

Of course we do. We're not stupid. We all nodded.

"Tyler, what was it like for you at home when your dad got drunk and hit you?" Hank moved his chair closer. His chair was the only one on wheels.

"It sucked," Tyler said softly, still keeping his focus on the carpet.

Hank's voice got louder. "Say more about that. How did it feel? How did it feel when your dad beat you, Tyler?"

Tyler blinked rapidly to keep tears from spilling onto his cheeks. "It sucked."

Hank slapped his leg. "C'mon, it sucked? You can do better than that. Did you laugh? Did you cry? Were you pissed? Shit, I'd be pissed if my old man beat the shit out of me. Christ, he was your dad. I bet he hit you all your life."

My hands began shaking. *Stop! Shut-up! Leave him alone!* I wanted to choke Hank to get him to stop. I tucked my hands under my legs.

Hank went on as he always did. His voice kept getting louder and louder. I wanted to cover my ears. "What did it feel like when you were a kid? What was it like before you got so damn tough?"

Big tears rolled from Tyler's eyes and he gulped. "I hated it. I felt like I did something wrong. Like I always tried to be good, but it was never good enough. I always did something wrong."

Hank suddenly changed. He moved his chair so his knees touched Tyler's, and then he softly placed his hands on Tyler's knees. He spoke gently, "It wasn't your fault."

Tyler broke down sobbing, which sounded like big hiccups as he gasped for air. Andy, the kid next to him on the couch, handed him a Kleenex. "I (gulp) just wanted to (gasp) die."

I looked away. I couldn't stand the raw pain, the air so thick with it that I couldn't breathe. I felt as if his pain was mine and realized I'd thought the exact same things that he'd just spoken out loud. *My dad didn't beat me, did he? He's hit me and thrown me around, trying to punish me. It was just me being punished. But I feel like Tyler does. But my dad didn't beat the shit out of me. Is it still wrong?*

I thought about the only time I ever saw my dad cry. I had a flash of a memory of myself as a little girl sitting on my dad's lap in my bedroom. He was apologizing for hurting me and saying he would never do it again. A tear had rolled down his right cheek.

What happened that day? I couldn't remember what came before or after.

But I did remember other days of my childhood clearly. I recalled the day my dad had thrown my brother off his chair at the dinner table for laughing. They knocked other chairs over in their struggle. My dad wrestled my brother to the ground. I grabbed Rebecca by the hand and ran with her downstairs to my bedroom. I held on to her while she cried.

"I'm scared," she sobbed.

I took her little, chubby face in my hands and looked into her big, blue eyes. "Becca, we have a mean daddy. Sometimes he can be nice, but other times he's mean. Do you understand?" She nodded her head. I cautioned softly in my nine-year-old voice, "We have to be careful of the mean daddy, okay? I'll protect you from the mean daddy, okay? You don't have to be scared."

Memories from my childhood flashed through my mind in group each time one of the other kids talked about theirs. The fragmented images bothered me. I willed them to stop but they were stronger than I was. I hated the way Hank attacked the kids and crumbled their insides.

In one of my daily private sessions with Hank, I challenged him, "Why do you always have to make everyone feel like shit?"

"Because kids like you guys have a lot of pain."

"But what's the point in talking about it and feeling like shit? I don't see how it does anything."

"I think you're just scared." He moved his chair closer to mine.

I shrieked, "Don't come near me!" Pushing my chair back against the wall, I continued, "Seriously, stay away."

"Whoa, whoa." He moved his chair back, further than it had been. "What are you so afraid of?"

I snapped, "I just don't like people in my space."

"Okay." He leaned back. "Kids don't run away if there's nothing to run from. Drugs help you run away. If you deal with what you're running from, then maybe you won't have to run anymore."

I do drugs because I like them. But why does it scare you to live without them? I just like my life better that way. Really? Do you really like puking, getting into trouble, losing time, and being up for days? It's not that bad. Oh yeah, do you really like the guys who put their dicks in your mouth when you're passed out in the back of a trailer someplace you don't even know? Shut up!

At that moment, I split into two completely distinct voices in my mind. The voices argued back and forth with each other. I don't know whose voice was the real me or if they both belonged to a part of me. I just know that two voices were born. They began a dialogue that would torment and haunt me until I sat with the barrel of a gun in my mouth, contemplating pulling the trigger to shut them up.

9

Remembering

It was hard to believe I could hate anything more than regular group, but I detested family group. Family group was the same format as regular group except that the families of all of the kids in treatment were brought in. Hank performed his usual rituals with everyone. I hated the way my family acted, like we were the picture-perfect Christian family. I was the only trouble in our house and if I got off the drugs then everything would be fine.

My mom would cry on the phone each time we talked, and I tried to get off the phone as fast as I could. "Heather, Satan has gotten ahold of you through drugs. You need to turn your back on him. Once he's out of your head, you'll be fine. But it's going to be hard because he's really got you."

There was a part of me that believed her. But I also knew I'd been messed up long before I ever started using drugs, so then that would mean Satan had been in my head since I was a little girl. If I completely believed her, I'd have to believe he'd possessed me as a very young child. I knew God was mean, but could he really be that mean?

Every Wednesday night, my parents and my sister, Rebecca, made the two-hour drive to Park Meadow to attend family group. My brother, Philip, never came because he still wasn't talking to me. He'd quit talking to me after Christmas the previous year because I'd accidentally punched my mom in the face that night.

It was hard to believe I could hate anything more than regular group, but I detested family group. Family group was the same format as regular group except that the families of all of the kids in treatment were brought in. Hank performed his usual rituals with everyone. I hated the way my family acted, like we were the picture-perfect Christian family. I was the only trouble in our house and if I got off the drugs then everything would be fine.

My mom would cry on the phone each time we talked, and I tried to get off the phone as fast as I could. "Heather, Satan has gotten ahold of you through drugs. You need to turn your back on him. Once he's out of your head, you'll be fine. But it's going to be hard because he's really got you."

There was a part of me that believed her. But I also knew I'd been messed up long before I ever started using drugs, so then that would mean Satan had been in my head since I was a little girl. If I completely believed her, I'd have to believe he'd possessed me as a very young child. I knew God was mean, but could he really be that mean?

Every Wednesday night, my parents and my sister, Rebecca, made the two-hour drive to Park Meadow to attend family group. My brother, Philip, never came because he still wasn't talking to me. He'd quit talking to me after Christmas Eve the previous year because I'd accidentally punched my mom in the face that night.

The night had started out very well. I came home for supper on time, which put a huge smile on my mom's face and made her eyes sparkle. She beamed to have the entire family sitting together around the table, since it seldom happened anymore. After supper, we all worked on a jigsaw puzzle together, laughing and reminiscing about family vacations we'd taken in the past. Next, we sat around the twinkling Christmas tree while Dad read the Christmas story to all of us. Afterwards, we all said prayers.

My family had a routine of going to bed early and Christmas Eve was no different. They started to get ready for bed at ten. I was anxious and decided it was okay for me to go out for awhile. I started putting my shoes on.

"Where are you going?" my mom asked, coming out of the bathroom, where she'd been washing her face.

"I'm gonna go out for a while."

"Heather, no," she cried, the new happiness disappearing from her face.

"Mom, I'm not asking permission. You're all going to sleep, so I'm just gonna go out for a while. You know I can't go to bed this early. I'll be back, don't worry."

"No, you won't. You never come back." Her eyes filled with tears. "It's Christmas. Why can't you just stay with us for one night?"

"I'll be here in the morning." I went to the closet to get my jacket. She looked as if she was going to cry but held back. She turned around and met my dad in the hallway as he was coming out of their bedroom.

"What's wrong?" I heard him ask her.

"Heather's taking off."

I had my hand on the doorknob when my dad pulled my shoulders from behind. I turned to face him.

"You're not going anywhere," he ordered.

"Yes I am," I countered.

The familiar battle followed. He yelled at me to stay. I screamed back that I was leaving. We wrestled back and forth, vying for control of the door. My mom stood behind him, pulling on his shoulders.

"Please, hon," she begged. "Not tonight. Don't do this. It's Christmas."

As always, he ignored her. He came at me again, ready for a fight. In response, I swung at him. At the exact moment of my swing, my mom stepped between us. Instead of connecting with my dad, I connected with her face. Her mouth dropped open. She stared at me in shock, bringing her hand up to her nose. She looked at me as if I had just taken a knife and plunged it into her heart.

I felt as if I was in a movie. My dad stood frozen behind her. I had to get away. I flung the door open and ran into the night. Crisp air met my lungs with a sharp pain. I took off sprinting down the street, my feet pounding against the icy road. My throat burned and my lungs ached, but I ran until I couldn't run anymore. I stopped, leaning over, gasping for air. Snot mixed with tears dripped onto my jeans. *I'm crying.*

I felt on the verge of hyperventilating, like I did at cross-country meets when I forgot to take my inhaler before the race. *I just punched my mom. I'm a fuckin' monster. What the hell is wrong with me? Calm down, Heather. Just breathe. I need to get high.* I fumbled in my pocket, searched for coins, and discovered I had enough to make a phone call. I decided to walk up to the booth outside of the phone company and call my friend Jay to come get me.

A car turned a corner and the headlights moved toward me. I didn't realize it was my brother's blue Mustang until he was almost directly in front of me. He slammed on the brakes and jumped out of the car.

"Get in the car!" Philip demanded, pointing to the passenger side.

"No." I took a step back.

"What the hell is wrong with you?" He stepped towards

me and grabbed both of my arms. "For God's sake, Heather, just get in!"

"No!" I yelled. I jerked my arms free and swung at him wildly with my fists. He wrapped his arms around me in a tight bear hug.

He hissed in my ear, "I am not Dad. This is your brother, remember?"

I went limp in his arms. "Okay, let me go. I'll get in."

He walked me to the car and I slid into the passenger seat. He got behind the wheel and drove a few blocks without saying a word. Finally, he declared flatly, without turning to look at me, "I don't know how you do it. You come home for one night and end up punching Mom. You've got Dad pissed as hell, storming around the house, and Becca's locked in her room crying."

"I'm sorry. I didn't mean to do it."

"Look, just come home." Philip turned a corner, still focused on the road. "All you've got to do is apologize and everything will be fine."

I replied hotly, "I'm not gonna apologize. It wasn't my fault. Dad shouldn't have come at me."

"Christ, for once, can't you just give in?"

No, I can't. If I say I'm sorry then that means I'm admitting to being the bad one. Like it's all my fault. He'd win again. I won't do it.

He stared at the road and I stared out the window at all of the passing trees covered with snow and icicles. After a few minutes, he broke the uncomfortable silence. "What else are you gonna do?"

"I'm gonna go find Strom and . . . "

He interrupted. "Get high all night?"

"Well, yeah."

He slammed on the breaks, sliding on the ice before the car stopped. "Get out!"

"But I . . . "

"Get the fuck out of my car," he hissed through gritted teeth, finally turning to look at me.

I opened my door. "I'm sorry. I really am."

"You're a fuckin' loser. Go get high with all your loser friends. You make me sick." He motioned to my door. "Go! I can't even stand to look at you."

I slid out of the car slowly. He reached for my door and pulled it shut before peeling off. I stood there on the side of the road, waiting to see his taillights turn around and head back towards me, but they just kept getting further and further away. I went in search of a phone booth to make my call.

That was the last time we'd talked. After that it was as if I ceased to exist, like he'd somehow erased me from his mind completely. I wanted him to come to family group, but I was too scared to invite him for fear he'd say no. Neither of my parents said anything about his absences.

Becca came every time because no matter how I acted, I was still her big sister. Her love for me was unconditional. She sent me cards and wrote me long letters begging me to get sober and telling me how much she missed me. It was hard to read them because she never tired of telling me I was the best sister. She sat in each family group silently. Her eyes were video cameras recording everything to play back later, to try to understand.

There were two types of parents. There was the type that spent all of their time crying and wallowing in guilt at their children being in treatment because they felt completely responsible. Hank would work with them at easing their sense of responsibility while also challenging them to be accountable. The second type seemed oblivious to having played any part in their child's dysfunction, but after going one round with Hank they quickly realized they'd been involved in and affected by what their child had been doing. They soon turned into the first type. Most of the time, if both parents were there, they'd each take turns talking, alternating between blaming each other and blaming themselves.

My parents didn't fit into either type. They were the only couple in the room that wasn't divorced or remarried, and it was entirely my responsibility for being where I was. My dad did all of the talking. My mom sat next to him quietly, with her hands folded in her lap and a smile on her face. My sister and I occupied chairs on either side of the couch my parents sat on.

The night Hank began focusing his attention on him, my dad declared, "I don't know why you're asking me questions. She's the drug addict. Talk to her."

"Well Mark, we just want to get an idea of what things are like at home." Hank clacked his fake teeth together as he spoke. "It helps us to understand how we can help her and what problems we're up against."

"Problems? She's the problem," my dad snorted. I saw my mom touch him lightly on the knee. "There's nothing more to understand."

Hank turned to look at my mom. "How do you feel, Carol?"

My mom smiled back at Hank with one of her plastic Christian smiles and looked up at my dad, waiting for him to speak. "My wife feels the same way I do. There wasn't any problem with Heather or anything else until she got into drugs."

Hank raised his right eyebrow. "I find that hard to believe."

My dad straightened his back and glared. "I really don't care what you think. You don't know anything about us."

The room got quiet. Every adult and kid in the room stared at us as if they were watching a suspense movie on TV. *Here we go.*

Hank smiled. "You're right. That's why I'm asking questions. I don't understand why you're being so defensive."

My dad pressed his lips together and made a sound like a horse sputtering. "Listen, my daughter is a drug addict. She is completely out of control. My family has nothing to do with it. She's had nothing but a good Christian upbringing by two parents that love her."

I looked over at Becca, trying to get her to meet my eyes so I could somehow send her a message that it was going to be okay. She intently stared back and forth between my dad and Hank. She looked terrified. My head began to swim and swirl, feeling as if it was going to roll right off my neck.

"Your daughter is very angry, or haven't you noticed?" Hank challenged, scooting his chair closer.

Knock it off, Hank. You're gonna piss him off. Just shut up. His usual tactics were not going to work with my dad. I'd known this before group started. There was no way he was going to get my dad to talk about anything other than how messed up I was.

"Of course I have," my dad huffed. "She's on drugs. They've messed up her mind. She was never angry before."

Yes, I was! He's lying! I was angry all the time. I clenched my teeth together.

"Well, I find that very hard to believe," Hank challenged. "Your daughter is too pissed to not have a reason. I . . . "

"Listen, buddy." My dad narrowed his eyes to slits and leaned forward. "You need to talk to *her.* I'm done. You leave me and my family alone."

They locked eyes with each other as if they were two kids having a stare-down. *Do something, Hank. Say something.* Someone coughed. Hank clasped his hands together and cracked his knuckles. He opened his mouth and shut it again.

Then he asked, "Anyone have any feedback?" He turned around in his chair, looking at the others. No one said anything. *My dad just silenced a whole room.*

"Well, let's move on then."

My family continued to come every week. We sat in every group, but were never counseled again as a family. I watched the other families work with Hank. The endings were always happy no matter how much pain came before. If Hank couldn't help us, then we were hopeless. In his private sessions with me, Hank had tried many times to get me to talk about my family and my childhood. After his battle with my dad, he tripled his efforts.

"What was it like growing up in your family, Heather?"

My standard response for almost anything: "It sucked."

"Your dad seems pretty frightening. Are you afraid of him?"

You are. He shut you up. What do you think? "No, I'm not scared of anything."

"Well, I'd be scared of him," he continued from his position behind the desk. "Does he make you mad?"

"I'm only pissed 'cause he blames everything on drugs," I blurted out. "Like everything was so fine before or something. Yeah, I used to not get into trouble. I was a good little fuckin' girl. But ya know what? I've wanted to die since I was eight years old. I used to daydream about hanging myself from the swing set in the backyard."

I should not have just said that. Damn. Why'd you do that? I don't know, it just came out. I wasn't thinking. Watch your mouth. An image of me as a little girl swinging up and down on the metal swing in my backyard flashed through my mind. I wore my ripped jean shorts and my favorite blue tank top. I flew up and down, staring at the back of the house, singing a song I'd heard on the radio. I only knew the line, "Even though inside I feel like dying, you know you'll never see me crying." I just kept singing the words over and over again, pumping my legs back and forth, trying to get myself to go higher.

Hank's voice broke into my memory. "Heather?"

"What?"

"Where'd you go?"

"I'm right here," I responded, shifting my weight in my seat.

"Well, I was asking you a question and you just disappeared." He leaned forward.

"I guess I just spaced out," I mumbled.

"Do you space out a lot?" He brought his arms up to the desk and rested his chin on his hands.

"I don't know." My head swam, as if I'd just been shoved underwater. Everything looked fuzzy and his voice was muffled and faraway.

"I'm just gonna ask you. Does your dad abuse you?"

I suddenly rocketed from Hank's office to Keith's red truck a few years before. I was sitting in the passenger seat. We had just left my parents' house and were headed out of town to cruise the back roads while we drank beer. Keith had been silent since we'd left my house.

Then he spoke. "I need to ask you a question." He took a left onto the first gravel road and pulled over on the shoulder.

What now? "What do you want to know?"

He shut the car off. "I want you to tell me the truth. This is serious. Promise me you'll tell the truth?" He turned to look at me with his brown eyes.

I nodded. *Here we go again. Christ, how many times do I have to tell him I'm not cheating?*

He cleared his throat, "I don't really know how to ask . . . "

Maybe this is serious. I waited for him to finish.

"Okay." He exhaled, taking both of my hands in his.

Ohmigod, he's gonna ask me to marry him. What am I gonna say?

He took another deep breath. "Does your dad fuck with you?"

I stared at him. "Well, yeah. You already know that. He's a controlling prick."

Keith looked down at my hands. "That's not what I mean. I mean does he mess around with you? Like, you know. I mean . . . Christ, does your dad fuck you?"

It took a moment for his words to register in my brain. I jerked my hands away. "What? Ohmigod. I can't believe you just asked me that. You're a sick fuck! I . . . what the . . . I . . . "

"Settle down." He reached for my hands again and I pulled them away. "The only reason I'm asking you is because I see the way he looks at you. Every time we walk into your house he checks out your tits and ass. He stares at you like I do, but he's your fuckin' dad. It's sick."

I felt puke rise in my throat. *He sees the way my dad looks at me. Maybe I'm not crazy. But I've got to be crazy. But I don't know. He sees. What does it mean?*

"So, does he?" Keith whispered. "Because if he does, I'll kill the bastard."

This can't be happening. This isn't happening. This can't be happening. I felt the life leaving my body, my brain pulling the plug and bringing me to a place of numbness and nothingness somewhere in the sky. I closed my eyes tightly then opened them slowly, back in Hank's office. He was sitting in the chair next to me with his hand on my shoulder. My legs were pulled up to my chest and my arms wrapped tightly around them.

Hank spoke into my thoughts. "You've given me enough of an answer."

Did I talk? I don't remember talking. I was just thinking. What's going on? What did I say? What the hell is happening? Get a grip, Heather. You're losing it. I don't remember how our session ended or even leaving Hank's office. What I do remember is being back in my room, sitting on my bed in a trance, twisting and turning a wire hanger until it snapped. Robotically, I broke it into small pieces. Then I watched myself rub the sharp end up and down my arm rhythmically until my skin was raw and started to bleed. As if someone had flipped a switch in my head, I rubbed harder and harder and faster and faster until my arm was a bunch of jagged lines creating a twisted web on my arm.

I came to with a jolt. *What did I just do? I don't know, but it felt good. Shit. Clean it up. People are gonna think you're a freak. Stupid ass, why'd you do it on your arm? How are ya gonna hide that? Don't worry. What did I just do?*

I jumped up from the bed and frantically collected the pieces of wire hanger. I buried them in the garbage underneath papers and trash. I walked to the doorway, trying not to let any blood drip onto the floor or get on my shirt. I peeked my head out and saw there was no one in sight. I sprinted to the bathroom. I stuck my arm underneath the faucet, watching the water slide off my arm like liquid rust. I blotted it dry with a paper towel over and over.

I felt calm as I walked out of the bathroom and back to my room. I took a long-sleeved shirt from my dresser and put it on. I lay down on my bed, crossing my arms across my chest the way vampires sleep in movies. My breathing relaxed and my head cleared. The memories were gone.

It's going to be okay, I told myself over and over again until sleep came.

A few days later, Hank came to my room and knocked at the door. " I need to talk to you. Meet me in my office in five minutes."

I knew the minute I walked into his office that something was wrong. Instead of sitting in his usual position behind the desk, he paced back and forth across the room. I sat in my usual spot in the right-hand corner of his office, across from the desk.

"I need to tell you something. As a counselor and as part of my job, I had to do something because it's required by law." He continued to pace anxiously in front of me. "I am a counselor and part of my job is being a mandated reporter. What that means is that if I am told about abuse going on, or if I suspect it, then I have to report it to the authorities. I want you to know how much I have struggled and agonized over having to do this. First and foremost, I have struggled because you have been one of the most untrusting kids I've ever had to work with. It has taken so long for you to open up in the least. You're at the very beginning of talking. I didn't want to jeopardize that. Second, I've debated trying to get around reporting it because you haven't exactly told me that there is abuse going on. Personally, I don't think you are even aware of a lot of things. I think you've been running from the truth for so long that you don't even know what the truth is. But your reactions to your family, and the things you say, send me millions of messages that you have been abused. You show every single sign. I had to go with my gut."

I sat quietly in my chair, absorbing the words he'd just spoken, registering them without any emotion. I felt like I was a computer downloading information. Hank always said "abuse," not what kind of abuse, but something in me had immediately known the first time he said it. He sat in the chair across from me. His face and eyes looked soft and warm.

"So, what are you saying?" I asked.

"I'm telling you that I made a report to the authorities in your county that said I suspected abuse was going on in your home." He looked at the floor. "I don't know what they'll do with it. What happens from here is completely up to them. As much as I didn't want to, I had to do it or I'd risk losing my job. Do you understand?"

I nodded my head in response, even though I didn't understand. I understood what the words meant, but I felt cut off. It was as if he was speaking to me about somebody else. I was not the girl we were talking about.

"Are you angry with me?" he asked.

I shook my head no. I couldn't talk.

"Do you have any questions?"

I shook my head again.

"Are you okay? Is there anything I can do?" he asked. His eyes were wet and glossy.

"I'm fine," I said softly, not recognizing the sound of my own voice.

"There is one other thing." He sighed. "Some people from the county might be coming to talk to you and ask you some questions. They might not, but I just want you to be prepared."

"Okay," I replied. "Can I go now?"

"Are you sure you're okay?"

I nodded. I walked back to my room in the same trancelike state I'd been in a few days earlier. *What in the hell is going on? Abuse . . . I don't wanna talk about my family. I wanna get high. There's nothing. What will my mom say? Nothing is wrong with my family. Everything is wrong with my family. Ohmigod, if people come, what do I say? You say nothing. I'm crazy. All of this is crazy. What is happening? This isn't happening.*

My eyes turned to my closet and the wire hangers inside. *It worked last time. Shut up. It's sick. Remember how good you felt?* Quickly, I jumped up from my bed and threw open the closet door. I grabbed a hanger and frantically tore it to pieces, hurriedly scraping the jagged edges along my arm. *I still feel crazy. Rub harder. This is insane. Rub harder.* And I did, this time bringing more blood. With each trickle that left my arm, the pressure in my head subsided a little until all the thoughts that I didn't understand were gone.

10

Dave

I thought I was going to be one of the kids who had to stay at Park Meadow for nine months. When Hank brought me into his office and told me I was being released after only two, I was surprised and elated.

"I *really* don't think it's a good idea for you to leave. We recommended you stay in extended care for at least another six months, but there's no one to pay for it."

My heart skipped a beat. *I'm getting out! I'm gonna be free!*

"The best we can do is set you up with a really strict aftercare plan." Hank pulled out the folder from his desk that held my file. "You're going to be monitored very closely by your probation officer. He'll be giving you drug tests. You'll have to go to at least three AA or NA meetings a week and . . . "

"Man, I hate those meetings," I interrupted.

Every few weeks we had people come to Park Meadow from Alcoholics Anonymous, droning on and on about how everyone needed to find God or else they'd drink again. Their stories were far too similar to the stories my mom used to tell me about how her and my dad used to drink and do lots of drugs until they found God.

"I don't care if you hate those meetings," Hank said sternly. "It's the only way you'll stay sober."

"Shit," I muttered, slumping down in my seat.

"You are also going to be enrolled in an aftercare program at New Hope Treatment Center . . . "

I interrupted again. "Aftercare program? I'm done."

Hank raised his eyebrow and clicked his teeth together. "You haven't even gotten started. You'll go there three nights a week."

"I can't," I explained. "I got kicked out of that place."

Hank smiled. "I spoke to Dave Bateman. He's willing to have you back now that you've completed a treatment program. He'll be your counselor once you leave."

I challenged, "And what if I don't do all of this?"

"You'll end up getting sent away again."

When I returned home, I was expected to step back into my life as if nothing had changed. My parents acted as if I'd gone away to treatment and gotten fixed. But my entire concept of the world had been shaken at Park Meadow. I'd look around at my family and wonder who these people really were. My head twirled and spun every time I walked through the door.

My dad's eyes followed me everywhere. I couldn't get away from the thick tension of his stares. It was like we were engaged in a silent war of I-Dare-You-To-Speak. My head hammered with anger each time I returned one of his looks. I'd evolved from hidden haughty eyes to open eyes of hate. However, I refused to give any energy to questioning why I was so angry. It felt too dangerous to go there directly.

My eyes followed my mom everywhere as she bustled around attending to her daily routines and chores. I searched her face for clues to what was going on. Did she know what Hank had said about our family? Did she know about the report? If she knew, why wasn't she saying anything? Did she hate me for it?

There was so much I didn't understand. If Hank had made the report, then why was I still at home? Was it only a matter of time before someone showed up at my door and took me away? Would they just take me? What about Becca? I couldn't even bear to think about Becca. And Philip? He never even acknowledged that I'd been away. That was how my family functioned, but now I questioned the conspiracy of silence that Hank had broken, that I'd somehow taken part in.

I didn't know what was real. Everyone around me continued to believe and behave as if nothing was wrong in our house. It made me wonder again if I was the crazy one. Nobody ever came from the county to get me. I didn't know what to do or how to feel, so I did the only thing I knew how to do. I started to get high.

Hank's threats had been real. My life was filled with court regulations and restrictions. I attended aftercare at New Hope Treatment Center for a week, then promptly quit going. I didn't go to any of the Alcoholics Anonymous or Narcotics Anonymous meetings that were required. Each week I had to go down to the courthouse and pee in a cup. Each week my THC and amphetamine counts were off the charts. I got into trouble with the law for drinking underage, being high, breaking curfew, shoplifting, stealing, and having drugs and paraphernalia on me.

I began living from court date to court date. Each time I appeared, the judge ordered me to stay sober and follow the rules of my probation. My punishment was hours upon hours of community service, which piled up quickly because I refused to do them.

I'd spent the majority of my time at New Hope and Park Meadow wanting to get high, desperate to return to some sense of normalcy. But once I got out, it was as if I couldn't get high enough. All the physiological responses took place but the magic seemed to be gone. Instead of filling my void, I was left feeling emptier.

As we sat in a small hotel room, junkies filling every inch of space, I announced to Strom, "They brainwashed me in treatment. I feel all weird, like I can get high, but not really."

"Here." He passed me the picture he'd taken off the wall. He'd heaped the glass with piles of different colored powders. We'd been passing it around the room for the last five hours. "This is good shit."

We balanced the picture on our laps. I took a chunk of yellow powder and dropped it into the beer I was drinking and then finished the beer quickly. I stuck my finger into the white powder and rubbed it all over my gums. I reached for one of the rolled-up dollar bills and brought my face down to the long trails, filling my nose with the familiar burn. I passed the picture to the next junkie in line on the bed.

I felt the mixture of coke and heroin tingling through my body. My gums numbed, as if they couldn't hold my teeth in place. I broke out in a wet sweat. For a second, my stomach heaved, threatening to come up, which signaled I was getting off. My heart started to race and for a second my mind was clear. But as quickly as the good feelings came, they were gone. I looked around the room, anxiously eyeing all the tall, skinny men rambling on and on to each other while their pupils danced back and forth.

I'm the only girl. So, what does that mean? Maybe I shouldn't be here. These people are old. Don't talk like this. This is where you belong. But what if I don't? Shut-up! If you don't belong here, you don't belong anywhere. Quit thinking this way. I can't help it. I don't even know these people. Big deal. You don't need to.

My eyes darted to the bathroom door, slightly ajar. Through the crack I could see movement. A tattooed arm with a belt tied around it. *Maybe that will do it.* I jumped up from my spot next to Strom. He grabbed my arm and pulled me back down next to him.

"Where are you going?" he asked, streams of sweat dripping down his face and falling off the crest of his chin.

"To the bathroom."

He shook his head wildly. "You are not gonna stick a fuckin' needle in your arm. Do ya hear me? If I ever catch you shooting that shit, I'm cutting you off. Seriously. You'll kill yourself. I know you."

I felt the excitement of anticipation leave me. I knew if Strom said something, he meant it. I couldn't lose my supply.

I reached into the nightstand next to the bed, pulled out the blue Gideon Bible, and stared as the words crossed and swerved in front of my eyes.

"You gonna save us all?" Strom asked, looking at me with empty eyes. Without a word, I took my lighter and brought it down to the pages, igniting them. The chatter in the room stopped and everyone stared at the Bible in flames on my lap. A guy standing in the doorway started to cry like a baby. A voice yelled from the corner, "Shit. Make her stop. That's fucked up." I kept on burning the pages, watching them disappear into ashes and float around the room.

Someone else cried, "She's freakin' me out."

Strom grabbed his beer and poured it onto the fire. He took the charred remains from my hands and set it back on the nightstand. "Why'd you do that?"

I shrugged my shoulders.

People began asking me why I did the things I did. Why I started things on fire, or all of a sudden threw whatever I was drinking at the wall, or at someone's head. There were times in the car with Strom when I'd roll down the window and climb out to sit on the edge of the car door. Other times I'd whip open the door and stick my feet out, laughing hysterically as I threatened to jump.

The truth of the matter was that I didn't know why I did the things I did. From out of nowhere, I'd be grabbed by a powerful anger and an overwhelming compulsion to destroy something. I didn't know where these outbursts came from or how to stop them. I started to believe my mom again, that Satan or one of his demons possessed me.

The only rule I followed was meeting with Dave Bateman every week. At first, I dreaded our meetings but for some reason I felt better every time I left. An inner peace and happiness radiated from his pores. He talked to me like he was talking to another adult, genuinely concerned. His mom had died when he was ten and he shared what his life was like when he'd been using. At one point, he'd almost blown his head off, but he'd been sober for almost ten years.

He was married and had five kids. Their drawings and pictures covered his tack board. Whenever he spoke of them, his eyes filled with love and his chest puffed with pride. He seemed so put together, so real, alive and genuine. A part of me was scared by his energy, but another part was intrigued and attracted by it.

By this time, I was convinced I was going insane. The two people in my head waged war against each other constantly and never shut up, no matter how much I willed them to. I felt like I couldn't trust anyone. I didn't know who I was anymore. My mind was filled with blank spaces where memories should have been. I didn't want to think but that was all I seemed to be able to do. My head pounded with confusion I didn't understand, and my anger had turned into a volatile rage that scared me.

I was afraid to tell anyone what was going on, but one day I whispered softly to Dave, "I think I'm crazy."

"What? I didn't hear you."

I cleared my throat and tried again. "I said I think I'm crazy."

A wide smile spread across his face. "I don't think so. I think your head is filled with chemicals that don't work anymore. You've lost control and you're trapped. That would make anyone feel like they were nuts."

"But you don't know what goes on in my head. There's like two different people talking to each other. They have actual conversations back and forth."

"You're not crazy. You're just a junkie. Sorry to disappoint you. It's a lot easier to be crazy than to be a junkie." He smiled.

I whined, "But it was never like this before."

He laughed loudly. "Of course it wasn't. It never starts out that way. Every junkie reaches a point where the drugs quit working."

There was no denying the fact that using had taken a turn on me that I'd never expected. For so long, drugs had been the only things that made me feel good and alive, and those feelings were gone. Now I lived the same day over and over again. It terrified me.

There had to be some way to reverse whatever was happening. Each day I dumped an entire buffet of chemicals into my body. I did lines, smoked weed like cigarettes, dropped acid, and smoked dope with a mission to prove they still worked. But to my dismay, I discovered I couldn't get any higher. I was as high as I was ever going to get. I needed more, but there was no more to be had. I'd done every drug and there would be no more first times.

More and more, I avoided people other than to get or sell drugs. I wasn't interested in pretending to be friends. I rarely slept and my mind was gripped by paranoia. I trusted no one except Strom. I spent most of my days and nights locked in Strom's bedroom at the house he'd rented in the country. The shades were drawn at all times, with candles providing the only light. There was a mattress on the floor against the wall in one corner and piles of dirty clothes in another. The only piece of furniture was a stereo that filled the room with music at all times.

"Heather, you need to rest," Strom said early one morning.

We never slept anymore, but we had to rest our bodies by keeping them still or they'd physically shut down. We'd lay our aching bones next to each other on the old mattress, listening to the band Live playing through one more time on the stereo.

"I've got some weird rash all over my legs," I announced.

"Don't worry. It's nothing. It's just the red in your veins. Your circulation is all fucked up." He rolled over to face me and propped himself up on his elbow.

"You ever get tired of this?" I asked.

"It's our life, sweetheart. We don't have a choice. Only the good die young." His eyes saddened as he stared down at me.

"Sometimes I think we're already dead."

He stared at me blankly. "We are." It was times like this that made me realize how much I loved him, because he could put away the act.

"Do you think there's a God?" I asked, sitting up to face him.

He didn't even take a moment to think of his response. "Yes, and he hates us." He took a long deep breath as his eyes filled with tears. "I don't wanna talk about this shit. You freak me out when you get all deep."

I started looking forward to my meetings with Dave, although I always pretended like I didn't want to be there, like it was a big inconvenience. But for an hour in his office, I felt like I wasn't a lunatic. Unfortunately, every time I left the confines of his office, my mind became cluttered with chaos again. When my head started spinning really fast and I thought I might snap, I began comforting myself by telling myself I'd be able to talk to Dave soon. I just had to hold on until our next appointment.

I began telling him stories about crazy things I'd done to see how he'd react. He'd told me time and time again that he cared about me and I was stuck with him, but part of me still didn't believe him.

"How was your weekend?" he asked on a Tuesday.

I reported nonchalantly, as if I was making a statement about what I'd eaten for dinner, "I slept with a guy that has HIV."

"Really?" He tilted his head to the side. "Why'd you do something like that? Did you use protection?"

I shook my head. I'd never used a condom. Drugs were my birth control. I'd lost so much weight that I didn't get periods anymore.

"Do you want to tell me about it?" he asked.

I shrugged. "Well, we were having a party at Red Oak Park. It's like this huge nature place in the woods. The police came and I took off with Chris. We drove around for a while and then headed back to the park. I fucked him in the weeds like ten feet from his girlfriend. She was yelling for us the whole time. How crazy is that?"

"How do you know he has HIV?"

"His ex-girlfriend told me. He's a slut. Like two years ago, him and his buddies had a competition to see who could fuck the most girls. They had a stupid point system and everything. I guess he got it then. No one will touch him now. Well, except for me."

Dave frowned. "That makes me so sad."

I swallowed and looked out the window behind him. *There you go. I'm a slut. A fuckin' whore. How do you like me now?*

"I still care about you," he announced. He had an uncanny ability to answer the questions I was asking in my mind. It was frightening.

A few days after one of our sessions, I ended up at detox. I don't remember getting pulled over but the police report said we fled from the cops. The driver got a DUI, I got hauled to detox, and Strom walked away unscathed. What I do remember is coming to in the backseat of the squad car, my rage boiling. I felt like a caged animal. As soon as the door opened, I took off as if a gun had just been fired, like my life depended on getting away. Amid red lights, the officer ran after me and tackled me to the ground. When he lifted me up, I kicked him with all of my might right between the legs. He dropped me and fell to the ground moaning.

I ran blindly again, hollering and screaming as if physical chains still bound me. My heart felt like it was beating on the outside of my body. My brain howled. Cops got behind me and surrounded me on all sides. As I watched myself from above, I kicked and flailed about like a mustang that had just been captured from the wild. It took four officers to get me into the building. They carried me by my arms and legs down the familiar baby blue hallway. A metal door unlocked, then they took off my handcuffs and threw me inside a cell. I spat at them, cussing and hollering as they locked the door behind them. Then I picked up the thin mattress, the only item in the room, and threw it against the wall. I screamed to be let out, pounding on the steel door until my knuckles bled and I exhausted myself. Then I sat in the corner hunched over, biting my nails and rocking back and forth.

Is this really how you want your life to be? They told you it'd get worse. How fun is this? This is your life. It's always gonna be this way.

My stomach heaved and I violently sprayed vomit all over my lap and arms. I puked until globs of blood came and created a nasty design on the green and yellows. I threw up the blood until nothing else came, and then kept right on gagging.

"Please God, let me die," I begged out loud. "I can't live like this."

The next morning staff unlocked me and allowed me to come out of the room. A guy I'd seen around before came up to me. "Man, you are one crazy chic," he laughed. "We were all sitting in the smoke room last night while you screamed bloody murder coming down the hall. I've never seen so many cops needed just to bring in some scrawny ass little girl. You really put up a fight, huh?"

I nodded and smiled.

He winked at me. "But here's the funny thing. This morning when I got up, I peeked through the glass into your room, and there you were all curled up in the fetal position and actually sucking your thumb. The bad ass sucks her thumb while she sleeps." He tilted his head back and roared.

Mortified, my face grew hot. "Fuck you. I'm going to take a shower."

The next week I went to see Dave at our normal time. I told him all about my detox experience, omitting the facts that I had been so ill and prayed to die. I boasted about the fact that it had taken four cops to get me inside.

"I didn't know why I was so pissed. But Strom told me the next day that when we saw the cops, we ate all the crank we had, and man we had a ton of rocks. I can't believe we ate it. Shit, it's no wonder I was out of my mind," I boasted.

He seemed unimpressed. "What kind of trouble are you in now?"

"God, too much. The stupid fuckers put me on a court ordered curfew. I have to be at my house at ten every night and I can't leave until eight. That's messed up," I snorted.

"Well, I can't blame them. They've got to be getting tired of you. Christ, how many times have you gotten arrested in the last two months?"

"I have no idea. I've lost count. My P.O. and everyone else in the stupid system is throwing a fit 'cause I kicked the cop.

They're trying to get me for assault on a police officer or some shit like that."

Dave rolled his eyes. "You kicked him?"

I smiled proudly. "Well yeah, but still it's not like I actually assaulted the dude."

He moved his chair back against the window. "Have you passed any of your drug tests?"

"Nope." I crossed my legs. "I haven't passed one. I tried to tell them I took diet pills, but I don't think they believe it. I've tried everything to pass those stupid things. I even drank that black tea and man . . . "

"Why don't you just quit getting high?" He stood up and walked towards me.

"Are you serious?" I asked. *He better not turn on me now.*

He hopped up on his desk, swinging his legs in front of me. "I want you to listen to me and hear what I'm saying. Okay?"

I nodded.

"I like you. A lot. I mean that. You have to know that by now. I know you're messed up and I know you need help. But I can't help you if you keep getting high. I . . . "

"Why?" I interrupted.

"Because I'm not helping you. I'm keeping you sick. Your life is a mess. You're like a huge gaping wound. You go out and bleed all week and then come in here for me to put a Band-Aid on it. Then you go out and do the exact same things over and over again."

I sat back in my chair, pulling my legs up to my chest. *You can't leave me now. There's so much I wanna tell you. You help me. See, he's just like everyone else. He's had enough of you.*

"You look like you're going to cry," he said softly, moving from the desk to sit in the chair next to me.

A softball-sized lump lodged in my throat. *Don't cry. Don't cry. You'll be fine. You don't need him. Yes, I do. You never should have trusted him. I don't want to lose him.*

"Can I hold your hand?" he asked.

I nodded, unable to speak. I stared at the design in the blue carpet, searching for some sort of a pattern hidden in the fabric. He took my hand and held it in his. The clock on the wall ticked. *Say something. Please.*

"Here's the deal," he began. "If you quit getting high, we can still meet."

My voice squeaked out like a little girl's, "What if I can't?"

"We'll start small," he replied, dropping my hand. "Will you look at me?"

I turned my head towards him, peeked at his eyes and quickly dropped my gaze to the floor. My hair fell over my face. He reached out and slowly tucked it behind my ears.

He presented his negotiation. "We meet on Thursdays. For the three days before you come to see me, I want you to stay clean and sober. You can do whatever else you want to do, but from Monday until after we meet, no drinking or getting high. Can you do that?"

I nodded.

"I want to hear you say it."

"I can do it."

11

No Saying No

I had never imagined not getting high, but I believed that if I wanted to badly enough or if I had a good enough reason, I could stop. I took my promise to stay sober seriously because meeting with Dave was the one bright spot in my life, and I didn't want him to cut me off. I met with him on Thursdays and every Monday I'd wake up determined not to do any drugs. I'd stay in bed as long as I could, take my time in the shower, and draw out the dressing process. I'd be ready for the day with nothing to do. My entire life revolved around getting, selling, and doing drugs. Without that, I was lost and there were only empty hours that seemed impossible to fill. The day stretched out endlessly in front of me. I found myself wondering what people my own age did to fill their time.

Cleaning my room seemed to be the only activity I had. When I ran out of things to clean, I'd rearrange my room. If my mom hadn't been so meticulous, I would have moved out into the other rooms in the house to continue my frenzied cleaning.

Once I'd cleaned my room, I'd sit on the edge of my bed and reach down to pull out my Ziploc bag full of green buds. I'd stare at it, rolling the plastic around in my fingers over and over again. I'd open it up and sniff the sweetness. I'd go to tuck it back under the mattress but before I could, an argument would begin in my head.

Pot's not a big deal. Really. It's nothing. Just smoking a little weed isn't like really getting high. It doesn't count. I mean you're still basically sober. But Dave said nothing. I'm sure he didn't mean weed. Yes, he did. You know he did. Well, still. I'm just smoking weed. It's still better than doing what I usually do. It's improvement. Shit, he'd probably be proud of me. Anyways, there's always tomorrow. I'll stay completely sober tomorrow.

The game was on. I'd leave my house and end up at Strom's. Once I smoked weed, I got thirsty so I had to have a drink. I didn't even think about it. I'd just grab a beer from the fridge or my bottle of Captain Morgan. Before long Strom would start chopping up lines to get ready for the day. He'd slide the mirror towards me. I began staring at the lines before I'd do them.

I don't have to do it. You know you're gonna do it. Yes, but I don't have to. I just want to. I've already ruined staying sober today so I might as well. It's not like today even counts anymore. Next week I'll do it. Next Sunday. I'll stop.

The next week would come all too quickly and it was the same as the week before. I considered lying to Dave about it but could never bring myself to do it. I was sure each time I came to see him it would be the last and he'd finally tell me to get lost.

Once, after I'd hung my head and mumbled I hadn't stayed sober at all, he suggested, "How about just trying to stay sober and clean the day before you come to see me?" I agreed. *One day isn't a big deal. I can stay sober for one day.*

On the day before our meeting the following week, I began to feel my skin crawling. I scratched my arms as I paced back and forth in my bedroom, treading a worn path on the blue carpet. Everything in my room reminded me of getting high and I kept staring at my mattress, knowing my stash was only a few steps away. I had to get out of there.

I called up Strom, telling him to meet me at our designated spot.

I just need to get out of the house. I'm not gonna get fucked up. I'm not gonna do anything. I won't. I can't.

No matter what he was doing or where he was, Strom always picked me up. Sometimes I'd have to wait for a few hours, but he'd always come. Strom had a job to do, and he was strangely fulfilled by taking care of me and teaching me his secrets. I in turn kept his secrets. All of them. I got to see the man behind the hard exterior and masks. I'd held him in my arms while he cried.

He pulled up on his motorcycle and I hopped on. He handed me a bottle. "Tuck this. I picked it up for you on the way."

I tucked the bottle of Captain between us, assuring myself I didn't have to drink it today. I'd put it in the cupboard when we got to his house and drink it the following night. We made a few drop-offs before we reached his old house. We never used the rotting front porch because more than one person had fallen through. The back door led us into a kitchen with old pizza lying on the counter, and macaroni and cheese crusted in a pan on the stove.

We walked into the living room, which consisted of a big pool table and ratty couches. A few bodies occupied the couches, each guy staring straight ahead. We walked by them to the bedroom. They didn't seem to notice as we walked through. We shut the door of his bedroom behind us.

"It was crazy here last night. Those dudes are from Stillwater. They were so messed up last night. They all got wives and are scared to go home all geeked out." Strom laughed. "They've just been sitting on the couch like that for hours."

He pointed towards his mattress, at the mirror covered in piles lying next to it. "That's why. Remember like a month ago when we got that shit from the Mexicans? Well, I got it again."

"I can't," I replied, turning around to play with the stereo, flipping through the CDs.

"Got a piss test tomorrow?" he asked, moving around me.

"Somethin' like that." I took out the CDs and started putting in new ones.

"Shit, girl. You're missin' out. This shit is like pink." I listened to him snorting.

Pink Floyd filled the room. I turned around and walked towards the spot where Strom sat on the floor with the mirror in his lap. He blinked rapidly as tears streamed down his cheeks. Sounding as if he had a pound of snot clogging it, he said, "God, my nose is fucked."

Don't do it. Don't do it. I knelt down next to him. *Stop. You're staying sober. You don't want to do this. Stop.* I picked up the tooter on the mirror. *You're staying sober. Don't do it.* I brought my face down, taking it all in. I brought my head up, my eyes burning and my throat constricting.

We stayed in his bedroom for the next two days, only leaving to go to the bathroom or change the CD. People came in and out. I didn't go home, which wasn't unusual, but I missed my appointment with Dave. Hunched over in the corner, by the stereo, I silently took whatever was passed in front of me. I was locked in my head, thinking the same thoughts over and over again.

I can't stop. I can't. I can't stop. I really wanted to. I did. I can't. Not even one day. I'm sixteen. I'm a junkie. I can't stop. I can't.

Somewhere along the way I'd crossed an invisible line that meant I could never go back. I knew I'd keep getting high in the same manner you know that every day you'll have to go to the bathroom.

Every night in the secrecy of my bedroom, silent sobs gripped and shook my whole body. My love affair with chemicals had turned into a nightmare I couldn't wake up from. I'd traded in my teenage years for an education on the streets and an opportunity to get high everyday. I'd given up every relationship from my childhood that had meant anything. Those I called my friends were only fellow junkies I knew nothing about, other than that they liked to get high as much as I did.

For highs, I'd turned my back on everything I used to value. The worst part was that drugs no longer even made me feel good. They'd betrayed me. I was sure I was as low as I was ever going to get, but things kept right on spiraling downward. I kept getting into trouble with the law and I knew it was only a matter of time before I got sent away again.

During this time I met Chad, who'd just moved to town from Arizona. He was at a party where I stopped by with Strom to make an exchange. We'd ending up staying there all night, and Chad and me hit it off. He was really funny, and he let me shave off his long hair in the early hours of the morning.

I thought being involved with a guy would make me feel a little normal. I hadn't been in a relationship with any man since Steve. Besides, Chad made me laugh and I'd been having a hard time finding anything to smile about.

So I called him up a few days later and asked if he wanted to go out to Strom's house with me. I walked to his place, not far from mine. He rented the basement of his aunt and uncle's house until he could save up enough money to get his own apartment.

I knocked on the door.

"Come in."

I opened the door, stepping into the entryway of a split-level house.

"I'm downstairs."

Downstairs, he met me in the hallway then led me into his small bedroom. The waterbed took up almost every inch of space. Clothes were scattered randomly on the floor. I perched on the edge of his bed.

Feeling cramped and confined, I said, "Let's go."

"What's the big hurry?" he asked, sitting down next to me

and putting his arm around me. "I want to take a shower before we leave."

"Well, get to it then," I said, shortly. "We're supposed to be at Strom's in an hour."

"Settle," he said, moving closer, practically sitting on top of me. "What's your deal with him anyway? I mean I know he keeps your nose supplied, but he's a loser."

I moved away.

"Hey." He scooted closer. "Sorry." He wrapped his arm around me again.

Great. He wants to mess around. No way. The only way I ever had sex was when I was wasted. It was the only time I could tolerate someone touching me. Otherwise the very thought of it repulsed me.

"Chad . . . " I sighed. "Get in the shower so we can go."

He reached for me and pulled me towards him, squishing me against his chest. I could smell chicken noodle soup. Then he buried his head in my neck, slobbering me with his wet tongue as if I was water and he was the dog.

"Knock it off." I pulled away.

"C'mon, don't be playing games," he said, cocking his head to the side to look at me.

I'm getting out of here. This is not going to happen. I stood up, feeling his clothes under my feet and kicking them away. Then he stood, towering above me. Suddenly my stomach flipped over. I didn't have enough oxygen. He stared at me for an instant, then threw his arms around me and tossed me on the bed. He jumped on top of me, pinning me down.

"Stop it. You're freaking me out," I cried.

"You're such a tease," he sneered, looking into my eyes without seeing me.

"I'm not. Knock it off. I don't want to do this," I demanded.

He brought his mouth towards mine. I clenched my teeth together and pinched my lips shut. He thrust his tongue through my lips, pushing it against my teeth. I jerked my head back and forth, wanting to scream but knowing that if I did, he'd gain access. *No! No! No!*

He gripped my wrists with one of his hands, bringing my arms above my head while he unzipped his pants with his other hand. I closed my eyes, not wanting to see what came out.

"Stop!" I cried. "Please Chad, don't do this. Please, don't. Please."

It was as if he couldn't hear me. His eyes bugged out of his head and a bead of sweat formed on his forehead as he peered down at me. I screamed as loudly as I could. He clasped his hand over my mouth, muffling the sound. I couldn't breathe. I bit his hand and he jerked it away.

He laughed. "Go ahead and scream. Nobody's here. No one can hear you."

I could see the excitement growing in his eyes. I wriggled my body underneath his while he laughed. In one quick movement, he reached down and ripped out the crotch of my shorts, then pulled my underwear to the side. He pried my legs apart with his.

"Please stop," I begged. "Please."

He refused to look at me. He took his dick and shoved it inside of me in one powerful thrust. I felt my insides ripping and tearing apart, as if I might be splitting in two. I cried out and felt my head begin to swim.

Don't fight him. Don't move. It will only make it worse. You've been here before. It'll be over soon. Don't fight. He violently thrust in and out of me while I stared at the ceiling, watching the ceiling fan move around, getting lost in its spin. He yelled as if he was in pain, arched his back, and collapsed on top of me. I could feel his heart thumping against my chest and smell his stench of chicken noodle soup. I lay there lifeless and immobilized under him. Suddenly, he pulled out of me and jumped up. He hurriedly zipped his pants.

"I'm sorry," he muttered, looking at the floor. "I'll take a shower and then we can go."

He turned around, walked out of the room and down the hallway to the bathroom. I sat up, listening for the sound of water pounding and the shower door shutting. Once I was satisfied he was in it, I leapt off the bed, sprang up the stairs, flung open the door, and ran into the sunshine. I ran through all of the neighbors' yards, not wanting to go on the streets where people had a better chance of seeing me.

I don't remember reaching my house or going downstairs. I just remember sitting on the toilet and seeing the blood between my legs. I got in the shower, furiously rubbing the washcloth all over my body to get rid of his filth, even though it stung and burned. I scrubbed between my legs.

In clean clothes, I curled up in my bed, pulling the covers over my head. I lay in my bed for the rest of the day in darkness, listening to music and wanting to die.

The next day, Strom asked, "What happened to you yesterday?"

"I went to Chad's to wait for him to get ready. I guess he thought I wanted to have sex, but I didn't. Anyways, he did and . . . "

"What the hell do you mean by that?" Strom interrupted.

"Well . . . I mean . . . like I said no but . . . I don't know . . . "

"You mean he raped you?" he demanded.

Quietly, I responded, "I guess you could say that."

He jumped up from his spot on the floor. "Get up. C'mon."

"What are you gonna do?" I asked.

"Don't worry about it." He marched out into the living room, where Jen and Rich sat next to each other on the couch. "Jen, I want you to bring Heather to the parking lot of the Main Motel in like two hours."

As he motioned for me to sit next to her, I said, "Strom, really, it's not a big deal."

"Not a big deal?" he yelled, the veins in his forehead bulging. "Nobody fucks with you. C'mon, Rich. I need you to drive."

Rich jumped up and followed Strom out the door. I sat down next to Jen, though I didn't know her very well. She'd started to come around a lot lately with her boyfriend, Rich. She never really said too much.

"What's going on?" she asked.

I shrugged. We sat in silence, staring at the images on the TV until it was time to go. She drove a big blue Cadillac covered with rust spots. We turned the corner into the Main Motel parking lot. I spotted Chad's blue jeep parked next to Rich's brown Tercel.

"Ohmigod," I cried. "Turn around. Get out of here!"

"What? Strom said . . . "

"I don't fuckin' care!" I yelled. "Please, leave."

She heard the desperation in my voice and whipped the car around skillfully, leaving the parking lot. We sped away and took the nearest gravel road out of town. I was shaking. *Chad must have denied the whole thing. Strom must've believed him. They were gonna call me a liar.*

Jen handed me a pill and pointed towards her water. "Here,

take this," she said. "It'll calm you down." I took the pill and gulped it down with water. "What's going on?" she asked.

Figuring she deserved an explanation for my behavior, I replied, "Chad kinda raped me."

"Kinda? That shit doesn't kinda happen," Jen snorted, throwing her black hair over her shoulders. "That fucker."

We drove in silence for a few moments, each of us lost in our own thoughts. Then she said softly, "I understand why you had to get out of there."

"You do?"

"Believe me. I get it." She lit a cigarette and took a long drag. "It's like when my uncle messed with me and my mom found out. All these people came from the county to talk to me and I freaked out. I don't know why. It's like you want someone to do something, but when it happens it's like you freak out. You get all tweaked, like they won't believe you."

She understands. Ohmigod. She gets it. "Yes," I gushed. "It's like when I saw Chad's car there with Strom's. I know Chad denied it and I freaked that Strom would believe him, ya know? I couldn't handle that."

"I believe you," she said, her long, pale fingers ashing her cigarette. "Men suck. Always wanting a piece of ass, and they'll take it any way they can get it. Happens to me all the time. The fuckers."

Later on that night, I found out that Strom was going to make Chad kneel down, kiss my feet, and tell me he was sorry. Before the parking lot, Strom had enticed him to a gravel road in the country by promising to get him high. Once they were there, Strom had pulled out his nine millimeter and held it against Chad's temple. Strom threatened that if Chad ever touched me again, he'd kill him. Chad had wet himself.

After that day, I shut down completely and became a spectator of my own life, as if I was watching a movie. I didn't care what happened to me. I wanted to die, but I'd been taught that people who committed suicide went to hell and burned forever. So I was trapped, biding my time, and hoping the next funeral I attended would be my own.

I kept going to see Dave every week, but I couldn't talk to him anymore. I felt worse each time because the happiness he exuded was out of my reach and always would be. He suggested I check myself into treatment. I toyed with the idea, but couldn't bring myself to do it. However, the decision was made for me when I went to my next court date in September.

I sat on my aluminum chair at the big wooden table, with my parents on the left side of me. Rubin Harris, my probation officer, was on my right and next to him was the district attorney. Behind the table, my social worker and Guardian ad Litem sat whispering to each other. I didn't know what either of them did on my legal case and didn't care to ask any questions to find out. In front of us towered the judge's massive desk. He got a comfortable, black padded chair. To his side sat the old lady with gray hair and glasses perched on the tip of her nose, who frantically typed everything being said.

I slouched in my chair, vaguely aware of the sound of Rubin's voice telling the judge what trouble I'd gotten into since my last court date, and all the things I hadn't followed through with. The judge would give me more community service hours that I wouldn't do, and sentence me to go to meetings that I wouldn't attend. It was the same boring routine and I'd lost interest long ago. The rap of the judge's gavel startled me.

From his position above me, the judge said loudly, "Heather, I'm talking to you. Do you understand what a stay of sentence means?" I shook my head. He frowned down at me. "I need you to answer."

I coughed, sitting up straighter in my chair. "No, I don't understand."

"This is how it works. The court takes all the charges you've accumulated and puts off sentencing you for one year." He spoke slowly and purposefully, enunciating each syllable. "Provided you don't accrue any new charges, or violate your probation in any way for the next year, the charges will be dropped from your record. You must comply with all of the court's requirements decided upon today and not get into any trouble."

What sort of requirements? What did I miss? I looked over at Rubin for some sort of a clue, but he just stared back at me blankly.

"Do you understand everything I have just said?" the judge asked again.

"If I don't get into any trouble for a year then all of my charges are dropped, right?"

"Yes, but the other part is you must follow through with everything we set in place today. Rubin has recommended long-term chemical dependency treatment and I agree with his recommendation. From here on out, you must follow through with whatever Rubin deems to be appropriate for you. If you don't, we'll be back here in court." His voice echoed through the empty courtroom. "Frankly, I hope that doesn't happen. I am getting rather tired of having you sit in front of me."

"What happens if I screw up?" I asked.

"You'll be charged with everything, and we'll be looking at a long-term correctional placement for you," he said firmly. "Anything else, Rubin?"

"No, your honor."

"Court is adjourned." He tapped his gavel on the desk and we rose from our seats.

Within a week, my parents were driving me to New Hope Treatment Center again. Rubin had made arrangements with

Dave for me to go back in. We pulled into the parking lot of the big brick treatment center, which by now was very familiar to me. Silently, we walked down the sidewalk to the door where we'd be buzzed in. I had a half-ounce stuffed in my shoe to get me through my stay. Suddenly, without thinking, I stopped and pulled the bag out from my sock. I walked up to the garbage can next to the door and tossed my bag of weed in, then hurriedly rang the buzzer before I changed my mind.

12

Empty Mirror

I'd become a trained professional at performing as the character of Heather. It had taken me years to perfect, but I had it down. I knew all the rules that governed her behavior; when I was seven,

I sat at my desk in my bedroom and wrote all of them down. The first and most important rule was quite simple. It was the foundation, which kept all other rules of the character in place: *Don't let anyone know if they hurt me.* If people know they hurt you, it's like giving them more power. Not being hurt was the one piece of power I had ahold of. The second rule: *Don't trust anyone.* My mom had claimed to be honest, but I'd watch her watch things happen and then deny she ever saw them occur.

"I don't know what you're talking about Heather," she'd said on so many occasions. "That never happened."

When my cat Tiger pooped on the floor, my dad took him outside to the vacant field and shot him. Whenever I'd say something about not being able to believe that my dad shot my cat just because it pooped, my mom would laugh and say, "Oh Heather, quit exaggerating. That never happened." Even though she was standing right by my side, right next to me while we watched him walk up the driveway with his rifle resting on his shoulder.

I'd learned I couldn't trust my parents and this rule had translated easily to the streets. No one could be trusted there because I knew that if I had a bag of dope or money, anyone would stab me in the back without a second thought.

I didn't feel emotions; at least I showed the world none of them. If you showed emotion, you were weak and got hurt. I cut off every painful emotion before it could start. Anger was the only emotion I could show because it had the power to scare and control other people. No one could ever get close to me, because I knew it was those who loved me the most that could inflict the most pain.

I'd played this Heather role for so long, I no longer knew it was a character. Angry and hostile, I moved around the treatment center ready to fight if provoked in the least. I was cold and aloof too, evading all serious talk. I heard the same things in group that I'd heard so many times before.

"Heather is so negative. She threatens my sobriety."

"I'm scared of Heather. She's got such an attitude. It seems like she doesn't really want to be here."

But I knew I was in trouble when Bobby, who happened to be in treatment at the same time as me, came running down the hallway to my room. He stood in the doorway because boys weren't allowed in girls' rooms. "Heather, your bag is at the front desk," he exclaimed. "I think they're kicking you out."

I jumped up from my bed and ran down the hallway with Bobby to the nurse's station. Leaning over the desk, I spotted my black duffel bag lying next to one of the chairs. I turned around to see Dave and the other adolescent counselor, Janice, walking towards me, neither of them smiling.

"Come with us." Dave pointed to the door leading down the stairs to the office.

I followed them through the doorway, looking over my shoulder at Bobby, whose eyes looked sad; it had been comforting being in treatment together. In Janice's office, I took a seat in front of the desk while Dave shut the door behind us. Janice sat on the small blue love seat across from me and Dave sat down in the chair next to her. Both faced me head on.

I crossed my arms. "What's going on?"

Janice looked towards Dave. He said, "You're going to have to leave. We called your probation officer. He's going to come get you and take you to a group home. You'll . . . "

"Are you serious?" I sat straight up in my chair.

"You can't follow the program," Janice said softly.

Dave declared, "It's not fair to the other kids here who are trying to get better."

A red light exploded in my head. "Fuck you, Dave! You're a damn liar. Always saying you care about me and all that bullshit about helping me. Now you're just gonna kick me out on the streets. Fuck you!"

He jumped up from his chair, chewed on his bottom lip, and narrowed his eyes. I'd never seen him mad before. His chest puffed up and he strutted back and forth between the door and his chair. For a second, I was afraid he was going to open the door and leave. Finally, he sat back down in his chair, taking deep breaths.

"Listen, you really piss me off. I love and care about you. More than you probably even know, Heather. I've gone to bat for you many times. If anyone is in your corner, it's me. You would've been kicked out of here a week ago if it wasn't for me fighting to keep your ass here. I keep telling the staff to just give you a chance, that it will take some time. But you give nothing but attitude.

There's nothing more I can do. It's up to you, and you seem perfectly content to destroy yourself. It breaks my heart, but I've got to let you go."

That familiar lump lodged in my throat. I fixed my gaze on the carpet. The room was silent except for the sound of our breathing and the ticking of the round clock on the wall. I couldn't find my voice.

Dave broke in, turning to look at Janice. "Okay." He stood up. "Let's sign the discharge papers."

My voice suddenly squeaked out. "Wait."

"What?" Janice asked.

"I don't want to leave." I didn't recognize the sound of my own voice.

Dave sat back down in his chair and crossed his legs. "Why?"

"Because . . . I . . . I just . . . " My tongue seemed to swell to massive proportions in my mouth. "Because I'll die out there."

As I spoke, it occurred to me that I was telling the truth. I didn't want to leave. Both Janice and Dave stared at me, waiting for me to go on. I couldn't.

"Let's talk about it," Dave said. "Tell me more."

I took a deep breath and began. "If I leave here, I know I'll get high. I don't know how not to. I'm afraid if I leave here I'll never get sober, and I want to see what it's like."

Once again I fixed my gaze on the carpet. I could feel their eyes still boring into me like I was sitting there completely naked. I wanted a blanket to wrap around me. I brought my knees up to my chest.

"I think that is the first honest and real thing I've ever heard you say," Janice commented. "This is the stuff you need to be sharing."

"What are you willing to do?" Dave asked next.

I shrugged my shoulders. "Anything, I guess."

"Okay. Then let's start talking, right now. Let's talk about your family and why you do everything you can to get out of that house."

I don't know what happened next. I know I talked and they must have thought I did well because I was allowed to stay. But it was one of my mental blank spots. Whenever things got intense or I felt scared, I went to some place in my mind and couldn't remember what happened. Anything dealing with my family was sure to cause it.

About a week later, I was sitting in my room drawing when Dave knocked at my door.

"What?"

"It's Dave. Can I come in?"

"Sure." I focused on the drawing I'd been working on since the night before.

He walked in and stood behind me at the desk, looking over my shoulder. "Nice." I continued working on the curve of the person's nose while he stood behind me. He continued, "Heather, some people are here to see you."

I turned around in my chair, finally looking up at him. "What people?"

"Well . . . " He cleared his throat. "There's a sheriff and two social workers. One of them is just a social worker, and the other one is a victim's advocate."

My mind immediately shifted into panic. "What in the hell are they doing here?" I jumped up from my chair to face him.

"I made a report to the county that I suspected abuse was going on in your house. They're just here to help. All you've got to do is talk to them like you're talking to me. They just want to ask you some questions. I'll be with you the whole time. Okay, honey?"

"No!" I screamed, grabbing a book from my desk and hurling

it at the wall. "I won't. You can't make me. Ohmigod, I am not going down there."

He pleaded softly, "C'mon. Don't make this difficult. I know you're scared."

"Fuck you," I yelled. "You don't know how I feel! Shit! Fuck! God dammit!"

I grabbed my pencil and furiously stabbed it through my paper. *This can't be happening. This isn't real. No one will believe you. They'll talk to your dad. Mom will say you're lying. What if they believe you? I'm crazy. I lied. I told the truth. This isn't happening.*

"Let's go. C'mon, they're all waiting. You have to do this," Dave coaxed, moving towards me.

I pulled away and grabbed a chair, quickly flipped it over, climbed onto my desk, and then jumped onto my bed behind it. Curling myself into a tight ball in the corner between the wall and the bed, my thoughts took over. *This isn't real. Just make it stop. Go away. Everyone needs to leave me alone.* Dave took a step towards me.

"GET AWAY FROM ME!" I yelled. He stopped in his tracks.

"Sweetie . . . "

"Don't call me that! Leave me alone." I wanted to grab the pencil and stab his eyes with it to make him stop looking at me.

He stood silently while I breathed rapidly in and out, hunched in the corner. He stood there for a long time, hoping I'd change my mind and go downstairs, but I couldn't. He had no idea how terrified I was. I'd only talked to him about my dad because I was trying to make sense of all the craziness in my head. I never wanted this to happen.

"Okay," he said quietly. "I'll tell them you refuse to come down."

He turned and left my room. As soon as he shut the door, I jumped off my bed and crawled under it to hide. Flat on my back, staring at the wire mesh inches from my nose, I pretended I was in a coffin, just like I used to do under my bed at home when I was little. I was dead, in some sort of a peaceful sleep. My space was transformed from wire springs holding a mattress to the top of a wooden coffin lined in purple satin. The hard floor became a soft cushiony pillow holding my dead body, while I slept in a world different than the one I was in.

Even though he made a report to the county, I kept opening up to Dave. I fought a constant battle between my character and myself. Without my character, I felt as if I had no self. I'd look into the mirror above the small sink in my bathroom and wonder who the person staring back was. I felt no connection of any sort to her.

Nights were the hardest for me. Either I couldn't sleep at all or I woke up screaming from nightmares. As soon as I was awake, I quickly pushed away the nightmare images. But then the nightmare nights became sleepless nights. One night, lying in my safe place, I contemplated untangling the wires from the springs above me, to make a noose so I could hang myself in the bathroom. I didn't care if I was going to hell.

Suddenly Dave's deep voice broke into my thoughts: "Hey." I turned my head to see him lying on his side next to the bed, peeking in at me. "Bad night again?" he asked tenderly.

I didn't respond.

"Wanna come out from underneath there so we can talk?"

I shook my head.

"Do you want to hold my hand?"

I shook my head again.

He stuck his arm underneath the bed and stretched his hand out to me. "Will you at least take hold of my pinkie?"

I reached out and hooked his pinkie with mine.

He sighed. "You're not alone in all of this, sweetie."

We lay like that for a long time. That's when I decided that he'd be the one I'd let see me, or rather the me that wasn't there. I'd give him a small amount of my trust and see what he did with it. It felt good to let someone else have a peek into the inner workings of my life, a place uncharted by anyone besides me. I realized that I didn't know what to do with myself, or with the chaotic mess that was my life, so I started to let Dave make some decisions for me; I realized I didn't know how to.

First, he decided it would be a good idea to not have any contact with my dad for a while. "There is way too much there for you to work through right now."

I nodded my head. "But what about my mom?"

"I'll take care of it," he assured me.

Still, I was surprised when my mom showed up for the following session alone. Once we were in family group, Dave instructed me to ask her if we could have a relationship without my dad being involved. I did it, even though I was scared to tell her that I didn't want to see or talk to my dad; I knew it would hurt her. But Dave sat in the chair next to me the entire time, squeezing my hand tightly, and I borrowed his strength as my own. I was surprised again when my mom agreed to not talk about my dad, and not make me see him.

On the days I could have visitors, my mom came by herself as well. One day, as we sat outside at a picnic table, she began the talk. "Heather, I need to speak to you."

I nodded.

She had some look in her eyes that I'd never seen before. "Well . . . see . . . um . . . I don't really know how to do this . . . "

"It's okay. I'm listening." My palms were sweating. My heart started to thump.

"Well, all the questions . . . Everyone asking me about whether you've been abused . . . "

Who's asking her? What does she say? Ohmigod . . . Stay here,

Heather. Don't go anywhere. You need to hear this. Listen. Don't leave. Stay.

It seemed like hours passed before she spoke again. "Well, I know everyone thinks it's your dad. They think he sexually abused you." She paused, watching my face for an answer. I stared at the initials carved in the picnic table. "Well, I asked him. He cried and said he never touched you. I have to believe him."

Of course she has to believe him. That's nothing new. He cried? I can't believe she even asked him. He knows? He knows?

"Heather . . . " Her voice broke into my thoughts. I looked up. "Is it your dad?"

How do I answer? I don't remember things. I don't know anything, Mom. I want to say no, but so many things say yes. I feel yes. I just don't know. "Well . . . see, there's weird things I remember . . . I can't really explain. Pieces. Weird shit goes on in my head. Dad looks at my ass."

"What kind of things?" she probed.

I sighed. "I don't know. Like I was so scared of a monster in my room at night when I was a kid, someone coming into my room at night. Then everything goes blank. I have really bad nightmares about gross things. He tickled me and touched me underneath my shirt . . . "

"Heather, I'm sure it was an accident."

We sat in a silence that threatened to overwhelm me. "I'm just trying to figure it all out," I blurted.

"I don't understand why you have to figure it all out. Why it even matters." Now her eyes were angry. *Is she mad at me? Why is she mad at me? What have I done?* "I mean, my grandpa sexually abused me, and it's not like it affects my life or anything. Besides, even if it did happen, we have to forgive. Christ teaches us to forgive. Even if your dad did do something to you, I forgive him. God forgives us."

Fuck God. Fuck his forgiveness. That's it? You just forgive him? What about Becca? My head pounded.

"Do you have enough cigarettes for the week?" she asked next.

I walked away from our visit in a daze, not quite believing that the conversation had occurred. I related the details of it to Dave, but it seemed as if I was telling him a story about another girl. He sat in the chair next to me, putting his arm around my shoulder. "I'm sorry, honey."

Sorry? What is he sorry for? I'm sorry I ever talked about it. So shut up. No more talking about Dad. But I . . . shut up. There is no reason to go there. You just get crazy.

Normally, kids stay in treatment for twenty eight days, but I stayed for fifty four. Dave kept getting me extensions from the county, but eventually the day came for me to leave. It had been decided that I would go to River East, a halfway house in the Twin Cities, for three months. The place was kind of like treatment, but not quite so strict. I was terrified to leave Dave.

"I'm so proud of you," he said as we drove up the long gravel driveway to the halfway house. I always got uncomfortable whenever he said anything nice about me, so I stared out the window at River East, a small white plaster building next to a church. He parked the car in front and turned to me.

"I want to give you something. Now don't laugh, 'cause it's kind of cheesy." I smiled as he took off the white sweater he was wearing and handed it to me.

He cleared his throat. "Whenever you get lonely and think nobody cares about you, just put this on and think of me giving you a great big old hug."

I took the sweater, blinking back tears that threatened to spill down my cheeks. "Thank you." Dressed only in a red T-shirt, Dave rubbed his arms as we walked in. A big man with a huge belly and chubby cheeks greeted us, sticking out his pudgy hand to me.

"I'm Bill," he declared. "C'mon, I'll show you around." He waddled in front of us. We followed him through the building lined with linoleum-like school cafeteria floors. Bill showed us the room where group was held every night, and he led us down a flight of stairs to the big dining room and kitchen. Every kid had a chore to do and everyone rotated cooking duties. The guys' rooms were all downstairs and I wouldn't be allowed in any of them. We headed back up the stairs as Bill explained that I'd be bused to the alternative high school nearby.

"All of these are girls' rooms." At the end of a long hallway, he opened the door to a white room with brown carpet. There were two beds, one on each wall. "And this is your room. You're lucky. You only got one roommate." Half of the room was completely bare except for the bed and nightstand. My roommate's side was covered in Coolio pictures. "I'll leave you two alone to say good-bye." Bill shut the door behind him.

I turned to look at Dave, clutching his sweater in my hands. He put both of his hands on my shoulders. "You'll be fine without me." His big blue eyes grew wet and glossy. "You are going to do great here. Everything is going to be okay."

"I'm gonna miss you," I stammered.

"I'll miss you, too." He pulled me into a tight hug. I breathed in his familiar scent and held on tightly, not wanting to let him go. "I love you and I'm so proud of you. I'm only a phone call away."

I love you, too. I couldn't say it, but I knew it was true. He slowly pulled away and cleared his throat.

"Okay." He coughed. "I'm gonna go. I'm just gonna go."

In two seconds he was gone and I was standing in the same place, still holding onto his sweater.

Jylinda was my roommate and for the most part we got along as best as two teenagers sharing a room can. She was a little younger than me and had created her own character, which was similar to mine. We were in a constant competition to prove who could be the toughest, and I didn't have a hard time competing. However, when the lights were turned off at night I was gripped by fear, empty and alone.

On Jylinda's nights, we listened to Coolio or Snoop Dogg as we fell asleep, and on my nights we listened to the Beatles or the Grateful Dead. I'd lie in my bed and strain my ears for the sounds of her falling asleep. I got very good at listening for the exact slow rhythm she made when she was sleeping deeply.

As soon as I knew Jylinda was asleep, I reached underneath my mattress and pulled out Dave's sweater. I'd wrap it around me as if his arms were inside of it giving me a hug. Sometimes I swore I could still smell his scent lingering in the soft fabric. Many nights I cried silent tears into it but—no matter what—I made sure I was the first one awake in the morning so I could quickly hide it underneath the mattress until night returned.

13

Second Chances

By the time I got out of River East, I had almost five months of sobriety. It felt like a lifetime. I'd become skilled at staying sober in an institution, but the real test would be in the outside world.

Shortly before my discharge, a CHIPS petition was filed in my county. I didn't know what it was. All I knew was that I'd be going to a foster home. I thought it had something to do with me being bad, but I found out later that it stands for Child in Need of Protective Services. My foster home was an hour away from my hometown.

Yvonne, my foster mom, was the opposite of Mrs. Morrison. At first I didn't know what to think of this middle-aged widow. She was over six feet tall, with wide shoulders and a big chest. Her gray frizzy hair stuck up haphazardly all over her head. Her face, lined with wrinkles, also bore a skin disorder that spotted her face with weird blotches and bumps. Behind her rather ugly exterior flashed warm and attentive eyes. I was impressed by the fact that she married a black man in the fifties, which had to mean she was a brave woman. She had two grown daughters with families of their own and Jewel, who was only fifteen. Jewel lived in a small house in the backyard, her own retreat from the foster kids. Yvonne had bought her a red convertible to drive around, even though she wasn't old enough.

The first day I arrived there, she laid down the rules. "Here's the deal, kid," she began in a deep and husky voice. She swayed in the rocking chair across from the couch I sat on. "I've heard an awful lot about you from your P.O. and your social worker, and most of it hasn't been that nice. They say you're nothing but a hellion and probably won't last more than two weeks here before I get sick of you. I've heard all this stuff about how you're disrespectful and will tell me to fuck off. Well, we're gonna get one thing straight. If you tell me to fuck off, I'll tell you to fuck off. I don't take any lip. Got it?"

I nodded my head, shocked.

"Okay. Just so you know, I've had lots of tough girls in my home. I've had every kind of girl come through here, so you don't scare me in the least." She sipped her tea and then set it back down on the end table next to her chair. "You're probably wondering why the hell I do this, huh? It's pretty simple. Kids in foster care have never had a nice home or they wouldn't be in foster care. I just want to give every kid who comes through here a chance to experience what it's like to have a good, safe home. I feel like it's my job to provide that."

I didn't know what to say. *How can she be so hard and soft at the same time?*

"You're a druggie, right?" She kept right on rocking her chair.

I laughed at her choice of words. "Yep, but I've been clean for almost five months."

She clapped her hands together. "Good for you. Honestly, I don't know anything about all those damn drugs. They seem just silly to me. I don't understand what possesses people to do them. You're the expert. There's nothing I could teach you about them that you don't already know."

I nodded my head, listening carefully.

"This is how I see things. You already know what's going to

happen to you if you start using again. No one can keep you sober. I know that much. It's got to be your choice. Drugs are your business, not mine. I just have one request and that is if you decide to start using drugs again, you don't bring them into my house. What you do when you leave here is up to you, but I don't want that shit in my house. Okay with you?"

"Sure," I replied.

"Basically, it's pretty simple. You respect me and I'll respect you."

Yvonne treated me as if I was an equal. I never felt as if she looked down on me. There were things she didn't understand, but she was always quick to ask questions rather than criticize. She was blunt and expressed her emotions and thoughts openly, always encouraging me to do the same.

I loved living at Yvonne's. I shared her with two foster sisters. Kushi was eighteen and had been at Yvonne's since she was twelve. She'd been adopted from an orphanage in India when she was a baby. Her adoptive brothers beat her severely and she was removed from the home because her adoptive parents continually refused to stop them. Kushi was beautiful, with smooth brown skin and long, shiny black hair that flowed down her back. Even though she looked like an adult, she saw the world through the eyes of a child and always would. Most of the time, she thought like an eight- or nine-year-old. It was impossible not to love her.

Kushi was Yvonne's prized product of a good, loving home. She puffed with pride every time she talked about the condition Kushi was in when she first got her. She'd been out of control with boys. They took advantage of her developing body because she didn't understand it was wrong to lift up her shirt and let boys touch her breasts. Yvonne had carefully schooled her in manners and the appropriate ways to interact. Kushi adored Yvonne and was eager to please. "Mom says that after Jewel graduates, I can live in her house." Her eyes sparkled. "I get to live back there. All by myself. I can decorate however I want. She says I can."

Courtney, my other foster sister, was fourteen and had been with Yvonne for a year. She was a continuing frustration for Yvonne because no matter how much attention and love was lavished on her, she refused to accept it. Courtney had been removed from her home because her dad had been forcing sex on her since she was nine. When I looked in her blue eyes, I felt like I was staring into the eyes of a very old woman. It would take a long time for her soul to recover. Courtney wasn't much older than my younger sister, and she looked up to me in the same way my sister did. I hadn't been there long before she started dressing and talking like me.

"Looks like you've got yourself a little Heather," Yvonne commented one day.

I didn't mind, but I did get tired of her stealing clothes from my closet. I would have gladly lent them to her, but she never asked. Courtney didn't have the ability to ask for things. She hoarded clothes in her room and stockpiled food from the kitchen under her bed and in her closet.

Each of us had our own room and I felt like a princess. My room was next to Courtney's and across from Kushi's. It had slanted ceilings and a huge queen-sized bed in the center, topped with a black silk comforter and matching red and black pillows. I had my own TV and phone. There was even a red and black artist's desk in the corner. I'd wanted a black and red room since I was little. It was as if Yvonne had known me before we ever met.

I didn't realize how unsafe my home was until I lived with Yvonne. People say you don't know what you have until it's gone, but my experience was the opposite. I didn't know what I didn't have until I got what I had at Yvonne's. When I walked through the doors I didn't feel a sense of impending doom like I did at my parents'. I didn't have to be constantly alert and aware of everyone's presence or subconsciously hold my breath at all times. There was never the suffocating anger underlying interactions. Anger was freely felt and freely discussed.

I also didn't have to cover up my body and try to hide from peering eyes. I could use the bathroom in private with no one intruding on me. When I showered at home, my dad had a habit of sneaking into the bathroom, standing on the toilet, and dumping cold water over me. My mom always said it was his way of joking around, just like when he pinched and slapped my sister's ass, or mine.

My mom came to visit occasionally. Sometimes she brought my sister, who was now being home-schooled for some reason. I didn't look forward to my mom's visits because things seemed so odd between us. Sometimes she had all sorts of questions, and said things that didn't make any sense to me. "I knew something was wrong with you when you were young. I knew someone was messing with you. But I really think it was the neighbor boys who messed with you. I just think you put your dad's face onto it."

She'd bring up weird stories that I didn't remember, like the day my screams sent her scurrying downstairs. "I ran into your bedroom. And there you were on the ground with your dresser on top of you. Your dad was pulling it off you as you screamed. I remember being shocked because you never cried or got upset when you got hurt. So I knew if you were making a fuss, then something was really wrong. But the weird thing was that you were naked underneath your dresser. You weren't screaming because you were hurt, you were just screaming for your clothes. What happened that day?"

I searched my memory for a recollection of some sort, for any small piece, but came up with nothing. It was the same way when she asked about me being left alone with my dad while she was up north. "Did anything happen then?" she asked. Once again,

I just shrugged my shoulders and mumbled that I didn't know; I couldn't even remember being left with my dad. The truth was that I didn't remember much of anything before I was ten. I was always happy when my mom left. I wanted to leave everything about my old life behind.

Everything in my new life was foreign, as if I'd been cut out from an old picture and pasted into a new one that didn't resemble anything familiar. I missed the rigid structure and rules I had when I was at River East. As much as I'd fought against them at the time, when they were gone I missed them. I felt like a baby who'd just learned to stand and was suddenly expected to know how to walk.

My feelings of being lost and misplaced were magnified when I started attending school at the Alternative Learning Center. Part of my probation was that I attend school, and I hated it. The ALC was at the far end of the regular part of the high school, separate from the mainstream kids. We weren't supposed to interact with the regulars, like we might have contaminated them. I sat in the same classroom with the same kids from nine until noon every day.

There were three groups of kids and I didn't fit into any of them. One group consisted of teen mothers who already had their babies or were expecting. These girls spent time at their desks eagerly focused on the work packets we were given. Then there was a bunch of Latino kids who spoke Spanish and broken English. They stuck with each other and rarely spoke to anyone else. The final group was the kids who were just like how I used to be. Most of them had gotten kicked out of regular school and could never go back. They came to class with red eyes, reeking of booze.

Yvonne observed my depressed mood each time I came home from school. She'd be sitting in her white wicker rocking chair, drinking her tea and waiting to hear about my day. "It's gotta be hard for you," she said one day. "I can see you're lonely and I wish there was something I could do. I'm sure you've got to get sick of hanging around an old bag like me."

I laughed, which made her break into laughter. I loved to make her laugh. She had this contagious giggle that went on and on as her eyes lit up. She'd actually laugh until tears rolled down her cheeks. She never pressured me to talk about anything I didn't want to. But she was right. I was lonely, like a five-year-old on the playground watching all the other kids play, wanting to join in, but not knowing how.

I'd been attending aftercare meetings at New Hope the few months since I'd gotten out. There was a girl, Kasey, who went to the groups and Dave was always encouraging me to be friends with her. Dave and I had kept in contact while I'd been at River East by writing and talking on the phone. He'd even driven up to see me a couple of times. Since I'd gotten out, we talked on the phone every day. It wasn't unusual for me to call him at home in the middle of the night or for him to call me. I knew it was against the rules for him to give me his home number but I didn't care as long as he didn't.

I began making efforts to talk to Kasey, a tall, skinny girl with short blond hair who'd gone through treatment about a month before I had. Peanut was her name on the streets when she was using. She was trying desperately to get rid of Peanut and become Kasey.

While we stood outside of the treatment center smoking, I asked, "Why do they call you Peanut?"

She shrugged. "I don't really know. They just do."

I burst out laughing. "You have a nickname and don't even know why?"

She had a contagious laugh of high squeals and hiccup sounds. "I never thought about it. That's funny."

We started hanging out together outside of aftercare groups.

Neither of us had any clue what to do with our time. We quickly took to doing anything that would cause us to feel a rush. Shoplifting became a favorite activity. There was a definite high as we successfully walked through the doors of a store with stolen merchandise. We each got a new wardrobe and anything else we wanted that way. We raced her grandma's car up and down Main Street. Sometimes we drove into things. Along the interstate, we pulled up our shirts, flashing the truckers. At night, we climbed the walls of buildings and flipped cartwheels on the roof. We were constantly in search of the next daring activity to outdo the last one.

I hadn't had a girlfriend in a very long time. Kasey lived with her grandma and we alternated between sleeping over at her grandma's and sleeping at Yvonne's. It was almost like we were normal teenagers as we munched on Oreo cookies late at night and lay side by side in bed, whispering and giggling until the sun came up. It was at night that we let our guards down, shedding our tough skins to become frightened little girls. Kasey and I became inseparable.

I kept nothing from Dave, dropping in at the treatment center all the time. Sometimes we sat in his office and talked, but we spent just as much time in the gym shooting baskets, playing endless games of Horse. At first, when my friendship with Kasey began, he'd been very encouraging. He'd laugh at the tales I told about our escapades. But he seemed to be getting less amused about the things we did. "Heather, if you're going to act, talk, and spit like a junkie then you might as well go all the way," he'd say. As always, I was desperate to please him and have his stamp of approval on my life so I assured him I understood, even though I didn't.

I met another friend, Sam, through the aftercare meetings at the treatment center, too. I was elated to learn that his parents were enrolling him in the ALC for the rest of the year. Finally, I had someone to hang out with during school. We both were artists and our teacher, Erin, encouraged us to develop our talents. She worked out a way for us to be able to use the art room alone every other day for an hour. We were in heaven there.

One day Sam was using rubber cement to glue pieces of tile onto a board. He complained, "This stuff reeks."

"Shit. That's nothing. Have you ever huffed it?" I continued trying to get the background on my painting just right; I'd been trying for a week.

Sam raised his head from his work. "Huh? Huffing? I don't get it."

"You've never done it?"

He laughed. "Uh, no. I'm not a freak."

"Shut-up." I gave him the finger, smiling. "You'd be surprised. It's a trip. You get this like vavoom sound in your head."

"Really?" He stared at the big tin can. "How do you do it?"

I put down my brush. "You just pour it into a bag. Then you take the bag and hold it on your mouth and nose like you're hyperventilating." I demonstrated with my hands and an imaginary bag. "You just make sure to hold the bag tight and breathe in and out as fast as you can."

He clapped his hands together, looking around at the empty room. "I wanna try it."

I looked at him. "Seriously? We're supposed to be sober."

Sam winked at me and smiled. "It's not like it's a real drug, Heather. It's just messin' around." He stood up and pushed his chair under the table. "C'mon. We've only got like fifteen minutes. Help me find a bag."

I got up from my seat and rummaged through the art supplies closet with him until I found a Ziploc bag filled with stencils. I dumped the contents into another bag and shook it out.

"This'll work," I exclaimed.

I walked back to our table, unscrewed the top of the can and dumped the thick goo into the bag. Sam stood by the door, watching. I walked over and handed it to him.

"Take it into the bathroom," I whispered, even though there was nobody around to hear me. "Do just like I told you to."

He grabbed the bag and skipped out of the door. Back at the table, I picked up the lid to screw it back on. *Stick your face in there. What? I'm not sticking my face in there. It's not a big deal. Christ, it's rubber cement.* I shook my head, trying to stop the thoughts.

But before I even knew what I was doing, I stuck my face into the jar. The stickiness clung to my chin and forehead as I took a few huge breaths. Then I jerked my head up, shocked and repulsed. After quickly screwing the lid back on, I shoved the can down the table, away from my arm's reach. My head felt dizzy, like I'd just gotten off a roller coaster. I tapped my fingers on the table, staring at my picture, unmoving, dazed.

It seemed like it took forever before Sam stumbled back through the door, clutching the bag in his left hand. He had a goofy grin plastered on his face and his eyes were slits, like he had just smoked a lot of weed. "Shit," he said, speaking slowly. "Everything looks like a cartoon."

The voices urged, *Get out of here. Run. Run.* But I couldn't move.

Sam burst out laughing, clutching his sides. "Ohmigod, ohmigod. I hear it. I hear that vavoom in my head. Agh, shit! This is nuts."

Mechanically, I stood up and moved towards him. *What are you doing? I know what I'm doing. No, you don't. Stop. Think about it. Shut up.* My actions were slow motion as I took the bag from his hands, then brought the bag up to my face, pulling it around my mouth and my nose. *What are you doing? Shut-up, this doesn't count.* I breathed in and out like I was running a race with my breath. The fumes invaded my lungs with a strange burn. In two minutes, I was high.

I grabbed Sam's hand with my empty hand. "Let's get out of here."

We ran out of the room and hit the nearest door. The sunshine struck my eyes, crisscrossing in waves. We headed across the street to a church, where we sat down next to each other on the steps. The bag of rubber cement passed back and forth between us until we blacked out and lay on the church steps, unconscious.

Addiction is like having a monster living in your mind. By staying sober, I hadn't fed the monster any food for almost six months. I'd made it weak, but huffing the rubber cement just that one time had reawakened my monster. As soon as I fed it, it attacked and set out to destroy me.

I called Dave that night, fully intending to tell him what I had done.

"Dave, I have something to tell you . . . " I stammered. My hands were sweating and my throat felt tight.

After a long period of silence, he asked, "What do you have to tell me?"

What do I say? Tell him it was an accident. "I kind of got high . . . "

"How do you kinda get high?" I could hear the edge in his voice. "Is that like being kinda pregnant?"

See, he's mad. He told you that you'd get high. You just proved him right. He's gonna leave. He's sick of your shit. You're such a fuck up. "Well, I don't really know how it happened. Me and Sam, ya know how we go to the art room everyday? I think I told you that, didn't I?"

"Get to it," he snapped.

I swallowed and let out a deep breath. "Well, we were using the rubber cement and it's in this big can. Anyways, I had to put the top back on it and while I was doing it, I like got dizzy. I think I breathed it in. I don't know if I did it on purpose, but I felt weird afterwards. Kinda strange."

He laughed. "Heather, you didn't get high. Fumes will do that to you, even a little bit. One time when I was painting my bathroom, I felt a little weird. I had to go outside in the fresh air for a while, but it's not like I got high. Next time just turn your head away. It's not like you stuck your head in the can or something like that."

I laughed. "You're right. I guess I'm just being paranoid."

From that point on, each night when Dave told me he was proud of me, I cringed inside. My secret ate away at me. I decided I should just get drunk so I could tell Dave I'd relapsed. The details of my relapse wouldn't matter. I could start over with a clean slate. If I could make a decision to start using again, then I could just as easily make the decision to stop.

On our way to group the following night, I declared to Kasey, "I wanna get drunk. We should get a bottle."

"Are you serious?"

"It's not like we're gonna do drugs or anything. I just wanna get drunk. Just once with you, to see what it's like." I couldn't look at her. *Leave her out of this. What kind of a friend are you? She doesn't really want to be sober. I'm doing her a favor. Helping her along.*

Driving over the railroad tracks, she lit a cigarette. "I don't know. I'm kinda scared."

"C'mon. We always talk about how much fun it would have been to use together. Let's just do it. It'll be fun."

I turned to look at her. She stared ahead and her forehead creased.

"Kasey," I called to her seductively. "You know you want to. But hey, if you're too scared, I understand."

"I'm not scared," she declared hotly, taking the dare. "I can get someone to buy us a bottle."

Once I was drunk that night, I wanted to smoke pot. Kasey tracked down the friends she'd stayed away from while she was sober. I decided it was okay to do it because I'd already relapsed, and I might as well make it a good one. I'd tell Dave about my relapse after I'd smoked pot.

Soon Kasey and I became two friends who got wasted together, instead of two friends staying sober together. Each time I used, I convinced myself it would be the last time, that I'd go talk to Dave the next day. The next day would come and I'd put it off for one more day. Before I knew it, the days turned into weeks. I quit going to aftercare groups at the treatment center because I didn't want Dave to see me. I knew he'd take one look at me and know.

Then my cover was blown. As she pulled into Yvonne's driveway to drop me off, Kasey announced, "I talked to Dave a few days ago. I'm going back into treatment to do a relapse program."

I tapped my fingers anxiously on the dashboard. "When?" If she had talked to Dave, then he had to know I was using, too. There was no way she hadn't told him. She stared out the window with the back of her head to me. "Today."

"Today?" I exclaimed. "Why didn't you tell me?"

She coughed nervously. "I was afraid you'd talk me out of it. I didn't want to tell you I couldn't handle all this. I hate this shit,

Heather. It's like I'm right back where I was before and I can't stand it."

We silently blew our smoke out the windows in thick white clouds.

"I should probably get going," she said, staring at the center of the steering wheel, still refusing to meet my eyes. "I still have to pack."

I nodded and opened my door. I wanted to give her a hug, tell her I understood and that I loved her, but I couldn't. I'd reverted back to the character of Heather, and showing emotion was not part of her makeup. I turned to look at her. "Call me?"

She shrugged. "Sure."

She drove away without looking back. As I watched the car disappear, I knew I'd soon become a name on her list. The list you have to make in treatment of all of your using friends that you can't hang around anymore.

Without Kasey, I didn't have any connections in Pervis, so I couldn't get high. I knew it'd only be a matter of time before I had to talk to Dave. He'd force me to get sober, and I had to get as much oblivion as possible before then. I resorted to huffing household products again, but it didn't take long before the cheap buzz wasn't doing anything for me. I wanted the real thing. So I called Strom and planned to meet with him the next time I was in town to visit my P.O.

I met him at the park across the street from his parents' house. He looked exactly the same as before. His brown hair was greasy and sticking up. His skin still hung from his face, creating three rolls of chins when he looked down. He gave me a hug. We sat across from each other at an old picnic table as he began packing a pinchie full of pot for me.

He looked up from the rolling. "It's been awhile."

I took it and started to smoke. "Yep."

"So where do you live now?" He stared at me, probably looking at me the same way I'd looked at him. *Do I look different?*

"Pervis," I replied, exhaling.

"Hmm." He dug another pinchie out of the pocket of his jeans and began packing it for himself.

Don't you want to know where I've been? It's been almost a year since you've seen me. Haven't you wondered? I waited for him to ask questions, but none came. We sat in silence, smoking our pinchies, pretending to be interested in something in the park. *I've forgotten how to be with him. Or maybe this is how it's always been. But I thought we talked?*

"How you been?" I asked.

He shrugged his big shoulders. "Fine. Ya know. Same old shit. Different day."

I smiled. "Yeah . . . "

"Anything exciting going on?" he asked, tapping his fingers on the top of the table.

"Not really."

"Oh . . . " His voice trailed off.

The silence stretched out between us. Finally I spoke. "I should get going. I gotta meet my mom soon. She's gonna bring me back to Pervis." I stood up.

"Well hey, it's good to see ya." He stood, too. "You shouldn't be such a stranger."

I smiled at him. "I won't . . . Hey, I don't know anyone where I live and I can't get anything. I don't have any money, but do ya think you could give me a bag?"

Before I even finished, he was digging in the pocket of his jeans. He handed me a baggie with green buds.

I tucked it into my pocket. "Thanks."

He shrugged. "Don't mention it. It's only weed. If you need anything else, lemme know. Gimme a call, whenever."

It was surprisingly easy to step back into my old life, as if I'd never been gone. Calling up old friends and connections, it struck me that no one asked me any questions. I'd been away from the scene almost a year, but it was like no one had even noticed. I thought being sober had destroyed the character of Heather, but in no time at all I was back to the performance.

It was harder and took more planning to get hooked up because I was a town away. I started staying out all night and skipping school. I didn't go to any of my aftercare meetings. I avoided Dave at all costs. At Yvonne's, I avoided everyone. I just wanted to be left alone.

Finally, Dave cornered me on the phone. I was the only one home and I'd been waiting for a call from Strom so I answered it when it rang.

He didn't even bother to say hello. "When are you gonna be done getting high?" There was no room for me to lie or change the subject.

"I . . . uh . . . I don't know." *What do I say?*

"Do you have any plans to get sober again?"

Do I? I don't know. Tell him yes. "Yes. It's just hard."

"Well, why don't you give me a call when you've made up your mind? I'm not gonna watch you destroy yourself." He hung up without saying good-bye. I clung to the phone until it began to make the busy signal.

Waiting for Yvonne to get home, I paced my room. When I heard her come in and turn on the TV, I walked slowly down the stairs. *What are you doing? You're gonna bust yourself. Stupid ass. Shut up. You don't want to do this. Yes, I do.*

I stood at the end of the stairs and cleared my throat to get her attention. "I've got to tell you something."

She picked up the remote and turned the sound down.

"I'm getting high again," I blurted out.

She looked at me without an ounce of surprise on her face. "I know."

"You do?"

She nodded. "I may not know a lot about drugs, but I'm certainly not an idiot. It's pretty obvious, kid. You're different. You're moody and irritable. Plus all sorts of strange people keep showing up on my doorstep."

I sat on the couch. "How come you never said anything?"

"I wanted you to come to me when you were ready. I talked to Dave about it when I first started getting . . . "

"You talked to Dave? What'd he say?" *He's probably talking shit behind your back. Shut up, he isn't. I bet he is.*

"He said to be patient and let you have your own consequences." Yvonne folded her hands together.

What the hell does that mean? Is he going to leave me? Is that my consequence? Everybody knows.

"Why didn't you do anything?" I was surprised at the sound of anger in my voice.

Yvonne raised her eyebrows. "Really Heather . . . What can anyone do to make you quit getting high?"

We sat in silence for a few minutes before I spoke again. "I'm scared. My world is falling apart again."

She reached over and squeezed my knee. "I still love you. You'll get through this. I know you will. You've just hit a rough spot. It'll get better again."

I wanted to believe her, but maybe I was so far gone that I was never going to be okay. I had a beautiful home, living with safety and security for the first time in my life, and I was risking losing it. I'd lost the first real friend I'd had in a long time. I'd been given a chance to go back to school, and I blew that, too.

I began attending groups again and going to meet with Dave whenever I got a chance. We started to talk on the phone again every night. I didn't believe I could get sober without him, and he didn't make me try. When things were okay, we played basketball in the gym or sat outside the treatment center at one of the picnic tables, playing cards and smoking. When things were bad, we'd stay in his office with the door locked. He'd sit next to me, holding me in his arms and rubbing my back.

Sometimes we stayed in his office really late at night. One particular night I couldn't reach Yvonne on the phone to come pick me up. When Dave offered me a ride home, I jumped at the invitation. He popped Tom Petty into the tape deck while I stared out the window, looking at the stars and wishing we could drive forever.

His voice broke into my thoughts. "Come here."

He patted the spot on the seat next to him. Without a thought, I slid over next to him. Then he invitingly lifted his arm. I laid my head against the side of his chest as he wrapped his arm around me. Breathing in his familiar scent, I closed my eyes. *I belong here.* We didn't speak. It was like he could talk to my soul without using language. He moved his arm down and wrapped his fingers on the side of my lower stomach, squeezing me softly. Then he gently rubbed circles on my side. I opened my eyes.

I want him to touch me. Ohmigod, Heather. You can't think this way. But I couldn't stop it. My body was alive with tingles I'd never felt before. A rush of energy flowed from my head down to my toes. I wanted to reach up and bury my face in his. My cheeks were on fire and I was thankful for the darkness. At that moment I knew I was in love with him. I'd known for a long time that I loved him, but this was different. Somewhere along the way, I'd fallen in love with him in a way I didn't even know I was capable of.

When we pulled up to the stop sign a block from Yvonne's house, he turned to look at me. "You better slide over. I don't want Yvonne to think your CD counselor is goofy, but first you've got to give me a kiss good night."

My heart thudded. I lifted my head up and brought my lips to his mouth, kissing him very softly and then scooting away quickly.

With a strange look in his eyes I'd never seen before, he said quietly, "I didn't mean like that. I meant on my cheek."

We never talked about it, but things changed between us after that night. I was afraid each time he looked at me that he'd see how much I loved him. I knew I was not supposed to love him like I did. I was terrified he was going to go away and leave me so I tried to keep my feelings a secret.

One night, as we walked outside the treatment center smoking cigarettes, he suddenly announced, "I want you to meet my wife."

I felt like he'd just slapped me in the face. I knew he had a wife but I'd never seen her, which made it easy to pretend he was just mine. We walked to the front driveway of the treatment center as his wife pulled up in a red minivan. He opened the passenger door and said, "Kathy, I want you to meet Heather," pointing back to me.

With a small face and long, flowing blond hair, she was beautiful. *I hate her.* "Hi, Heather. I've heard so much about you."

"Hey," I replied. In the back of the van, three young faces smiled at me. "I'm going back inside."

I tried to pretend as if nothing had changed and that everything was okay, but I couldn't. I was plagued by the idea that I was only trying to stay sober so I could have Dave in my life. It nagged at me constantly. Each day I was sober, the thing that kept me from throwing it all away was knowing that I couldn't be close to Dave if I was getting high. I didn't care enough about myself to stay sober, and there would come a day when Dave would move on with his life. He had a life that existed without me, a family and children he belonged with. I was just a kid he was trying to help. I didn't have anyone or any place where I belonged.

Dave had told me many times about other treatment staff

cautioning him about being so close to me, and they'd also expressed concern about my unhealthy dependence on him. If I told him how I was really feeling, it would confirm their concerns and he'd have no choice but to leave me.

My anger returned with momentum. I'd finally found someone I loved but I'd never be able to have him. God had played a cruel joke on me. I wasn't staying sober because I wanted to. I was staying sober because I wanted him. If I couldn't have Dave, then I didn't want sobriety. After all, it really wasn't my sobriety, it was his.

14

Back in Hell

Our monthly visit was almost up. For the last hour, I'd regaled Rubin with my usual stories of going to AA meetings, working a part-time job, and doing well in school. None of which were true, but I hadn't gotten into any trouble for a long time so they sounded believable.

"Oh," Rubin suddenly exclaimed, reaching into his briefcase. "One more thing to take care of before I leave." He pulled out the familiar plastic container with a red seal on the cap. Handing it to me, he said, "It's been awhile, so I figured it's time. Can you go for me real quick?"

I sat on the toilet with Rubin waiting directly outside the door, my heart sinking. When he got the tests back, my drug count would be off the charts. I'd been using all my favorites on a daily basis for months. It'd be a probation violation, which meant all my charges that had been put on a stay of sentence would come reeling back into my face. I'd been caught within weeks of my time being up. As soon as Rubin drove away with the bottle, I rushed to Dave's office.

I cried out, "They're gonna lock me up."

Dave no longer expected me to stay sober, and for some strange reason he was okay with it. We still talked almost every day and I stopped in at his office frequently. From his position behind the desk, Dave declared, "Not if you check yourself into treatment first. They don't know how long you've been using. For all they know, you've been sober this whole time. If you check yourself into treatment, it'll look like you just had a relapse, realized your mistake, and decided to do something about it."

"Can I come back here?" I asked eagerly.

"We're too close," he replied, shaking his head. "I can't go back to being your CD counselor."

"What do you mean?" *Can't go back?*

He stood up and walked over to sit in the chair next to me, like he'd done so many times in the past.

"C'mon, Heather . . . " He brushed his hand softly across my cheek. "You know as well as I do."

I do? What do I know? I don't know anything.

My head swirled. He took my chin in his hands and tilted my face towards his. I took in a deep breath. *Ohmigod. Is he going to kiss me? No. God, you're losing it, Heather.* He brought his lips to my forehead and kissed my skin softly before pulling his head back.

He spoke in a deep, husky voice, a voice I hadn't heard before. "I crossed the line of being your CD counselor a long time ago. Somewhere along the way, I've fallen for you. I hate myself for it, but I can't deny my feelings. They're there. I love you in so many different ways."

I looked away from his intense stare. *He loves me, too? He can't. I can love him, but he can't love me. Can he?* I'd fantasized so many times about this moment. How he'd take me into his arms and tell me he was in love with me, too. But now that it was happening, my stomach tightened into a knot and I wanted to get up and run out of his office as fast as I could. I kept my eyes averted until I could leave.

As always, Dave had a plan for me and I followed it. He took me to a place called The Portico, an extended care treatment center for women; though it certainly didn't look like any treatment center I'd ever been to before. The sprawling mansion in the middle of a residential area showcased immaculate old Victorian furniture. I sat next to Dave in the director's office without opening my mouth. The director was older, with gold glasses perched on the tip of her nose.

"Heather really needs your help," Dave explained. "I understand this is an adult halfway house and she's only seventeen, but she doesn't fit with the adolescents. She's chronic and I really think you could help her."

The woman looked at me and back at Dave. "Well, normally we don't do this, but I suppose we can make an exception. If she's really serious, I want her here tomorrow."

"Not a problem," Dave responded eagerly. "I can talk to her social worker and get a Rule 25 going, and I'll bring her myself."

He took care of everything. He called my social worker, Ruth, and made arrangements for me to go in the following day. Then he brought me to Vivian's and explained the situation to her.

"Are you sure this is what you want to do, kid?" Vivian asked, turning to look at me once Dave had finished speaking.

No! I'm not sure about anything. I nodded. She peered at me, trying to read my thoughts, but I kept my gaze focused on Dave. If he said it was what I needed to do, then I would do it. *Maybe he wants me to live with him when I get out. Stop it! He's married for God's sake. You're being an idiot. You can't get sober just 'cause of him. It's never worked before. Whatever.*

At eight the next morning, Dave returned in his station wagon and my bags were packed once again. Saying good-bye to Vivian was harder than I thought it would be. Somewhere inside me a small voice told me it was never going to be the same.

"I'll be here waiting for ya when ya get out, kid." Vivian

hugged me tightly next to her chest as I breathed in her familiar vanilla scent. "You're welcome in my home anytime."

I didn't want to be at The Portico because I didn't even know if I wanted to get sober again, and I was so sick of failing at it. Plus, there was another part of me in turmoil over Dave. I couldn't quite shake the feeling that it wasn't right for him to be in love with me, too. But I loved and trusted Dave and he said I was special, so maybe it was okay. Still, one voice resounded over and over, interrupting my thoughts: *He's old enough to be your dad. You're only seventeen.*

I decided to go through with The Portico, even though I didn't know if I wanted to be sober, because I did know I didn't want to be locked up at some boot camp. I'd done treatment many times, so I knew what was expected of me. Soon, though, it became glaringly obvious that I didn't belong there. Not only was I the youngest person, I was the only person funded by the county. All the other women came from a foreign world of wealth. They'd never had to steal or sleep with crusty old men to get high. They just blew thousands of dollars from their trust funds. They'd never been in any serious trouble with the law because they all had rich daddies or husbands who hired really expensive lawyers to get them off. They wore sparkling jewels on their fingers and a few had even been flown to treatment on private jets. They'd been to the Betty Ford Clinic and Hazelden, luxury resorts compared to the places I'd been. I was Goodwill clothes among designer labels.

Other than group, I spent most of my time in my room. I had a roommate but we didn't talk. For that matter, I didn't speak to anyone unless I was spoken to, and even then I kept my responses short. I'd been there for almost a month when staff called me into a meeting with the director.

I sat alone in a chair up against the wall, while they all faced me in their own chairs: seven women neatly dressed and immaculately made-up, staring at me.

The director began, "Heather, Mary's jewelry is missing."

I didn't give her a chance to finish. "If you think I took it, I didn't." I had no desire to steal from any of them. Stealing was exactly what they expected of me and I would never have dreamed of giving them the satisfaction.

While looking around at the others, my counselor proclaimed, "You'll never get better if you can't get honest." The others all nodded their heads in agreement.

"Look," I replied hotly. "I don't know who took the jewelry, but it wasn't me."

The fat blond in the corner snipped, "Why are you being so defensive?"

"Shit. I . . . "

Martha, the fattest one of them all, interrupted. "Please don't use that language."

I snorted, "I guess I forgot where I was. Have you ever thought maybe someone else did it? Oh, of course not. It couldn't have been one of the princesses."

All eyes bore silently into me. I went from one pair to the next, trying to send my hatred towards them through some sort of visual telepathy.

The director let out a deep sigh. "Since you refuse to be helpful, you might as well go. We'll let you know what we decide to do with this matter."

I stood up, holding back an urge to toss my chair at them. I stormed into the hallway, where a few old women didn't even pretend to not have been eavesdropping. They sneered at me and I sneered right back. I made my way up the winding staircase to my bedroom and plopped down on my bed, staring at the ceiling.

Before long, I heard a knock on the door and Jill walked in.

She was the technician who had taken me to detox the week before. I wasn't wasted, but staff had been convinced that I was. Once I'd gotten there, I'd passed every sobriety test, but staff made them keep me there overnight. Now Jill was holding my duffel bag over her shoulder and I didn't have to guess about the decision that had been made.

"You're being discharged. You'll be going to jail. Your mother agreed to pick you up. She'll be here in ten minutes." Jill tossed my bag to me. "The police have already been called and they're waiting to pick you up if you don't leave quietly."

I didn't know what to expect when I arrived at the courthouse with my mom. She hadn't said a word during the half hour drive. I thought we'd march straight into the court, but instead we headed down the familiar flight of stairs leading to Rubin's office. Rubin sat in his usual spot behind the desk but his small office was crammed with bodies. The bodies of my committee—the ones who made decisions in my life—occupied the rest of the chairs. To Rubin's right sat Renee Hewitt, my Guardian ad Litem, appointed by the judge a couple of years earlier. She was supposed to be my voice in the courtroom, whatever that meant. Trying to be the cool one, she was the one who picked me up from detox and gave me cigarettes. Next to her, Lynette chewed on a toothpick. Renee had introduced Lynette to me as a friend she thought might be helpful. But her cover had been blown when Lynette gave me her business card with the title "Victim's Advocate" in glaring black letters across the top. I was not a victim and I didn't know what an advocate was, but I certainly didn't need one.

Judge Asfeld sat next to them, dressed in plainclothes rather than his black robe. As always, he twirled his glasses in his hand. I'd come to the conclusion that they were merely a prop. Ruth Dorff, my social worker, was next in line. Her arms folded on a pregnant belly that stretched out so far it looked painful. Next to

Rubin, she'd been part of the committee the longest. She took care of all the funding for placing me, always perturbed that I didn't express gratitude for her efforts.

"Well hey, isn't this nice that we're all back together again?" I joked, sitting next to Rubin as my mom slid quietly into the chair beside me. Nobody cracked a smile, not even a fake one. This was not going to be good.

Rubin cleared his throat. "Here's the deal, Heather. We've reached the end of the road. For the past few years, we've given you every break imaginable. Rather than punish you, we've repeatedly tried to help you." He paused, making eye contact with everyone else in the room.

"You reach a point when you realize you've done all that you can do, and we've reached that point." Everyone nodded. "We've run out of options and we've all reached an agreement. First of all, you are free to live wherever you choose. We're not going to put you into another placement. Basically, you're on your own. In six months, you'll be an adult."

"I don't get it," I interrupted. "I'm free?"

This time Judge Asfeld spoke. "Well, you're free from the adolescent court system. We're closing your social service file and your CHIPS petition. From this day, everything will be handled by corrections and we're going to begin the process of transferring you into the adult correctional program. You've used up all your chances. Once all the paperwork is completed and filed, you'll be tried as an adult when you break the law, and punished in the same manner as one. You're almost an adult now and we're just speeding up the process."

I took his words in slowly, letting each of them sink in. "So . . . I'm not going back to Vivian's?"

Ruth smiled. "Nope." I wanted to punch the smug look off her face.

"Where will I go?" I asked, looking towards Rubin.

He shrugged. "Wherever you want. However, you are not allowed to leave the state. You'll have to find a place to live."

Ruth jumped in again. "It's no longer our responsibility."

For so long, I'd wanted out of the claws of my committee's constant orders, threats, punishments, watchful eyes, demands, and relentless questions. I'd spent many hours dreaming about being free, but I'd just been let go from their restraint and I felt lost. They'd made the decisions for my life. I didn't know how to. *Where will I go? What will I do? I'm gonna end up in prison.* I looked over at my mom, but she stared at the floor, refusing to meet my eyes.

Rubin slid a document across his desk to me. I signed on the dotted line next to their signatures and it was over. The committee filed out of the room. I followed my mom back up the stairs, feeling a powerful sense of impending doom. *I'm not gonna make it.*

"Well, I suppose you can stay in the back bedroom for a few days until you figure out what you're going to do," my mom said softly as we pulled out of the parking lot.

I didn't want to go back to living with my parents. I hadn't seen or spoken to my dad in almost a year. I didn't even have a bedroom in their house anymore. A year before, they'd gutted out my bedroom in the basement completely, redone it with pink carpet and flowered wallpaper for Becca. Her old room had become the storage area for all my mom's arts and crafts supplies. Even though Philip's room was downstairs and empty since he'd left for the Navy, she made no offer of his. I'd sleep in the room filled with boxes of overflowing fabric and lace. My presence had been completely erased from their house and I doubted my mom wanted to revive it. I couldn't blame her; I was officially an outcast and would soon find out what it was like to be homeless.

I wasn't homeless in the traditional sense of the old men who wander the streets talking to themselves, drinking cheap wine out of brown paper bags, but I had no place to go and nowhere to call my home. So I succumbed completely to the ever-present desire to destroy myself, immersing myself fully in chemicals. I knew they didn't work anymore, but I didn't care.

Every time I thought it couldn't get any worse, it did. I have no idea how many days and nights I spent driving with Strom from sunup until sundown because neither of us had anywhere to go. His house had been condemned and he was in the same spot as me. We became wanderers from trailer to trailer, from one apartment to the next, and off to the next dark basement as we dropped off drugs. It would have made sense to save the money for a down payment or first month's rent, but as quick as it came into our hands it was gone. All we had to show for it was bloody noses, aching bones, and vacant eyes.

Strom had the luxury of being able to go home to his parents' house to crash when he couldn't take it any longer. I tried going home but it wasn't any comfort. I'd lie in the bed my mom had moved into the back bedroom, among boxes of crafts, longing for sleep but unable to relax. At home, my skin crawled and there never seemed to be enough air. My parents' bedroom was right next to the room I used, and I could swear I heard every breath my dad took.

Put a pillow over his head. Just do it. What about mom? She's a light sleeper, she'll wake up. Who cares? Your life is over. So you go to prison. I don't wanna go to prison. Who ya kidding, you're gonna go to prison. It's only a matter of time. Do it. Besides, you can just kill yourself afterwards. Where's the guns? The guns? Ya know, he hunts. Stick the rifle in your mouth. I can't. Yes, you can. No, I can't. You're a fuckin' wimp. Some tough girl you are. I'm losing my mind. It's already gone.

The voices had grown into personalities all their own. I couldn't control them at all anymore or shut them off. They screamed constantly. I don't know what happened other than that my brain broke completely. But I still had enough sense to know I couldn't stay at my parents' house. The voices controlled me, and I didn't really want to kill anyone. So I came up with a plan. I needed a car that was my own so that when Strom had reached his limit of sleepless days and nights, I could go to my own car.

My parents had tucked away a thousand dollars for each of us kids as graduation presents. I only knew this because my brother had gotten his money when he graduated. I came home one day when I knew my mom would be alone. "Mom, do you still have the money for my graduation?"

"Yes, why?" she asked, instantly suspicious.

"Well, I was thinking if I'm ever gonna get my life together, I'm going to need a job. And I can't get a job without a car."

"I'm not giving you the money. You'll blow it all on drugs in a week."

"Listen Mom," I pleaded. "I have to have a car if I'm going to work. I have to be able to get there."

"That money is a reward for graduating from high school. That's why we saved it."

I looked at her. "C'mon, mom. Really. Do you actually think I am ever gonna graduate high school? I mean, Christ, it's my senior year right now. Can you honestly tell yourself that's gonna happen? Let's be real for just one second."

She stared back at me, looking twenty years older than she really was. Her lip quivered and her eyes filled with tears. *Look what you've done. Look at her. How can you live with yourself? You're a monster. Do you hear me? A fuckin' monster! Shut-up. For God's sake, leave me alone.*

Finally she spoke. "I'll talk to your dad."

I went back a few days later and she handed me ten hundred-dollar bills.

"Thank-you." I moved to hug her.

She pushed me back, repulsed. "Don't you dare thank me. Just go before I change my mind."

Within a few days I had my own car, an '87 Duster with red padded seats and a radio—all I needed. I paid seven hundred dollars for it and blew the rest on dope, proud of myself that I didn't blow it all.

I finally had my own home. Whenever Strom had to leave, he dropped me off at my car. Many cold nights I curled up in the seat shaking, trying to quiet my thoughts. I had hoped the inner voices would stop when I was out of my house.

Did you hear that? They're coming. They're coming to get you. No one is coming to get you. You'll see. They want to kill you. They'll kill you. Drive. Get out of here. I did what they told me to, even if it made no sense. I drove endlessly, never getting anywhere but always moving. Somehow the voices seemed much more content when we were moving.

I didn't have money for food, and even if I did have the money, my stomach seemed to have forgotten how to complete the task of eating. Sometimes Strom would bring me to Perkins on a mission. He'd order and set a plate of food in front of me. "You have to eat." The most I could ever get down was half a bagel, and even that was hard to keep from coming back up.

I still went to my parents' occasionally for a warm shower, a clean set of clothes, and a chance to get rid of the fuzz on my teeth. I'd go while my dad was at work or sleeping. But it wasn't long until my mom confronted me, cornering me as I came out of the bathroom. "I can't watch you do this."

Holding any sort of normal conversation was becoming increasingly more difficult. "Wha . . . I . . . just . . . what did I say? I can't remember . . . I just . . . "

My mom screamed, "Just look at you. You can't even speak. You used to be so smart and now you can't even talk. I cannot watch you destroy yourself. You wanna do drugs, fine. Do drugs. Kill yourself, but not under my roof. I won't have you die in my house."

Shortly after her confrontation, she started locking the doors at night so I could no longer creep in when I needed to. I just kept on wandering, in and out of consciousness, in and out of different days that all became the same day. I completely lost track of whether it was night or day, where I was, where I'd been, what I'd done, who I'd been with, what drugs I'd done, when I'd slept, if I'd slept. I was back in that eternity of hell I called my life.

A few weeks later we were on our way to a memorial service for Bryan, another one of us to die. He'd crashed his truck drunk, flying out of the car. Like everyone else, he was dead on arrival. We'd been drinking all day in preparation for another service. It had only been a few weeks since we'd lost Piss Pants. He'd been given his name after pissing his pants on a bar stool at a local bar. I had no idea what his real name was.

I hadn't gone to the memorial service for Piss Pants, and didn't know anyone who had. Nobody wanted to be questioned about how he'd died. We never talked about that night, about the party, or how he'd left in a car with Hamilton and Justin and overdosed in the back seat of the car. We never mentioned how they'd left him on the front steps of a church. Even though Hamilton and Justin were the ones to do it, we knew that any one of us would have done the same thing. We never talked about Piss Pants because somehow speaking out loud makes what you already know become true, a reality that you can't take back.

I walked into the funeral home with Bobby and Strom at my sides. How many times would we be here before this nightmare face, heavily coated with make-up and unrecognizable. Thick paint couldn't quite cover the bruises; blue and purple shades still shone through. I followed his left arm down to a plastic hand. He'd lost his real one in the accident.

Bryan's eyes were closed and he looked peaceful. I realized I'd never seen him sleep, and certainly had never seen him look peaceful. I'd only seen him with dilated pupils overcoming any sign of color, eyes bulging out of his forehead. His blond hair was combed nicely, and I'd never seen that either. Usually his hair stuck up haphazardly all over his head from running his hands through it over and over and over again.

I wanted to feel something as I stared at him, but there was only a hollow emptiness. It dawned on me that I knew absolutely nothing about Bryan. We'd spent many days together but I didn't have any clue who this man was. I didn't even know his last name. He could have been anyone. The people I called my friends were only fixtures who sat next to me as we got high. It wouldn't be long before I'd be surrounded by junkies who would look at me just like I was looking at Bryan and like me, they'd feel nothing. I walked to the back of the room and leaned against the wall, chewing on the nubs of my fingers since my fingernails were gone.

In a few minutes, Bobby and Strom joined me. Strom pointed to the door and we quietly exited, greeted by cold winter air. We tried to be nonchalant but our walk was hurried. We got into the car and each of us reached underneath the seats to grab the beer. We packed our one-hitters full of the pot we carried in our pockets at all times, smoking in silence, staring out the windows, each of us in our private world. Strom started the car and the radio blared out. I drank another beer and smoked my one-hitter, trying to get lost in the thick voice of Tom Petty. But my mind refused to leave.

We reached a farmhouse on the edge of town. The familiar smell of body odor mixed with old booze, urine and puke hurled up my nose. But this time I wanted to gag. There were about ten bodies there with faces I knew. I sat in wetness and slime that still stuck to me when I moved further down the couch. I didn't bother to say hello to anyone, and no one said hello to me. The pool table was littered with cans and dirty papers. Someone had cut out Bryan's obituary and tacked it on the wall next to all the others, the overdoses and car accidents. Strom picked up a set of dice from the pool table and started to shake them in his hand. "Should we roll to see who's next?" The room filled with laughter. Any other time my voice would have joined them.

"What's wrong with you?" Bobby asked, plopping down beside me.

"Nothin'." They rolled the dice and laughed about whose number fell, then started their stories about how they would die. They were the same stories we told every time, one last hoorah and out with a bang. Normally, I'd tell my own fantasy about lying in a field under a tree with a creek running by, nothing but grass underneath and the blue sky above me. I'd shoot myself so full of dope that I'd go to sleep and never wake up.

But all I could think of now was that we didn't die romantically. We put guns in our mouths and blew our brains out. We died in car accidents that we caused, our hands severed. We stopped our own hearts from beating with chemical potions. When we died, we were easily discarded on doorsteps like bags of trash. I guzzled the bottle of vodka in front of me, but my mind still ran on.

"I gotta get outta here," I told Bobby.

Bobby didn't ask any questions. He just grabbed Strom and as quick as we had come, we were gone. Gone to another kitchen in another trailer park with a two-foot bong on the table. The owner of the trailer chopped up lines on a mirror and passed it around. When I declined, Strom looked at me as if I'd lost my mind completely. But the last thing I wanted was to be up for any more days than I already had been. I wanted my mind to shut down.

The conversation was full of the things we said we'd do, but never actually did. I hit the bong over and over again, drinking between each hit. Physically, my body was wasted but my mind was still sober. I hated it. I hated myself even more. The man across from me had raped his own daughter. We'd all read about it in the paper and had seen it on the news. This was what I called my family? I knew no one but Strom cared about me. The others would kill me if I had something they wanted, or if I stepped out of line. They'd rape me if they got the chance, and some already had.

I jumped up from my chair and ran to the bathroom, where I violently heaved into the toilet, wrapping my arms around the white bowl as it came in spastic waves. I couldn't get it out fast enough. I was contaminated with filth, disgust in every part of my body. I puked until there was nothing but blood and eventually that was gone, too. I dry heaved with every thought that went through my head.

The worst part was that no matter how much I hated my life and myself, I couldn't live any other way. This was where I fit until my number was rolled. Every day was the same and would always be the same. I knew in a way I'd never known before that I was in hell and was never getting out of it.

The one thing that had always kept me from committing suicide was the fear of hell. I'd spent my childhood terrified of the place. But at that moment, lying on the cold tiles of the bathroom floor with my head resting on the rim of the toilet, I realized I only had two options left. I could go on living in the hell of my life, or I could take myself to the next level of hell.

I stumbled out of the bathroom and asked Strom to take me to my parents' house, where I banged on the front door. My mom had always been a light sleeper and she came to the door quickly, frowning. "You look awful." I shrugged and moved past her. "You're staying here tonight?"

"Yes. I just . . . Mom, I can't . . . "

She patted my shoulder from behind. "Just go to bed. We can talk in the morning."

In the shower, warm water pounded my skin but I still couldn't get warm. In fact, I couldn't even remember what it felt like to be warm. My bones ached. I scrubbed my skin, trying to wash off the filth. I stuck my finger into the back of my throat, trying to grab the glob of goo that hung there at all times. I caught a piece of the slime, gagged and pulled it out in a long line, then watched the black mucous work its way through the small holes in the drain.

That's what you put in your body. You can't even get any more in. It's not working. You have to do something. Mom's pink Bic razor hung from the wire container over the showerhead. *Do it with that. But that never works. Cut deep. The razor sucks.* Methodically, I took the razor and scrapped it along my wrists, moving it up and down as if I was shaving my arms. I cut and crossed jagged edges. I bled, but not enough to do any real damage.

The gun. There's a gun in Philip's room. Use it. C'mon. Your life is over. I can't. Yes, you can. It'll be quick. I stepped out of the shower, dried myself, and put on the same dirty clothes I'd been wearing for days. I caught a glimpse of hollow eyes in the mirror. *That's not me. I'm not that girl.*

In the hallway, I put my head against the door of my parents' bedroom, listening for the sounds of them sleeping. I heard my mom's deep breaths and the weird clicking sound my dad made in the back of his throat. I walked through the living room and down the stairs, trying to keep them from creaking.

I didn't bother to turn on the light in my brother's room. My eyes adapted quickly. His room was exactly as I remembered it: the wallpaper with blue ships, posters of punk bands on the wall, the glowing edges standing out. I sat on the edge of the bed in a time warp.

Phil, where are you? Do you miss me? Do you ever even think about me? Do you remember when we were little and promised we'd always be best friends? I couldn't stop the tears anymore. Becca was across the hall in my old room. *What's her life like? God, she's got to be so disappointed. She's lost her big sister.* My eyes turned to the corner of the room where Phil's hunting rifle stood, propped in its black case. I picked it up and unzipped the cover, pulling the long barrel out, turning it over and over in my hands. It was longer than I remembered. *You should call Dave. I can't. Yes, you can. No, I can't. Remember what he said?*

A few days before, I'd stopped in at Dave's office. Instead of taking a seat next to me, he stood with his arms crossed tightly. As I started to sit in my usual chair he said sternly, "You have to leave."

I stood. "What do you mean?"

"Heather . . . " Two tears slid down his cheek and he gulped. "I can't watch you die any longer. I won't do it anymore. It's tearing me apart."

"What am I supposed to do?"

He said softly, "I don't know. But I'm just going to give you a kiss good-bye and then you are going to leave this office and not come back." He took my head in his hands, brought his face towards mine, and kissed me softly on the lips. Then he pulled back and motioned to the door. I hung my head and walked away.

Nobody cares. You have no one. I picked out the Pink Floyd CD from Phil's collection and slid it in. I programmed it to the song "Comfortably Numb," and pressed repeat before sitting back down on the bed. I put the end of the gun between my feet. It was long enough to come up to my face. I put my mouth over the cold barrel. My mouth fit around it easily. I rested my teeth on the metal and my hand on the trigger.

How do I pull the trigger? How the hell do I do this? Can I do this? You don't have the guts. Yes, I do. I just want to make sure I do it right. I don't want to blow half my face off and end up still having to live.

I sat in that position as "Comfortably Numb" played all the way through, over and over again. I was in a trance as the voices argued. *Fuck it. Pull the goddamn trigger, you wimp. Blow your fuckin' head off. But God hates me. What if I miss? What if I only blow half my face off? Do it. Quit thinking about it. But . . . Fuckin' do it.*

At some point during the night, a small meek voice joined the other angry voices in my head. *What if you got clean? I can't get clean. I've tried. I'm doomed. But what if you're not? What if there's another way to live your life? There's not. But what if? You've never really tried.*

Slowly, still in a trance, I put the gun back in its place in the corner. *Fuckin' wimp!* I didn't wait for the sun to rise. At five thirty my mom would be up. I got into my car and drove aimlessly. *I am so tired. I have never been this tired.*

A few days later, I had court, another hearing of some sort to take care of all of my paperwork, or maybe it was to charge me with something new. I didn't really know. I'd quit paying attention. *Maybe they're locking me up today. Who cares?* I walked down the long carpeted hallway and up the stairs to the waiting area outside the courtroom. Hunched over in a chair, shaking my legs up and down and rocking back and forth, the mantra repeated: *I'm tired. I'm so tired.* The big wooden doors swung open and the bailiff called out, "Heather. Heather Harrison."

I stood up, swaying to one side. I started to walk towards the door. Right before I stepped through, I stopped. The small voice returned. *Please. Please. God help me.* I walked down the aisle and sat in my spot at the wooden desk. The whole committee was there, sitting in their normal positions. As usual, Judge Asfeld towered above us. I disappeared into my thoughts, oblivious to the talk going on around me. "Heather," Judge Asfeld's voice broke in. "Heather, do you have anything to say for yourself?"

I can talk? They want me to talk? I hadn't been allowed to talk in court for over a year. I opened my mouth and heard my voice speaking, but the words weren't my own. They cried, "Please give me another chance to get clean. I just wanna get clean. I'll do anything you want me to. I'll go to jail, prison, whatever. I don't care. I'll do anything. I just need a chance to get clean. You have to send me somewhere. Please." *What is going on? Shut-up! Shut-up! Shut-up! What am I talking about?* The voices complained but I completely separated from my own thoughts and kept right on talking, begging the judge and everyone in the room to give me one more chance to get clean.

I don't know what happened next and I don't know why, but they took mercy on me. Rubin made arrangements for me to go to treatment within the next few days.

A few mornings later, I lay curled into a ball on the front seat, praying for the sun to rise. As soon as it came up, I was on my way back to treatment. I'd promised myself that when it came up, I was done doing drugs. The sun came up slowly. I turned my car on and began driving down the gravel road into town. *Get high. Get high. You can't get through this day without getting high. No! Shut-up! I won't.*

I slammed on the brakes, spewing gravel. I rolled down my window, letting bursts of searing cold into the car. I dug frantically in my pockets for my bag of weed and folds of crank. I threw them out the window. I reached underneath the seat, grabbing pipes and tinfoil in handfuls. I tossed them out the window. The wind caught some of the tinfoil and it fluttered through the air.

A primal scream tore out from somewhere deep inside me. I felt like I'd just ripped off my arm and tossed it away. I wanted to jump out of the car and frantically collect everything before it blew away. It took every ounce of energy I had left to put my foot back on the gas pedal.

15

Recovery House

Thirteen days before my eighteenth birthday, I checked into St. John's Hospital more exhausted than I'd ever been. To keep me away from the adults, I got my own private room next to the nurse's station. I crawled underneath the thin, crisp sheet, laid my head on the foam pillow, pulled the coarse white blanket up to my chin, and closed my eyes. I lay in that same position, unmoving, most of my days there, feeling as close to death as I could possibly be without physically dying. When I did get out of bed, I floated through lectures or group therapy.

After I'd been in the hospital for about three weeks, Rubin came to inform me that I'd be going to a place called Recovery House. I'd be monitored very closely because the court system was still unsure what to do with me. I accepted the situation without putting up a fight, even though the prospect of living in a house with twenty five other women disturbed me. Memories from The Portico rushed through my mind.

But the women at Recovery House were hard-core just like me, and except for the drunken housewives who never left the confines of their home, everyone had spent time on the streets. We were the women who'd lost everything, the ones the rest of society looked upon as the lowest form of human beings. So the only competition that existed among us was arguing over who had the worst life.

These women spoke openly, and when they cried, others gathered around to hug and hold them. I hated them. They were admitting defeat, no longer fighting the battle to be tough. I didn't want them to get near me. I'd let Dave and Yvonne get close to me and my worst fears had played themselves out. Both had been taken away from me, and I wasn't going to make the same mistake with these women. My toughness had kept me alive.

At night, one roommate, Crystal, curled up into the fetal position and cried harder than I had ever heard anyone cry before. "H-H-Heather?" she'd call out, lifting her head from the pillow. "Are you awake?"

I'd lie there in silence with my eyes closed. Every night she began to cry and every night she called out to me for some sort of comfort. But I couldn't bring myself to do it—to tell her it was going to be okay—because I really didn't believe that. Eventually Shaundra would emerge from her room and crawl into bed next to Crystal, curling herself around her small body.

"Oh, baby," she'd whisper in her southern drawl. "It's going to be okay. Really, honey, it's not that bad."

"I can't take this," Crystal would sob. "It hurts. It hurts so fuckin' bad and all I can think about is getting high."

"I know, doll. I know," Shaundra would coo to her, running her big, calloused hands through Crystal's dark hair. "Ya just gotta let the pain come. Ya just gotta let it move through ya." There were many nights when they cried themselves to sleep in each other's arms.

I knew there was no way I could be in a house with all lesbians, and it was beyond my comprehension that people could touch each other without any sort of sexual undercurrents to it. These alien women pushed me further into myself and increased my efforts at being unbreakable.

One day in group when everyone was being all touchy-feely,

I announced, "We're not all gonna make it. Seriously, statistically speaking, in five years only two of us are gonna be alive and sober. The rest of us are gonna be either dead or fucked up."

Jean jumped up from her chair. "Girl, I am so fuckin' sick of you. Shut the fuck up! Maybe you think you're gonna die, but keep that shit to yourself."

I cocked my head to the side and looked at the counselor, Carla. "Tell her, Carla. You know the statistics. I'm not lying. Tell her. Tell her the truth that very few of us are gonna make it out of this hell."

Carla's blue eyes grew huge. "Heather. Stop."

I jumped up from my chair, too. "Stop? C'mon, you want me to tell the truth. Isn't that what getting sober is about? We're supposed to tell the truth. That's what I'm doing."

Jean lunged at me with her arms outstretched. I ducked. Her big arms circled the air above my head. "You fuckin' punk ass bitch. I'm gonna shut your ass up!"

I stood up to her, pushing my small bony chest against her huge chest, feeling her breasts smash against me. I looked directly into her brown eyes and unflinchingly responded, "Bring it on. You can try to kick my ass but it doesn't change the facts."

Carla leapt from her chair, grabbing Jean's arm. "Jean, stop! Heather, sit down!"

Then Carla stepped between us, but we continued to glare at each other over her shoulder. Jean's nostrils flared in and out.

She hissed, "I'm gonna hurt her. Seriously. She needs to keep her negative ass mouth shut."

I spat at her, my fluid landing on her dark face. "I am not scared of you. I have yet to get my ass kicked by a girl."

Carla grabbed my shoulders with both her hands and pushed me back. "You need to stop. I mean it. In fact, you need to leave group."

"I don't . . . "

Carla yelled, "Not another word! You need to leave. Go to your room and stay there."

I laughed. "You're not my mom."

Carla pointed towards the door, her face a deep red. "Go. You don't leave now, Heather, and you're gone. That's it. You cannot act this way."

"Fine," I snapped. "Fuck all of you."

I stormed out and stomped loudly all the way up the stairs to my third floor room. There I threw myself face first on the bed, pounding my fists and kicking my legs like a two-year-old throwing a temper tantrum.

After that episode, the women began leaving me alone. They just pretended I wasn't there. Before, they'd ask me to go with them on their outings to the mall or the movies, but those invitations quit coming. I pretended I was unaffected by it, but in the silence of my room, when I was alone, I writhed in agony. I was clean but I felt like more of a mess than I'd ever been. The only relief came from cutting, and from burning my arms and legs with cigarettes, in a vain attempt to release the pain I felt inside.

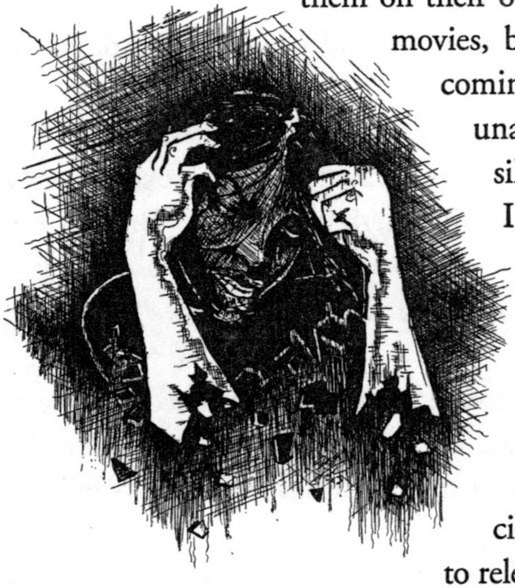

There was one phone in the house that we all had to share. There were never-ending battles over whose turn it was next. I was surprised one night when Crystal announced that the phone was for me. No one ever called me.

I picked up the receiver. "Hello?"

A husky male voice responded, "Hey, girl. Now this is gonna sound crazy, but I been watching you."

"Who is this?"

He spoke softly, "My name's Reggie. I'm your neighbor."

My neighbor? Did he mean the apartment next door? We'd been instructed not to associate with any of our neighbors.

"How the hell do you know my name?" I demanded.

"Look, before ya freak out, lemme explain some shit." He spoke hurriedly. "Ya know ole girl, Gerri? She stays at your crib, right?"

"Mmm-hmm."

"Well, see we kick it sometimes together and I been seeing ya in the parking lot and wonderin' if I could get to know ya. I asked her 'bout ya. She hooked me up with this number. See, I know how hard this shit you're going through is. I been sober six months myself. Hardest shit I've ever had ta do."

I was intrigued. "Really?"

I began talking to Reggie regularly over the next week. In the world of a junkie, a week is an awfully long time. I asked Gerri if he was an okay guy and she assured me he was. After we'd been talking for over a week, I agreed to meet Reggie for coffee.

I couldn't just walk over to Reggie's apartment because someone might be outside smoking and see me. I'd be in trouble for sure then. So I agreed to meet Reggie at the gas station. A tall, skinny black man opened the door and got into my car. He stuck out his hand. "Glad to finally meet ya, girl."

I took his big hand in mine. "You, too."

"Nice ride," he commented.

I shrugged. "Nothin' special."

"This is what I been thinking. I know we was gonna go to Perkins and have coffee, but how 'bout we just go to my place and

I'll make us some? 'Sides, then I can show you the pictures of my kids." He'd told me all about his two little girls many times. He was just starting to be able to see them again.

As I pulled out of the gas station, I said, "All right. But I'm gonna have to park a few blocks away, 'cause I don't want any of the girls to see my car."

"Cool," Reggie replied, turning up the sound on the radio and rolling the window down. I peeked at him out of the corner of my eye. He wasn't the best looking man I'd ever seen, but he was definitely attractive. I parked my car a few blocks away and we started walking towards his apartment.

Looking around nervously, he said, "We should go in the back door so nobody sees, huh?"

"For sure," I responded. "They're pretty strict about us not hanging out with the neighbors."

"Can't blame 'em. There's some crazy people livin' 'round here." He smiled broadly at me.

When we got close, we hurried towards the back of the brick complex, which was identical to the one I lived in next door. He opened the steel door and I rushed inside. He pointed down the stairs and towards the end of the hallway as he followed from behind. "Last one on the right."

I stood by his door while he dug in his jeans for the keys. When he opened the door, I stepped in and felt him standing behind me, shutting it. My eyes darted around the room quickly, taking in the dingy walls and the dirty, shaggy yellow carpet. It wasn't until I heard the sound of the dead bolt being latched on the door that I thought, *I'm in trouble.* My stomach twisted. I took a step forward. I could hear him breathing heavily behind me.

"You should make coffee," I said. I didn't turn around to look at him. *Be careful, Heather. You're in trouble.*

He didn't move. I walked forward to the middle of the room. A bird cage hung by the draped window. It was a big cage, but there was no bird. I pretended to be really interested in it while furtively looking around. The only other piece of furniture was a brown, raggedy couch with the cushions hanging off of it. Underneath it, I spotted a crack pipe.

"Ya know," I said, trying to keep my voice steady. "Maybe we should go to Perkins."

"Why? This is fine." His voice sounded different, lower.

"I'm scared I'm gonna get in trouble," I lied. "Someone might have seen me come in here."

"Oh, nobody saw you come in here."

He was behind me. I felt him without turning around to actually see him. There was not enough oxygen in the room to breathe. My heart thumped in my chest and my head swam. *Stay here. Don't leave.* I felt his hands on my hips. *This can't be happening. Stay calm. Stay here. Don't leave.*

He ordered, "Turn around."

I laughed a laugh that wasn't my own. "How come you have a bird cage with no bird?"

He repeated, "Turn around."

"Really, how strange is that? I mean a birdcage, but no bird. It's sad or something."

His hands tightened on my hips. He turned me around to face him. His eyes had changed. The pupils had grown larger and colder. "We didn't come here to talk."

Trying to move to the side, I said in a rush, "Listen, I gotta go. Really." He held me tight, squeezing his hands harder on my hipbones. I wanted to cry out, but I clenched my teeth together. *Don't let him smell fear. Don't leave.* "I didn't mean to give you the wrong impression. I should go. I really . . . "

His big mouth crashed down on mine. As he tried to shove his tongue through my teeth, I clenched them together until my jaw hurt. He jerked up and moved his head to my neck, licking all the way down to my shoulder. I pushed him back.

I yelled, "Stop. I wanna go home. I wanna go home now."

He lifted his head and tilted it back, laughing. "I told ya. Ya ain't goin' nowhere. You're mine now."

I smelled old booze seeping from his pores, mixed with putrid sweat. He crushed me against his chest. I pulled back but he was stronger, holding me in place with arms that were so long that they circled completely around me. I screamed. He grabbed my hair and snapped my head back.

"Shut the fuck up, bitch." His spit hit my face. I gagged. He slapped me across the face.

I struggled to get one arm free and pounded on his chest. I heard myself screaming from somewhere far away. He lifted me effortlessly and threw me over his shoulder like I was bag of cargo. I beat at his back with my fists and kicked at his stomach wildly with my legs. He carried me kicking and screaming into the bedroom, then threw me on the bed. I scrambled up and he tossed me back down as if I weighed nothing.

What happened next is a blur filled with pieces of awareness and pieces of empty, blank spaces. I fought him on the bed with everything I had in me, which only seemed to excite him more. I remember him pinning me on the bed and ripping my threadbare jeans apart as he breathed heavily in and out. I screamed until my throat was raw. No one came. Sometimes he'd slap my face with the back of his hand to shut me up. Other times he let me scream while he laughed.

As he struggled to get inside me, I writhed back and forth, trying to prevent it. I beat on his chest with my arms as hard as I could, trying to pummel him with my fists. It was as if he couldn't even feel me. At one point, I freed myself and tumbled from the bed, cracking my head on the heat vent on the floor and knocking myself out.

I opened my eyes back on the bed. He was back inside me, pumping wildly, slapping my hips, my shoulders, my thighs with his big hands. *He's going to kill me. He's going to kill me.* He finished and fell on top of me. I couldn't move under his weight. *Please fall asleep. Please fall asleep.* I listened so hard to his breathing that a ringing began in my ears. Outside the room, birds chirped. Just when his breathing became really relaxed, he raised himself to look at me.

His eyes had turned empty and dark, as if I was looking into a tunnel with nothing at the other end. He looked right through me, unseeing. I didn't exist in his world. He was shiny from the sweat that had dried on his body. My body ached and screamed out in pain. I throbbed between my legs, and a hammer steadily pounded on my skull.

He took off his shirt, revealing a lean, muscular chest, red from where my fists had beat on it. He was completely naked on top of me, though I couldn't remember when he'd taken his pants off. He reached down to play with himself, never taking his eyes off me. *He's going to kill me when he's done with me. No one knows I'm here. This is it. No, I don't want this to be it. I will not die this way. I will not.*

"Hey." My voice was raspy.

"I told you to keep your fuckin' mouth shut," he snorted. "You do what I tell you to. I'm not done with you."

"I know," I said, trying to sound convincing and forcing myself to look in his eyes. "I just thought maybe we could go in the living room."

"Nice try, bitch." He laughed, raising his arm again to strike.

I said quickly, "No, really. I'll suck your dick out there. Really. I will. I want to."

He stared at me for what seemed like minutes. "You better suck it good."

He got up from on top of me and jerked me up by my arm. "C'mon. Move." He slapped my ass from behind.

I walked into the living room. *This can't be happening. Yes, it is. Do not fuckin' leave now, Heather. You'll be in hell the next time you open your eyes.*

I tried to sound excited. "Why don't you sit on the couch?"

He walked over and took a seat. I stood in front of him. He grabbed my head with both of his hands.

I cried out, "I'll do it. I said I would."

I brought my head down to his monster. *Do it, Heather. You have to.* I put it in my mouth and began to perform, trying not to gag. He began to move with the motions of my mouth. I peeked up at him, never stopping what I was doing. His eyes were almost completely closed. *Now!*

I jumped up, grabbed his head with my hands, and slammed it against the wall. I dashed for the door, unlatched the deadbolt, and ran as fast as I could, not looking back. I darted through the hallway, whipped open the door and ran into the sunshine. I raced all of the way through the parking lot, back to Recovery House.

I hurried through the door and took the stairs three at a time. I shut the bedroom door and locked myself in the bathroom. I stripped off my tattered clothes and jumped into the shower. I let the scalding water scorch my skin. I took the soap and my washcloth, scrubbing my skin until it stung. And then I kept right on scrubbing, scrubbed on the inside with antiseptic soap, over and over. Halfway through, I dry heaved onto my feet and watched the yellow mucous slowly snake its way down the drain.

I don't remember getting out of the shower and going back into my room. I don't remember my roommate finding me naked on the floor while I ripped open the cuts and burn blisters on my arm with my fingernails. I don't remember the cops coming or the drive to the hospital.

But I do remember the hospital.

The small white room and two male doctors with long white coats.

Three male cops dressed in blue, standing against the door with their arms folded.

A detective sitting on the stool next to my bed, questioning me.

He looks down at the notebook on his lap. "So. You're a junkie."

I nod my head.

He snaps, "You have to speak your answers. I already told you once. We're recording your statement."

I clear my throat. "Yes, I'm a junkie."

"You live at Recovery House?"

"Yes."

"You say that your relationship with Reggie started on the phone?"

"Yes."

"Where were the two of you going?"

"For coffee."

"How did you end up at Reggie's place?"

"We decided to have coffee there."

The detective coughs. "So you don't know this man. But you decide to go to his house. Is that correct?"

"I guess." I stare at the white tiles underneath his stool. *Smooth gray cracks between them. Scuffed black shoes.*

"You say that he smokes crack. Is that correct?"

"Yes."

"How do you know that?"

"I saw the pipe."

"Did you see him smoke it?"

I shake my head.

He lets out an exaggerated sigh. Says, "Look, you need to speak."

The questioning goes on. And on.

"How'd you get the marks all over your arms? Did he do that?"

"No." *There are white tiles on the ceiling, too. This whole place is white tiles. Gray cracks between them.*

"Then who did?"

"I did them to myself." My voice is soft.

The room is still.

"Okay," he snorts. "So, let me get this straight. You're a junkie but you claim that you've been sober for three months. You talked to Reggie on the phone for a week. You met to go to Perkins. Then you went to his house. There was a crack pipe. Neither of you smoked. Then he raped you. Repeatedly. Allegedly. Have I got it right so far?"

There are little holes punched in the ceiling tiles. How many holes are in one tile?

I finally look at him.

He looks back with pure disgust, at something repulsive.

"Yes. That's right."

"Supposedly you screamed. The whole time. And no one in the building heard you scream. You performed oral sex which he didn't make you do. You ran back to Recovery House. That's when police were called. Now you are here, no semen inside you. All you have are cuts and burns all over your arm that you say you did yourself. And you want to press charges?"

I look behind him. One of the cops smirks. The one who forcibly held my legs open. So the doctor could insert the metal into me. The tall cop next to him picks something out from underneath his nails. They want to get this over with. Move on to people who matter. I am not one of them.

I vow no one will ever look at me that way again. It strikes me that I fought for my life. Which means I want to live. But not like this. Never again.

16

Calling all Angels

The police brought me back to Recovery House. Dawn, the head counselor, called an emergency group session in the main dining room to explain—from her position at the head of the two tables—that I'd been raped.

"The police arrested the man who did this to her, and I can assure you all that you are safe. The police are closely monitoring the house." Out of the corner of my eye, I saw her nod toward where I sat curled up, staring at the holes in my jeans. "I'm sure this will bring up past issues, and all of your counselors are available to talk to any of you who may need a little extra help in the next few days. I also want to stress how important it is that you are there for Heather."

I continued to study the holes in my jeans, trying to let the words sink in that I was the girl Dawn was talking about. She asked if there were any questions. No one said a word. So we stood, joined hands, and said the Serenity Prayer out loud, like we always did. Once we dropped hands, the girls formed a single line in front of me. One by one, they gave me a hug. I kept my hands at my sides, but for the first time I let them circle their arms around me. No one asked me what happened. They didn't need to, because my experience was their experience. One right after another, they came toward me. Some kissed the top of my head.

Some had tears that slid silently down their cheeks, as I let them cry the tears that I couldn't. Seeing the pain in their eyes mirroring my own, I suddenly didn't feel so alone.

After that, I was no longer an outsider. The other women welcomed me into the healing circle that I had watched going on around me for so long. I was committed to keeping the vow I made in the hospital and I realized that I needed their help to do it. But my growth was slow, awkward, and painful. For each step forward, it seemed like I took another two backward. My mood changed by the hour. My highs were so high that I felt as if joy would explode from my body. My lows were so low that I felt trapped in a thick puddle of mud with concrete slabs tied around my ankles.

When I felt good, I was a newborn baby taking pleasure in everything that came across my eyes. I could sit enamored by clouds for hours, aware of every breath coming in and out of my lungs, marveling at the fact that I still existed and was capable of thinking and feeling. I'd sit curled on my bed or under a tree at the nearby park writing, filled with a burning desire to somehow express the emotions and thoughts raging through my body and mind. My words filled hours and pages.

I was also in a state of mourning. Even though I was determined to begin a new sober life, it didn't take away the raw grief over losing the only thing that had made me feel okay. There wasn't a day that passed when the craving to get high didn't grip me in its stronghold. I also knew that underneath that grieving were much more treacherous hurts waiting for me.

My walls of defenses were slowly demolished. I rocketed from one emotion to the next without knowing why. My insides had been frozen for years and I'd reached the melting point where I gushed forth. It was impossible to fight the tears. I cried alone in the silence of my room, still unwilling to let others see me so exposed. The grief passed through me in waves. Each time I thought I'd die from the pain inside and made it through, I felt a little stronger for the next wave.

Each weekend, the mothers who still had any custody rights were allowed to have their children come stay for the weekend. Since I'd been in treatment and Recovery House, I'd been trying to rebuild a relationship with Becca, so I asked Dawn if my sister could come for the weekend. When Becca had come to visit me at St. John's, I hadn't been able to stop staring at her. Somewhere along the way she'd grown up and I'd missed it. She was no longer the chubby little girl with bouncy blond hair and big blue eyes. She was a tall, skinny teenager who'd traded in her glasses for contact lenses.

My mom brought her up to the Cities to drop her off the following weekend. It was awkward between us at first, but I wanted to get to know this stranger who was my sister. Conversation was difficult with Becca because she censored everything that came out of her mouth, like she was afraid one wrong word might make me break down and get high. But she liked the house and the other women.

On Saturday night, as she lay on the floor of my room in a borrowed sleeping bag, she asked, "You know this week when mom told you that I puked in my bed?"

"Yeah, I remember."

"Well . . . I didn't really get sick. I mean, I got sick . . . I puked in my bed. I puked . . . But, but that's not why."

"Were you drunk?"

"No."

I waited for her to go on. When she didn't, I pressed, "Well, what then? What are you talking about, Becca?"

"Well . . . I like . . . you know . . . "

I sighed. "Becca, spit it out. I told you I want us to be able to talk to each other. It's okay, whatever it is. I told you that I want to start being here for you. I mean it. You can tell me anything."

"Promise you won't tell mom and dad?"

"Whatever you tell me, stays with me," I assured her.

"I guess . . . I well . . . well I . . . I took a lot of pills . . . "

I sat upright in my bed. "You took a lot of pills *on purpose*?"

She responded softly, in that small voice I remembered from our childhoods, "Yes."

"Why?" *You know the answer. No. Please, no. Not her. Not Becca.*

"Sometimes I just don't wanna be here. You know? I just wanted to go to sleep and wake up in heaven. If it's so nice there, then I wanna go there. I don't like it here. But I puked . . . everywhere. I was so sick."

My heart had jumped into my throat, my pits already dripped, and my hands felt sticky. I cleared my throat. "Why do you want to die?"

Silence filled the room and stretched on endlessly. Finally she spoke. "I don't know." And I knew that she didn't.

How can I help her? There's so much I don't understand. "You should talk to someone."

"I can't talk to people," she said quietly.

"I understand. I hate it with a passion. But it helps. It really does."

Silence once again. I reached down and ran my fingers through her hair. I wanted to hop out of my bed, wrap my arms around her, and hold her like I used to do when she was a little girl. But she was no longer a little girl, and I was afraid of her response.

After a few minutes, she said, "I'm fine." Her voice had changed. "Can we go to the thrift store before mom picks me up tomorrow?"

"Sure," I responded sadly because she sounded like my mom. She'd just dropped a bomb and now she wanted to talk about shopping. Even though she'd been able to step around the damage, the bomb kept exploding over and over again in my head. It was worse in the morning when I had to let her go back home, knowing that she was going back to the house with talking walls, and fires in the kitchen that everyone pretended weren't burning. *What will happen to her? What is gonna happen to me?*

I locked myself in my bedroom until group time in the evening because I didn't trust myself. I was afraid I'd trick myself into getting high. By the time it arrived and I took my seat in the circle, I was crawling out of my skin because my voices screamed at me to get high, drink, cut myself, hit someone in the face, drive my car into a tree, anything that would take me away. I'd been telling them to shut up for hours and I couldn't hold it off much longer. Everyone had barely sat down when I spewed out the entire story about Becca. I didn't realize I was crying until Jean handed me a Kleenex. It was the first time I'd ever cried in front of anyone but family and Dave.

I pounded my fists on my thighs. "I want to get high! Dammit, I want to get fucked up so goddamn bad, I can't stand it." My chest hurt, like someone held my heart in the palm of their hand, squeezing it. "I think I'm having a heart attack."

Carla pulled her chair close to me. "Breathe, Heather. You're not having a heart attack. It's just feelings. You've just got to let them come. Don't fight them."

I pulled my knees up, wrapping my arms around them, and hid my face. Silent sobs shook my shoulders and wracked my body. The intensity of the pain nearly drowned me.

"Look up. Look at me," Carla ordered. "There's no going away. I want you here."

I lifted my head slowly to meet her green eyes. *Run! Leave! Get out! No. No, I'm staying. I'm staying. Leave me alone. Please.*

"What does it mean to you that your sister tried to commit suicide?"

I gulped. "I don't want her to die."

Carla's green eyes stared into mine. "It's more than that. C'mon. What else?"

"Because . . . Because . . . then maybe . . . maybe I'm not crazy."

"And if you're not crazy . . . "

I interrupted. "I *am* crazy! I'm fuckin' nuts."

Carla shook her head. "If you're crazy then you don't have to look at the truth. And the truth is that both you and your sister have some of the same feelings. Or maybe she's crazy, too."

"She's not crazy," I snapped.

"Well then . . . "

I interrupted again. "I don't want to talk about it."

Jean interjected from her seat next to me, "You brought it up."

I glared at her, wanting to jump up and have one of our fights. Instead, I looked away and began talking as fast as I could. "I've always thought I was crazy. Ever since I was a little kid. I can't even tell you all the weird shit that went on in my head. Way before drugs. My head is messed up. It's easy to believe I'm crazy. If I'm crazy then I don't have to believe . . . I don't have to think about . . . " I suddenly ran out of words.

"And what is the alternative to being crazy?"

Kids didn't want to die without having some sort of reason. I took a deep breath. "That some really bad shit happened in my house and fucked me up pretty bad." My voice grew softer, "Fucked both of us up."

I'd answered the question people had been asking me for so long. Bad things happened in my parents' house. The place was infected with a disease that I knew intimately but couldn't identify, even though I knew it was there. But the first words were out, and I could never take them back.

As my discharge date grew closer, it became obvious that I had to start all over in a different place. I'd have to live far away from everything and everyone I'd ever known: my family, my streets, my Strom, my fellow junkies, my trailers, all of it. Not one thing could resemble anything associated with my past. I knew this was my last chance.

My final weeks at Recovery House were spent preparing to live alone in my first apartment. But I don't think anything could have made me ready for the surge of anxiety and fear as I stood in the doorway of my new bedroom that first night. Smaller than my bedroom at the halfway house, my new room was empty except for the twin bed my parents had given me, pushed against the wall with my burgundy sleeping bag unrolled on top of it. A dresser that used to be my sister's stood against the opposite wall.

I was eighteen years old, technically an adult, but with no idea how to live in the real world. I took a deep breath and instructed myself out loud, "Just stay focused on getting through this night. That's all you've got to worry about."

I'd dreaded this moment because I knew sleep would be difficult. It had taken me months to learn how to fall asleep sober. Without chemicals, I'd lie in bed for hours with my mind racing, replaying random events from my life. Some nights the paralyzing fear would grip me, making my heart race. Sweet smelling sweat would ooze from my pores as all of my senses became keenly alert. The darkness carried ghosts of all the memories I'd tried to block out for so long.

I was already scared about graduating from the halfway house. I didn't know what to do with the freedom. My structured environment, and with it my safety, were gone. I could so easily trick myself into getting high. The selves in my head were slowing, becoming one, but many times they still did battle. It had been comforting to live with women who understood what I was going through, reassuring to know I wasn't the only one struggling to make sense of the contradictory messages in my head. But that night, my mind was my only company.

I yearned for my old room at the halfway house, for my small bed under the window that was always opened a crack for fresh air. I wanted the nightstand next to it that held my journal, along with the white alarm clock that woke me every morning at seven to go the telemarketing job I'd worked so hard to get. I wanted the walls covered with pictures I'd spent hours tearing out of magazines. I missed the stains on the ugly lime green carpet. I even missed the sounds my roommate made every night in the bathroom, sticking fingers down her gagging throat after eating bags of chips, cookies, and candy bars. It was hard to believe I could miss the sound of her puking into the toilet, trying to rid herself of her own demons, but at least her sounds were familiar.

I missed listening to twenty four women getting ready for bed. The sounds of toilets flushing and sinks running. Female voices calling out good night, the patter of feet on the carpet, doors shutting and lights turning off. The faint smell of cigarette smoke from someone smoking in her room because she couldn't wait until the morning when the alarm was turned off. I missed it all.

Nothing in this room was familiar. Each creak was new. The only movement was my own breathing. I walked towards my bed thinking about Linda, the overnight technician at Recovery House. I could call her and hear her voice if I needed to. She'd comforted me many nights when I couldn't sleep. I'd rise and slip quietly past the other rooms and down the stairs to the second floor staff office to find Linda smoking on the balcony off to the side of the office, the only one not wired with an alarm.

Linda was a big woman, like Vivian, over six feet tall with broad shoulders and a large chest. Her short gray hair, sprinkled with spots of white, closely framed her face. She wore a subtle red lipstick on small lips that moved so easily into a large smile.

I'd knock on the glass and she'd turn her face, smiling. Then I'd go stand next to her, leaning against the black railing, lighting one of my own cigarettes.

Her eyes focused on the stars overhead, she'd ask, "Another one of your nights?"

"Yeah," I'd reply softly.

In silence, she'd smoke her Virginia Slims and I'd smoke my Marlboro Reds, the smoke curling its way up to the sky in twisted spirals. She always left the conversation up to me, listening if I wanted to speak and keeping silence if I didn't.

After our smoke, she'd sit on the wooden office chair underneath the overhead lamp, and pick up her knitting from the end table. I'd sit on the floor at her feet, crossing my legs Indian style. Her small white dog, Sushi, would run to my lap with her tongue sticking out and her tail wagging, licking my hands and face. She told me every time I played with Sushi, "She likes you. She doesn't like everyone, you know."

Sometimes I'd tell Linda about my day. I'd tell her about silly fights that we girls had gotten into over using the phone, or what we had for dinner. She was intrigued by my stories about the AA meetings I went to every day. At other times, I'd tell her about getting high and how I couldn't understand how I could love it and hate it so much, all at the same time. Sometimes I even talked to her about my family and what it was really like for me growing up. Then there were the times when I was quiet, content to just be in her presence and play with Sushi. But no matter what I said or didn't say, I always had one request. "Will you sing for me?"

She'd set her knitting back on the table and reach under her chair for the instrument. "Of course, darling." It looked like a keyboard except it didn't have any keys. There was a volume switch on the left and a small speaker on the right. It had a bunch of lines across the middle that she'd tap and sweep her fingers across. The lines made beautiful strumming sounds under the touch of her skilled fingers. The first time she showed me the small white board, she'd explained, "I never learned to play the guitar or piano. Then I found this old thing and I've been hooked on it ever since."

Her voice, filled with emotion and power, boomed from her chest. She'd flip her fingers back and forth across the board in smooth, quick motions, tears dripping down her face and onto the board. But her eyes shone and her face glowed, like she had sunshine inside that seeped through her pores while she sang. I'd sit at her feet mesmerized. She'd written all the music and lyrics, filled with sweet words about a God who loved her beyond comprehension, a God so different from the one my parents worshipped. The only song she played that wasn't her own was "Amazing Grace," my favorite. I wouldn't notice I was crying until I felt Sushi's soft pink tongue on my cheek, licking away the tears.

Alone in my apartment, I longed for Linda's melodies. I sat on my bed, pulling my knees up to my chest, wishing I could believe God loved me. But I couldn't erase the image of a mean, heartless bastard grinning as he cast people into hell. I knew it was wrong to hate God, but I couldn't deny that I did.

One of Linda's favorite things to say was, "You're alive for a reason. God didn't bring you all this way just to drop you on your face." I recalled the first time I'd overdosed after just getting released from my first treatment center. Strom had promised to throw me a party. I hadn't been able to use drugs for three months, and every day I'd been away from them I'd counted the hours until my next high. It was the only thing that made treatment bearable.

Our party consisted of Strom and me sitting cross-legged on his only piece of furniture, a mattress in his dark bedroom.

The floor was covered with CDs, dirty laundry piled in one corner and moldy food and trash spilling out of a garbage can in another corner. The one window was covered with a dark sheet. A lamp burned dimly on top of the stereo, casting eerie shadows on the wall.

A buffet of drugs spread out in front of us: a mirror with chunks of yellow and white powder, an open bag of pot with sticky, green buds spilling out, my half-empty bottle of Captain Morgan and Strom's bottle of Windsor Canadian. We'd already been at it for hours. I grabbed the tooter and brought my face down into the powder, inhaling another line up my nose. The familiar burn in my nostrils made my eyes water and I grabbed my bottle to wash down the putrid drip in the back of my throat.

There was a knock at the door. A male voice called out, "It's Hamilton."

I looked towards Strom. He looked up at me and mouthed "eight-ball." I still remembered the routine.

"Come in!" I yelled back.

Hamilton looked like he'd lost ten pounds since the last time I'd seen him. His pale skin stretched tightly across protruding cheekbones. His vacant eyes bore black circles around them and sunk into his head. His black Metallica T-shirt hung on his body and his jeans sagged.

I started to chop a long line on the mirror. As he watched, Hamilton wrung his hands together and tapped his feet against each other. Strom eyed him from his spot in the corner. Hamilton took a seat on the floor across from me, rubbing his nose in anticipation. I pushed the mirror in his direction.

"Here you go," I said. "It's really good shit. You'll be up for at least two days, guaranteed."

His eyes lit up as he grabbed the tooter and brought his head down to the mirror. Strom dug in the wooden box that held his stash and pulled out a crumpled picture. He laughed at me. "Hey, look at this. You look totally geeked."

The photo showed my eyes bulging out of my head, about ready to burst out of their sockets. The blue was completely erased by dilated pupils. My matted hair stuck up on top from running my fingers through it over and over again. My yellowed skin was covered with filmy dirt, a result of days on acid. My mouth opened wide in a horrific yell.

Strom said, "That was the night we couldn't even figure out how to play Go Fish, we were so fucked up. 'Member?"

I turned away from the photo. "Christ, how could I forget? I look like I'm insane."

Bringing his face up from the mirror, Hamilton interjected, "Look like it? You are!"

"Shut-up. Do you like it or what?"

"Yeah, I want it. Gimme an eight." He stuck his hand into his pocket and pulled out a roll of bills.

"Well, gimme your money," Strom ordered, taking out a baggie from the stash in the wooden box. He handed Hamilton the bag and took his money, then tapped my arm. "Turn down the stereo."

I jumped up, and suddenly felt like I'd stuck my finger into a light socket, only it was ten times more powerful. Electricity surged through my body, shocking me. I arched my back and tried to yell, but no sound came. I fell to my knees as brown liquid sprayed from my mouth and nose. My heart felt like it was going to burst through my chest in a violent explosion; it was so tight I couldn't breathe. I clawed at my shirt, trying to rip it off. I could see nothing but white lights blinking everywhere in front of me. My last thought, before darkness overcame the white and I floated into nothingness, was *Please God, let me die.*

I shuddered at the memory of that night, at how angry I was

coming to in the bathroom with Strom by my side. There were so many times I should have died. Like the train. One night I'd told Linda the train story, figuring she wouldn't laugh at me. I was driving my parents' red Mazda truck, trying to get it home before five so my mom wouldn't know I'd taken it again. I was so wasted that I couldn't work my feet on the clutch. My vision doubled or tripled, and lights blurred in front of my eyes. I kept passing out at the wheel, weaving off the road, and then being awakened by the crunch of gravel on the shoulder.

I passed out one final time, only to be startled awake by the blare of a train horn and its white light glaring in through the window. I'd stalled the truck in the middle of the railroad tracks. The train roared toward me like a tornado, just yards from the truck. I instinctively covered my face with my arms as the thought flashed: *I'm dead.* At that moment, I felt a powerful force push the truck over the tracks as the reverberating thunder of the train sped past, its horn still blaring.

The truck was still not running, but I was over the tracks. I opened the door with shaking arms, my knees wobbling. I had to lean against the stalled truck, then looked down at my pants and saw that I'd wet myself. I felt completely sober.

After telling that story to Linda, she'd asked me, "Do you believe in angels?" I didn't know what moved the truck over the tracks, but alone in my new apartment that first night, I realized that Linda had truly been an angel in my life. I got down on my knees, a position I hadn't been in for years, and tears started.

"Dear God, I don't know how to pray. It's been so long and I don't even know if you're listening. I don't know why I'm still alive. But I've got to believe that you're keeping me alive for a reason. I can't have been through all of this for nothing." Gut wrenching sobs gripped my whole body. "There's so much I don't understand. About you. About me. About my parents. My life.

Why you let things happen. But I'm scared. I don't know how to live without drugs. I don't know how to not hate you. I've never been on my own like this. I feel like a lost little girl. I need help. I can't do this by myself. I've got to have some help or I know I'll never make it."

When I finally opened my eyes, I realized that my fear had left me and my mind was quiet. An overwhelming sense of peace filled my body. For the first time in my sobriety, I felt like there was a chance I'd be okay. I got up and crawled into my sleeping bag, pulling it up to my chin. I closed my eyes and took some deep breaths.

"Please . . . keep sending . . . me . . . your angels . . ." I murmured, drifting into a peaceful sleep.

17

The Beginning

I walk down the wooden stairs into the basement of a church. I'm never on time but tonight I'm early. I head straight for the table with coffee and grab a cup of the thick black liquid that always makes my stomach ache in protest. I think it's an unwritten rule at these meetings: the coffee must be terrible. I'm not a regular here, so I move through unfamiliar faces to an empty aluminum chair.

I spot Conrad, who acknowledges my presence with a wave and a slight nod. Last week, he asked if I'd tell my story at his annual club banquet. I've never shared my story and the idea troubles me. A story implies a beginning and an end, and I don't have either. What I have are pieces of images and words in no particular order. I watch my life and make sense of it all through videos I splice together to create some semblance of a whole. I constantly press pause, rewind, fast forward, and stop. What's changing now is that when I watch the movies of my life, more and more I can recognize that the girl in the videos is me.

I look down the aisle at five empty seats, where my Recovery House girls should be sitting: Maggie, Maria, Brenda, Tonya, and Tammy. We'd been a crew for the last year, a strange bunch that never would have associated with each other if we hadn't ended up in treatment at the same time. Maggie was two years older than me and my exact opposite. Whereas I'd taken my anger and thrown it in the world's face, she had eaten all of hers. Then there was Maria, an older version of myself, a 40-year-old speed freak who'd been shooting our favorite poison for twenty years. Brenda was a retired hippie who'd traded in her needle for a bottle of booze. Tonya had damaged her brain. On her good days she resembled a fairytale grandmother bustling around the house taking care of people, but on her bad days she stayed locked in her room, convinced everyone was out to get her in some elaborate conspiracy theory. Finally there was Tammy, the classic picture of an alcoholic housewife. While the rest of us had wreaked havoc in the outside world, she'd caused just as much chaos without ever stepping outside her front door.

We'd all gotten out around the same time and had made a commitment to stay together. Each Friday night we gathered back at Recovery House at five, where we held our own private group session. We all made it to one year of sobriety. Just when I thought we'd beaten the statistics, Tammy returned to the place we'd all worked so hard to leave.

Tammy was one of those people who came out of the womb with a day planner in her hand. If she said she'd be somewhere, she was. If she promised to call you back, she always did. When she didn't call me for three days, and even missed the Thursday AA meeting, I knew something was wrong. A few days later, my phone rang at four thirty in the morning.

No one ever called at that time of morning just to say hi. So my heart pounded as I said, "Hello?"

"He-H-Heather . . . " Tammy's voice sounded as if her tongue was trapped in a mouthful of marbles.

"Tammy, you're drunk!" I cried.

She slurred, "Yes. Yes. Yes, I am. I am."

My heart sank. I was speechless. I wanted to ask her why but

I knew that neither of us could ever really answer the riddle as to why we used when we knew better than anyone just how crazy it made us. It just was what it was.

When Tammy opened her door to let me in that morning, I tried to keep the shock from showing. Her usually neat blond hair was dirty and matted to the left side of her head. I'd never known she wore any sort of dentures but there was a huge gap where her front teeth used to be. The right side of her face was scratched and bruised. She clutched a dirty white bathrobe around her small body.

I reached out my arms. "C'm here."

She stumbled into my arms and held on, smelling like old booze and vomit. Silent sobs shook her frail body. I shuffled us into her apartment. Blinds shut tightly, blocking out any chance of light. Her immaculate apartment lay in ruins, the recliner tipped over and the couch cushions tossed on the floor. Empty pints of cheap brandy randomly marked the room. Ashtrays overflowed with cigarette butts that spilled onto the floor. The floor was covered in rancid puke and urine, and I tried to breathe through my mouth. My shoes squished on the carpet as I walked over to the cushionless couch.

"I'm so . . . emb . . . embarrassed," Tammy muttered, throwing her body down next to mine. I held her and rubbed her back gently as she mumbled incoherently. I didn't know what to do with this person next to me. I'd never been on this side of the scenario. Between sobs and disconnected words, I caught the names of her son and daughter.

She'd only been drinking for three days and already any semblance of her new sober life was destroyed. I felt the sickness in the room as if it was a real entity that could overtake me at any time. "Tammy, I don't know what to do. Can I call the halfway house for help?"

She nodded. Staff told me to take her to detox. She sobbed silently while I drove. In the emergency room, the breathalyzer read .42. The nurse shook her head. "A point four means you should be dead. I don't know how you walked in here."

Tammy's drinking set up a chain reaction. Before I knew it, I was meeting Maggie late at night in the Denny's parking lot to tell her good-bye. She was drinking again, and had recently done her first line. She'd already been arrested three different times and was running to Oregon to hide. Maria was next in line. Her doctor wrote her a prescription for Ritalin because he believed it would help her to mellow out. In the next twenty four hours, she filled a three-month prescription, boiled it up, and shot all of it into her veins. Then the part of Tonya's brain that was damaged took over the part that still worked, and she was committed to a state mental institution. Brenda stayed sober, but refusing to get hurt again, she cut herself off from any contact with the world.

Waiting anxiously on my aluminum chair for the meeting to start, I reflect on those statistics I used to spew out in group. At the time, I never imagined I'd be the one to watch the numbers play themselves out, that I'd be the one still standing. I feel a tap on my shoulder and turn to see Charlotte's face. I scoot over one chair so she can sit in the aisle.

She squeezes my knee. "Hey, kid."

I smile and watch her set her purse on the floor, turn off her cell phone, and begin the scanning routine. She scans the room in the same manner I survey every room that I enter. I met Charlotte early in sobriety, but only recently was I letting her get close to me. When I first met her, she terrified me. It was hard to believe I could be scared of a 60-year-old woman, but when she looked at me with her crystalline blue eyes it was as if she could look right into my soul. Like Linda, Charlotte could take my broken spirit into the palm of her hand, caress it soothingly, and give it back to me comforted.

Finishing her scan of the exits, entryways, those in front of us, and those in back of us, Charlotte asks, "Did you go to your therapist this week?"

I roll my eyes and huff an exaggerated sigh. "Yes, fuck her."

The court requires me to go to therapy. The legal restrictions are lessening, but I have a feeling the therapy rule will be the last to go. My therapist, Patti, had been assigned to me during my first month at Recovery House, so I'd kept her when I got out. I don't like her because she talks to me too quietly, like I might break if she gets any louder. I also don't trust therapists because of what happened with Dave. I couldn't picture myself falling in love with a woman, but I'd never thought I'd fall in love with Dave either, so I was real careful. Part of me knew that what happened between me and Dave was wrong; I was still even a minor. And if I can't trust Dave as a therapist, can I trust any of them?

Nonetheless, each week I show up and each week Patti tries to get me to talk about my dad. She expects me to just spill forth openly about my childhood. She doesn't understand that I still can't talk about him. Maybe someday I will, maybe not. The only thing I want to work on right now is taking away his status as God, that position he's held for too long, and never should have held at all. I want to kick him out, to make him become the mere mortal he is in reality.

In one of our sessions, Patti said, "Take away your anger. Just pretend for a moment that it's not there. What do you feel underneath it?"

I flipped through all of my newly discovered emotions, trying to settle on one that I could attach to him, but I came up with nothing. I didn't know what to feel besides anger. For so many years when I looked into his eyes, I was only aware of a seething desire to hurt him. Getting rid of my anger would require forgiveness, and I didn't know how I was supposed to forgive someone who'd never even admitted doing anything wrong, let alone apologized.

Each week, Patti also sends me home with a different book to read, always a book with some strange title about breaking the silence, getting in touch with my inner child, or healing the invisible hurt. When I get home, I bury it beneath other books on my shelves, making sure the title is hidden.

Charlotte nudges my elbow, breaking into my thoughts. Everyone stands as the meeting opens. I take her hand and grab the hand of the other person standing next to me. We recite the words of a familiar prayer, not one from my childhood. Then the chairperson begins going through a list of announcements.

The man leading the meeting looks like he used to be a linebacker in his day, but now all his muscle has turned to fat. His hair is really long and pulled back into a ponytail that trails to the middle of his back. He's losing the hair on the top of his head, and I think he keeps the rest of his hair long to stay in denial about that. After the announcements, he begins talking about his recovery program. He says beautiful words with his mouth, but I see the look in his eyes, a look I know not to trust. He probably goes home and beats his wife.

His eyes trigger memories. My mind wanders off to another day and another table. The table of my childhood kitchen with bright yellow walls. The only picture hanging in that small space. A murky orange background in the center of which stands a hideous tree, lumpy and dark. It's alive with evil. The branches become the arms of a skeleton that can reach out to grab me, or rip my sister out of her highchair. The black frame can't contain it. Evil infiltrates the head of the table.

I'd always wondered how my mom could go right on eating her dinner no matter what happened at the supper table. Even as a kid I remember thinking, *Why? Why does she just sit there?*

Recently, my mom had begun to give me small pieces of the answer, tiny pieces of truth, but I'd take anything I could get.

Each year in the fall my mom, her four sisters, and my grandma travel up north and spend the weekend at a hotel in a small town, where there's a huge craft sale. This year my mom invited me to go along and we had a room to ourselves. As we lay there in the darkness, listening to the hum of the heater, she asked, "Do you know why I always stayed up with you kids while you were sick?" Whenever one of us kids had gotten sick, she'd lavish us with care, holding our hair while we puked or putting a cool washcloth on fevered foreheads. One time, I had hives so bad that I scratched my skin raw, so she lay in my bed all night long, holding my hands tightly in hers so I couldn't scratch in my sleep.

"It's because when I was sick, my mom never took care of me. I had to be all by myself and those were some of the loneliest nights of my life. One night both mom and dad were passed out drunk and . . . "

"What? Grandma drank?" I'd never seen my grandma put a glass of alcohol to her lips.

She laughed. "Oh heavens, Heather. She was as bad of a drunk as your grandpa. They used to disappear for days at a time on benders. Back then you could do that. She just doesn't drink anymore because her stomach is completely shot and she gets deathly ill. Anyway, I got really sick one night and puked all over in the hallway on my way to the bathroom. I woke my mom up and told her I was sick. She just yelled at me to clean it up and go back to bed. I vowed then that if I ever had kids, I'd never make them be alone while they were sick."

"Was Grandma nasty like Grandpa?"

"She was just as bad, maybe even worse. You should have seen the fights they got into." She was silent for a minute. "You had the same violent temper as my parents when you drank."

Her comment surprised me because since I'd gotten sober she wanted to pretend that I wasn't an addict, and didn't even like to hear my apologies. She'd shrug me off: "Oh, Heather. Of course I know you're sorry and forgive you. But that was the past and there's no need to talk about it. It's all over now."

The sound of clapping brings me back to the present. A woman walks to the front of the room where the big man embraces her and thumps her on the back. He pulls away and hands her a sobriety medallion. With a huge smile, she cries. "Thank-you. Thank you so much. I can't believe I've stayed sober for ninty days. So much has changed in my life. I can't even find the words. I started drinking after I'd been sober . . . "

I can't focus on her anymore. Soon Conrad will introduce me to speak and my heart's beating fast. How do I explain my life to these people? Maybe I should just start with my desperate prayer outside of the courtroom. It seems like ever since then miracles have been happening, not the miracles in the Bible stories I read as a child, but things like surviving Reggie. And me staying sober seems nearly as dramatic as walking on water. I don't know how I've made it with so many wounds still bleeding. I just hold on and trust blindly that someday the wounds will become scars. Someday, but not today. For now, I still bleed.

Sometimes I have to just pretend to be okay. All I know is that if I get high again I'll die, and for the first time in my life I don't want to die. I've never really been alive, and I'm beginning to hope that I may become a whole person. I've held on to my suicide option though, because I'd rather blow my head off and chance going straight to hell than live in the hell of my addiction. Just keeping that option open is comforting somehow.

The woman has finished speaking and Conrad walks up to stand behind the podium. *Ohmigod. This is really happening.* He winks at me. "I'm honored to introduce our speaker tonight.

She's an incredible lady, a great example of the miracles that can happen if you just stay sober long enough to let them. I sat in many meetings with her in the beginning of her sobriety. Honestly, I didn't think she'd make it. But the person you see tonight is not the person that I used to sit next to in meetings. For one thing, her vocabulary has expanded. I've been a trucker for twenty years and things used to come out of her mouth that shocked even me."

The crowd laughs. I try to keep my throat from closing up. *Why did I say I'd do this?* Conrad continues, "Seriously, though. This girl should be dead, but God's got a plan for her. I've thoroughly enjoyed watching her grow and change. I'm constantly amazed and grateful to be a part of it. If she can stay sober, anyone can. I'm sure you'll get a lot out of her sharing tonight. So, with that, I give you your speaker. Heather?"

Conrad smiles and nods at me as the crowd claps. I stand but my knees wobble as if they might not be able to hold my body if I walk. All eyes turn to look at me. Charlotte reaches up and touches my hand. *Run. Get out of here. Run now!* That voice of fear is the only one I need to give me the strength to take a step past Charlotte and into the aisle. That voice is the part of me so scared to see and tell the truth that it would rather die. This one has been here since the beginning and will be here until the end, I am sure. All I can do is act against it. I take strides towards the podium, so far away.

Eyes bore into me and I can sense the questions. They wonder what a young girl, barely a woman, can possibly share with them that might touch their lives in any sort of meaningful way. They don't understand that although my body is young, it houses the spirit of a very old warrior. If they'd just look into my eyes, they'd be able to see that I've been places I wish I'd never been, seen things I wish I'd never seen, done things I wish I'd never done.

And even though I've returned from war, I carry the battlefields, and my fallen comrades, within me still.

I step up onto the platform. *You can still get out of here. Run!* Conrad hugs me and I try to hug him back, but it's not a real hug because I'm scared. In front of the podium, I adjust the microphone and face all the faces looking back at me. My voice catches somewhere in my throat. I can't find it. Then I realize that these people are not seeing the girl people used to shudder to look at. I'm not standing crooked and hunched over. I'm standing straight and tall. My eyes aren't vacant and hollow with dark circles encasing them. They shine brightly. My face isn't showing every bone, and my hair is no longer dingy and gray, or hanging in my face. My face is clear and fresh, my hair pulled back neatly. They can't see the young girl next to men ten years older than her, men who keep her high for a price she agrees to pay. They can't see that because I'm no longer that girl. I'm no longer a girl, but a woman. I'm no longer high, and my soul is my own.

I take a deep breath and rub the sobriety medallion in my pocket. Suddenly, I feel the eyes and the smiles of Charlotte, Linda, Carla, Yvonne, Hank, and other shadowy angels hovering over me. From inside of me, they form a new voice: *You have survived. Now thrive.* I look out at the eyes of the crowd, smile, and begin to speak. "Hi. My name is Heather and I'm a recovering drug addict and alcoholic . . . "

Afterword

This book started with me sitting in front of my computer with piles upon piles of old journals. I wanted to put together the pieces of my life, in the hope of discovering my own truth. My past was a series of blurred images, questions, blank spaces and confusion. As I went through the journals, I began to write my story. Slowly, it grew into a book. My motive to write, and the fuel that kept me going even when I wanted to quit, was the desire to find my truth and to claim it as my own.

In a few short weeks, I will have been sober for seven years. I've never gone back to live in the cities in which I grew up, nor have I had any contact with the friends I used with. Periodically throughout the years, my mom will tell me what she has read in the papers about those who have been arrested or those who have died. As far as I know, "Strom" is still alive. He's the one I miss the most and perhaps someday our paths will cross again, but even if they never do, he will always have his spot reserved in my heart. I have contact (though limited) with all the members of my family. I've accepted that I will probably always be the only one who has the courage to tell the truth.

I used to think that I would go to a really great meeting, or have an incredibly intense therapy session, or read an inspiring book and—in that one moment—all my hurts would be healed and I would move forward, leaving it all behind me. But just when you think you've cried the last tear, more rise to the surface. Grief is never truly over, but I believe my wounds have become scars and are no longer bleeding.

Sometimes I'm still amazed that I'm alive. My life has turned into something I never could have imagined. I got my GED, started out at a two-year college, and then transferred to a four-year college on a presidential scholarship. At the age of 23, I graduated from Hamline University in St. Paul, Minnesota (*summa cum laude*) with a B.A in psychology. Currently, at the age of 24, I'm attending the University of Southern Mississippi, working towards my doctoral degree in clinical psychology. On the outside, everything in my life has changed, but the most important piece of growth has occurred within my spirit. A lot of terrible things happened to me but the most painful was the damage done to my spirit. And today I can truly say that the biggest miracle God has worked in my life has been healing my spirit.

—Heather Harrison, December 21, 2003

Acknowledgments

There are so many people who have been a part of the process of my writing this book. But first and foremost, I want to thank God for keeping me alive long enough to have a story, despite my best efforts to destroy myself. Also, for all of the people he placed and continues to place in my journey to help, heal, and teach me.

The number of individuals who have made this book possible are too numerous to list, but I would like to take a moment to list a few who are the most important. I want to thank Carolyn for teaching how to show others my story rather than tell it. I am the writer I am today because of the things she taught me. I will forever carry her voice in my head as I write and rewrite. I want to thank Charlotte for her undying patience, for teaching me how to let others truly see me, and for being a source of constant strength in my life. I want to thank Blake for his help, his time, and his patience from the first chapter to the final chapter. Thank you for being a truly safe man. I want to thank Kasey for being my spiritual sister and providing me with strength and encouragement whenever mine ran low. Thank you for teaching me the true meaning of friendship and unconditional love. I want to thank Gail for all the work she put into making my story complete, and for sharing her story with me. Thank you for always answering my phone calls, even if it is at four in the morning. I want to thank Linda Ann, Vivian, Frank, and all of my other angels who worked miracles in my life. I want to thank all my fellow sisters in sobriety that helped me to stay sober. Finally, I want to thank Pastor Hale for helping me heal a part of myself that I never thought would heal. Without all of you, my story would not be laid out in these pages.

WORD WARRIORS PRESS

Word Warriors Press publishes trade paperbacks of memoir and reflective essays by authors primarily in their twenties and late teens. We especially want to hear new and emerging voices from people whose stories aren't often told in mainstream society, the stories that are all too common but that rarely get talked about or reported on the news. We believe in the power of this generation's truth-telling words to change the world. By publishing unheard voices, Word Warriors Press seeks to empower, educate and entertain those whom society ignores.

Word Warriors Press is unique in many ways. Upholding the importance of art, and of giving young visual artists a venue, we include pen and ink drawings in all our books. Young men and women are hired for all possible aspects of the business: from writing, art and proofing to web design. Social and political change begins with psychological change: a sense of individual and group power, and the realization that change is possible. Through its books and interactive website, this press hopes to help engender such changes. We invite you to visit our website for more information, for lively discussion in its forums, and to become a part of this process.

www.wordwarriorspress.com